THE BOOK OF
BUCKSKINNING

Edited by
WILLIAM H. SCURLOCK

REBEL PUBLISHING COMPANY/TEXARKANA, TEXAS

EDITORIAL STAFF

EDITOR:
William H. Scurlock

GRAPHIC DESIGN:
David Wright

COVER PHOTOGRAPHY:
David Wright

PUBLISHER:
Oran Scurlock, Jr.

ABOUT THE COVERS

First Printing: January, 1981
Second Printing: August, 1981
Third Printing: June, 1982
Fourth Printing: May, 1983
Fifth Printing: August, 1984
Sixth Printing: December, 1986
Seventh Printing: February, 1988
Eighth Printing: March, 1989
Ninth Printing: June, 1990

ISBN #0-9605666-0-0   Library of Congress Catalog Card #80-54597

Contents

DEDICATION

*To all modern day longhunters & mountain men
that cherish those bygone days and strive to emulate the old ways.*

Foreword

GROWING UP IN THE piney woods of East Texas, the outdoors contributed in large measure to my education. The lore of the woods, streams and lakes, along with an abiding fascination with the wonders of nature, have remained with me throughout my life. It is little wonder that after being hooked by the black powder habit, I should follow the primitive trail.

Buckskinning is an enjoyable activity. It can be a once a year adventure or it can be an every day activity. For most of us it is something in between. There is a feeling that you acquire which is not easily explained. It is certainly more than playing games and being a romantic. You find yourself wanting to recreate history, to live it. While few of us can escape the demands of life in the Twentieth Century entirely, we can withdraw as often as possible and wander the paths of the wilderness.

As for this book, we felt that it was needed. Buckskinning is the fastest growing segment of the muzzleloading sport. There are literally thousands of folks joining the ranks each year. Up to now about the only way to learn something about this activity was to go to a gathering of buckskinners or to know one personally. Our approach was to find a group of men who could express themselves and had the expertise gained from experience to do so. The men who have contributed to this work have been at it for a great many years and are imminently qualified to share their knowledge with you. They are not armchair authorities! Each one of them has been involved in the primitive game for years and all of them belong to at least one of the national buckskinning organizations. They are all active participants in the activities of buckskinning.

Whether your interest lies with the Eastern Longhunter or the Western Mountain Man you will find much information which should prove useful to you. If you are a "pilgrim", then it is our hope that this book will save you much time and effort in gaining the knowledge and skills of the game. If you are a "hivernant", it is our hope that you will gain much additional information which will add to your enjoyment.

But most of all, it is our wish that each one who reads this book will become more deeply committed and involved in what many have come to think of as "A Way of Life."

Oran Scurlock, Jr.
Publisher

v

The Philosophy of Buckskinning

by Dick "Beau Jacques" House

IN 1938, 11-YEAR-OLD Dick House came into possession of a well-thumbed, dogeared Francis Bannerman Sons 1937 catalog of Civil War and other military surplus. That same year, a Gettysburg guide gave him a minie ball from the Pickett's Charge field. The next year, his first muzzleloader was a $2 Civil War contract musket which had been chopped to halfstock. After service in World War II, education in journalism, and marriage to a hometown girl, House began collecting and shooting in earnest, mainly full and halfstock Kentuckies. He was a long-time member of the Ohio Gun Collectors Association, and helped found The Cleveland Civil War Roundtable.

In the early 60's Ford transferred him to Michigan. There, for two years, he was a member of Loomis Battery, a uniformed Civil War artillery unit. With them, he participated as a gunner in the 1961 centennial re-enactment of the First Bull Run.

Later, in California, his mountain-man interest was rekindled. His first novel, a mountain-man adventure, SO THE LOUD TORRENT, was published in 1977 by North Star Press, St. Cloud, Minnesota. For many years as Beau Jacques, he wrote "Smokepoles in the Closet" for The Buckskin Report. He has written other blackpowder articles; his fiction and nonfiction have appeared in "Far West", "True West", "Treasure", and in Norway's "Western" magazines.

His second novel, VENGEANCE MOUNTAIN, is soon to be published by Tower Books, New York. House is membership chairman and executive board nominee of The Western Writers of America, Inc. He is a special features editor for the MUZZLELOADER and is a member of NAPR, NMLRA, NRA, and the International Chili Society. Dick House is editor of employee publications with the Jet Propulsion Laboratory, Pasadena, California, the nation's leading unmanned space explorers, affiliated with NASA and Caltech.

1

TO UNDERSTAND THE CONSCIENCE of a buckskinner and the motivations which have brought about a legion of men, women and children who take pleasure in living in tipis and grimy 'skins, we first must put a collective finger on the pulse of that great social experiment called America.

If first we have a concept of what made America strong, and why it has lost some of that vibrance and resilience, then we may better understand what makes a muzzleloader man.

Buckskinning is a reaching out to get a firm grip again on cherished traditions and institutions which the years have eroded and corroded. It is God Bless America in raunchy buckskins squatting in front of a tipi, a latter-day Bridger and his Hawken stepping up to a firing line; a striving for substance, something to stick to the ribs, in a nation turned into plastic and where most of life is but an imitation of life.

It is finding again the Faith of our Fathers, not so much in a religious sense as in a moral sense.

It is a tiny but growing culture that searches for roots, something that probes deeply into the rich, lush land from which America blossomed and flourished. It is not so much a search for personal heritage as it is a quest for a cultural identity and integrity at a time when the limbs turn brittle and the leaves wither on the tree of American life, and its fruits have gone sour.

In a very large sense, America in the 1980s is an ashamed land.

Burglary runs rampant in a country where in the glory days the latchstring was always out; where we welcomed the wayfaring stranger to come in and warm himself, rest himself, and feed himself. In a single generation, we have come from a position of never locking our homes or our cars, to a timid, haunted paranoia in which everything is buttoned down in eternal fear that it will walk away the moment our backs are turned.

The nation is beset by personal and aggravated assault — armed robberies and rapes — by characters who slither out at us from the dark in a land that once prided itself that its streets and byways were the safest in the world — by day and by night.

We are appalled by corruption in high places — even at the very top — and of cheating the system, and it's dirt easy. Not only can you fight City Hall, but it's a pushover; you are only required to be moderately shrewd. The same type of con artist roams the streets victimizing vulnerable elderly white-haired widows.

This in a nation where not that long ago a man's word was as good as his bond.

That same American who cried, "Death before Dishonor," stood his ground against all comers, did not ask his neighbors nor his nation for a dole. When it came to making his own way with pride, he asked no quarter and gave no quarter. He was guided by two sound principles — the Golden Rule and that a job worth doing was worth doing well.

What came his way came by the grit and grip of his own two hands. He loved his family, stood by his wife, but if he learned of a neighbor's plight, his rest was troubled unless he stepped in to help.

Such is buckskinning; a search for truth in the face of national trauma. Idealistic though it may be, buckskinning seeks to develop a culture based on substance. Total fantasy that it may appear on the face of it, buckskinning, in truth, is a quest for reality based on simple, friendly, basic ways.

Back, then, to the basics.

Although it rejects out-of-hand the quasi-comfortable, blaring-stereo aspects of the 1980s, "outdoor life" and camping, the primitive style does not mean discomfort for the sake of authenticity.

2

Totally to the contrary.

A humble tipi is hardly a cramped, damp, dirty and cold hovel. The beckoning fire in the center ring is a place of warmth, both physical and spiritual. In its spaciousness, blankets, furs and robes are spread over the floor, welcoming the visitor to stretch out, relax, palaver, sing, and otherwise celebrate life — buckskinner style.

You know you are a buckskinner when the most impressive sight you can imagine is watching from afar a cluster of cone-shaped white lodges, some off-white from the smoke of a hundred rendezvous, and the laughter and joy that have enriched them. There they lay in a flat meadowland against the backdrop of trees and rolling country and, away off, the mountains; they nestle together in friendship and welcome, their sprays of tall lodgepoles extended like happy fingers in a welcome wave at the blue sky. Their covers may be gaily colored and decorated with "Injun sign".

Around them, 'skinners are busy with their own camp chores, helping a newfound friend "get his lodge up", or striding off for some shootin' or to make palaver. Kids in their own little sets of 'skins scamper and frolic and hoot with a freedom unknown in four walls and on city streets, or any place else in the world for that matter.

Your heart warms as you see women, in beaded, fringy 'skins or in calico, clustering together to exchange secrets as they did a century and more ago.

A typical buckskinner camp in no way compares with anything associated with the 20th century. The intent is to emulate a long-dead lifestyle; many of the so-called creature comforts are dispensed with — replaced with revived techniques a thousand times better and more enjoyable.

A dyed-in-the-wood purist rejects anything associated with here and now. An average rendezvous, though, will find an occasional camera — what better way to relive those golden hours than through the miracle of modern photography? (Cameras have even been seen encased in fringed buckskin!)

Almost any lodge will have an ice chest or two (probably draped with a buffalo robe to sustain authenticity); meats and other necessities for "vittles", and various libations must be kept chilled.

And even the most hardy 'skinner will allow the luxury of a cold beer or two. Or three.

You'll also know you're a buckskinner when the most precious sight in the world is down the browned top flat of a mountain-style rifle barrel, a perfect four-point line from eye through fine notch of rear sight, across the thin tip of front blade sight, spanning the distance on a precise line to a target, be it one of pelt or of paper.

Fire, too, is a sight — and a sound and a smell — that confirms a buckskinner. The conversation in a lodge takes its cue from the fiery action in the center pit. When the blaze is merry and bright, high and crackling, that's the time for the bright joke, the witty wisecrack, the "remember the time we . . ?" Then, the talk turns low when the coals just glow. Often there are lapses into silence as the eyes of those around the ring explore the depth of the dying fire, each occupied with his own deep

thoughts.

And, if something doesn't happen to kick up the fire to brighten the conversation, heads nod as the embers bury themselves under a heap of ash with an abiding warmth. The bedding, be they blankets, robes or bedrolls, beckons — for sleep, to a buckskinner, is another rich and precious experience, unlike that of any place else on earth or at any other time.

Unless the camp is up singing, dancing, making music and palaver and in general up at all hours for "shinin' times", sleep seeps in with the growing dark; the camp quiets, and the night's rest is the most beautiful of all. And it somehow breaks with the first glimmers of dawn — to be up and rejoice at another beautiful day "at rendezvous" — even though it may be raining!

You wake to a host of marvelous smells; your spirit soars at the musky aroma of powdery dust blended with dead leaves long gone to powdery mulch, of the smoke of a freshly revived fire, and an early bird's coffee aroma drifting to you on an early-morning breeze. Later in the day, you savor the smell of crushed, bruised green grass as you stretch out to prop your rifle on your elbows and take a long sight at something away off.

Or, when you're out alone, in intimate touch with a half-lost trail through moccasinned soles, hefting a good rifle, and a warm breeze at last flutters in the whang-fringe along your legs; it is the Air of Spring bringing new life to a world weary of snow and cold and sullen skies. It's that first warm breeze gliding down at you from a far-off range, reaching your nose and your skin and carrying the fragrance of rebirth and youth and promise.

A buckskinner's nose is also keen on the marvelous age-smell of fall, pleasantly cooling a summer-fevered skin; the smells that are not driven on the wind, but wafted on a soft fall breeze, suggesting the snows of tomorrow, but giving a warm richness right now — smells of leaves dying and going brittle, and of nuts and fruits maturing. And of the animals going for them as you watch through your gunsights — deer and squirrel and other game or varmints.

If you trap, the fall winds foretell a time when the furs along your line will turn rich and prime against the bitterness of cold and snow.

Your nose, tasting these smells, lures you to the deep, secret places in the Great Out There, to hunt or merely to savor the experience of being alive, and to hark to the music, the chants and the songs that only a forest or a mountainside can sing.

Buckskinning is shooting a rifle if only to smell the smoke, and to see it standing heavy, thick and pungent beside you or over you — a battleflag of the religious reloading ritual and of a shot well-placed.

It is the smell of that smoke, and the distinctive smells of cleaned-out fouling from a well-used barrel that have made you more of an addict than any noxious drug peddled in the slum or skidrow — and it is capable of imparting ten times the "high", with none of the harmful after-effects. In truth, the joy is yours forever.

Taste, too, enters into it. Savoring recipes of yore that your taste buds have been long deprived of — like, perhaps, 150 years. Yet when you taste them there is familiarity, recollection.

And small things. What can match the taste of a powderhorn plug pulled with your teeth to reload the way you've done it a thousand times over? And still the experience and the taste of the old plug is always fresh and new. Your plug has become saturated with your juices, all the while spending its life living intimately with blackpowder.

Touch and feel. The graceful satin feel of buckskins

A solitary buckskinner in an isolated camp enjoys a time that only such a camp can offer.

flexing with your muscles. Buckskin soothes a skin rasped raw by 20th century raiment; like a gentle touch from a soft hand, it massages skin and muscle with a therapy all its own. And moccasins. Soft. The earth caresses back with your soft, quiet tread. No vibrum-soled bulky and stiff backpacker's boot offers the communion with the trail of a buckskinner's moccasin. Of course, an occasional sharp rock can sting through the moc's sole — but whoever told you that life in the High Lonesome would be strewn with rose petals?

When you live the buckskinner life, whether in rendezvous with dozens of others, or on a lone trail all others have forsaken, the sense of what you are and what you are doing grows more acute. Senses heighten. The very air whispers of strange mysteries of a long-ago day; the sun that beats down to soften stiffened buckskins with sweat, the rain that pelts, and the winds that rip are the very ones that beat, pelted and ripped Simon Kenton and John Colter and Daniel Boone and Jim Bridger, and a thousand other nameless faces in buckskin.

Pivotal to all of buckskinning is the gun. It began with shooters wanting to get back to the basics. Back to the truth of the stalk and the hunt. Disillusioned by high technology trajectories and automated ballistics, many turned back to the gun that made America great — the muzzle loader!

Hollywood to the contrary, it was not the '73 Winchester nor the .45-70 Springfield that won the West. It was the muzzleloader. After it had won the East.

The muzzleloader has proved more durable than any tool of its time, and certainly more durable than those who thought they saw the passing of an era with the advent of breechloaders and smokeless powder.

Muzzleloading endured. Production of frontstuffers may have slowed dramatically sometime after 1860, but it never totally died out. It was still favored by men who enjoyed the distinctive slow, plodding, methodical aspect of loading — as well as the challenge of that lone shot at a target, animate or inanimate. Repeating cartridge rifles offered an opportunity for one man to virtually spray the landscape with a hail of bullets. While this appealed to some, for others, shooting would always take on the aspect of an art. And any kind of art in its true form is never hurried.

Historians contend that the American frontier was finally considered tamed about 1894. By the turn of the century, hunting had changed diametrically from a thing of survival to a thing of sport. Meat was cheaper and easier to come by off the butcher's shelf. And to hunt for the sheer thrill of the sport, the repeating breechloader was THE weapon. Unless a hunter was an indifferent marksman — and many were and are — if he could scare up game, the chances were good he'd bag something.

Meanwhile, muzzleloading continued quietly, existing largely out of the limelight. Competitive shoots still went on, many of them deep in one of muzzleloading's ancestral homes, the Tennessee hill country.

Much of the social life, at least where men were concerned, revolved around hunting and especially shooting. Tennessee's Sergeant Alvin York, America's most decorated World War I hero, picked up his

DRAWING BY DAVID WRIGHT

6

Large encampments offer a wide range of activities and numerous opportunities for fellowship with other buckskinners.

"shootin' eye" behind the crescent butt of a fullstock turned out "just down the road a piece". He learned at the side of old time shooters who never in their lives had held a breechloading rifle.

And there to record the events on film as well as to take part in them was a professional photographer named Walter M. Cline. It is fascinating in tracing the lineage of buckskinning and contemporary muzzleloading that the home ground of The National Muzzle Loading Rifle Association in Friendship, Indiana, is the Walter M. Cline Range.

But, to generalize, there is about where muzzleloading lay at the outbreak of World War II. About the only universal interest in frontstuffer guns was in their value as collectors' items.

With the end of that conflict, a strange phenomenon began to materialize on the American scene. It was called by many names, but the one that stuck was Leisure Time.

Up to about 1930, those who stayed down on the farm or the ranch generally put in a six-day week, and usually from sunup to sundown, and even a Sabbath

7

afternoon might have to be devoted to mending harness. For the city cousins, the routine was almost the same. The five-day week may have been reality, but the breadwinner still put in a ten-hour day. The only major change was that beyond that he got time-and-a-half pay.

The Great Depression, roughly the decade from 1930 to 1940, can only be viewed as a Dark Age in sport shooting. If a man had a job, he fought hard to keep it, leaving little energy for sports or hobbies.

If he didn't have a job, the same energies were dissipated in worry and struggle keeping a roof over the family's heads and bread and beans on the table. What hunting that was done had reverted back to a matter of survival; the meat was sorely needed at home.

Then the close of World War II ushered in a new age of prosperity and leisure. Nearly every American between 17 and 30 had been in uniform and returned from the mud of France and Germany or the sands of Iwo Jima drenched in glory. And he had done it with a gun in his hand.

The gun held no stigma; indeed, it was a thing of pride and glory. The shooting sports in America came into full bloom.

And so did collecting. It was no longer a rich man's hobby; working stiffs began developing enviable collections. Local gun shows flourished and the Kentuckies and the muskets and, yes, even the Hawkens and other plains and mountain style rifles emerged out of the cobwebs of attics all over the land.

A strange new urge, a compelling nostalgia was beginning to be felt in the bones of people interested in old guns. By some it was called Heritage — an interest in and a seeking out of the past. Despite the dull, dry dates and memorized recitations of the classroom, men began to find that history had allure and substance. Progress had been accomplished by flesh and blood men who put their pants on one leg at a time, got drunk and went to the bathroom like everyone else. A kinship with heritage developed.

A few of the collectors read up on the techniques of shooting the old timers, bought a Dixie Gun Works red-handled tong mold and a pound of Ffg black powder and tried a little paper-punching. Some even became bold enough to hunt with a muzzleloader. The lesser collector's guns of dealers like Abels and Flayderman were turned into shooters.

The Korean Conflict came and went, winding up in something of a Mexican standoff. There was hardly the glory of World War II, but there was little disillusionment either.

Along about then someone found a frontstuffer for a song, but the stock was in horrible shape and the lock was missing. The breech area and the bore were solid enough, and the rest of the furniture was intact. He learned that somewhere someone was building reproduction locks or had a supply of spare originals, and he sent off for one. While he waited for the mailman, he got a nice chunk of straight-grain maple and began hacking out a stock.

He was about to build himself a shooter.

(Mind you, the discussion here is in the most general of terms. To this tale of the "begats of buckskinning" there are, to be sure, isolated, remote exceptions. As

Above: Buckskinners enjoy competing against each other in the old time skills such as this shooting match.
Below: Jim Suffield blows down his barrel after his shot to extinguish any live sparks.

surely as first the powder then the ball, someone will read this and say, "That guy is talking through his hat! Hell, I was building muzzleloaders in 19 and 35!")

First it was mainly those antique gun dealers who catered to collectors who came up with the spare parts from old junker guns. As interest grew in shooting the old muzzle loaders which needed parts and work, here and there businesses sprang up filling that need. Prime examples that continue today are Dixie Gun Works in Union City, Tennessee, and the Log Cabin Sport Shop in Lodi, Ohio.

The interest grew through a relative handful of muzzle loading aficionados. The National Muzzle Loading Rifle Association has a long history of serving the blackpowder fraternity — but for many years it was small enough that most members knew one another by name!

The term buckskinner had yet to be coined. The Grand Old Sport still nestled in the blossom; it would yet be several years before it would come into full bloom.

Jeff Hengesbaugh (left) and members of the American Mountain Men (below) express their jubilation upon completing a four day ride over the Wind River Mountains of Wyoming.

Then a thing began to happen. The Ship of State started to spring some serious leaks. Someone once observed to this writer that with the assassination of John F. Kennedy, America suffered a nervous breakdown. What happened after that was a kind of creeping disillusionment not unlike the falling of a row of dominoes. Robert Kennedy was felled by an assassin's bullet; shortly another national leader in Dr. Martin Luther King was gunned down. America was so numb with shock that by the time a would-be assassin paralyzed Governor George Wallace and an attempt was made on the life of President Gerald Ford, the resultant national outrage was hardly a groundswell.

The heartbreak of the national disgrace of Watergate was interrupted only on the half-hour by the heartbreak of psoriasis. Daily, live from Vietnam, Americans were fed a monotonous menu of mayhem and MIAs — and somehow the guns of Southeast Asia became the guns of Kent State.

But guns, the logical thinkers said in response to the growing and stridently vocal anti-gun movement, do not kill people; people kill people.

Almost as if to prove the point, the buckskinner emerged. In no way, however, was buckskinning conceived as a protest or pro-gun movement. There are next to no political overtones, except an unswerving commitment to the Second Amendment.

Beyond that, buckskinners are gentle people. Their shooting contests are always good-natured, filled with tongue-in-cheek barbs. They love a winner, even if it is the other guy. They admire a well-made gun, and the competent use of it.

They hunt in the sincere belief that they will use as much of the kill as possible — meat, hides, horns or antlers, and other byproducts. They kill with the conviction that thinned herds guarantee an abundant life for the rest of the species.

Because the gun carries one single shot, they are painfully aware that the first shot must be clean and final; they get no second chance. Their compassion is at such a depth that merely wounding the game to limp off and die an agonized, unproductive death would be un-

10

It's all in the heart. Ralph Hooker on Boone's Wilderness Road leading a party of skinners. Mr. Hooker has twice walked this trail and once walked the Santa Fe Trail. He certainly proves the point that age is no barrier to buckskinning.

thinkable. When he learns of such an incident on the part of another hunter, a buckskinner becomes furious. This was the Indian way. It was adopted by the whites who moved into the Indian's territory and took on the Indian lifestyle. The Frontiersmen and Mountain Men along with the Indians, hated to waste anything since provisions were not that easy to come by when away from civilization.

Starting in about 1960, or perhaps a bit before, the models these men set were remembered and the cherishing of the mountain man's "way" began. Two types of men associated with the fur trade days set the pace for today's buckskinners.

First were those who built the rifles used to blaze the trails westward. Today's buckskinners look to the work of the old masters and see gunsmithing genius as well as something almost gone from the American scene — pride in individual productivity.

They designed their guns to last, and they built them to last. More than pride went into what they did; it was more than dedication to the principle of integrity. It was love in the form of incredible concern that the gun's owner would benefit. They knew that a man's life might depend on that gun.

Today, all across the land, riflesmiths are at work producing guns with a real pride equal to that of the old time smiths. With but a few exceptions, the designers and builders of guns for the buckskinner trade have taken up that fine old symbol of integrity in craftsmanship that characterized these men.

The second kind of 18th or early 19th century man who forms a model for buckskinners are the frontiersmen and mountain men themselves — the Boones, the Bridgers, the Kentons, and the Smiths.

By all accounts, they were a rough-cut lot, groomed that way by the abrasive environment, "sired by a hurricane, dam'd by an earthquake, and half-related to the cholera on my mother's side."

These were not men to follow the flock. They were rugged individuals who learned to survive by their wits, but of a moral character that could only be described as cast-iron. They were solitary, lonely men who could easily get through a year without hearing another voice — and rejoice that such was possible. Yet they could build such a kinship with a comrade that they could face death that the other might live.

In their own rough-cut way, they cherished, worshipped the supernal beauty they found in the wilderness. Like a cathedral, the mountains were hypnotically sacred, sanctified by the blood of their fellow hunters and trappers.

Like those hivernants of old, paramount in the buckskinner ethic is freedom — a freedom to expand his entire soul to take in the whole of the outdoors; the mountains, the valleys and rivers, the lush land, the barren land, and what it offers in magnificence as well as in threat.

It is meeting God where many of them believe God intended to be met. In a nation where freedoms are sloughed off like dead skin, the buckskinner finds true and fulfilling freedom in a primitive existence in a primal wilderness.

That great mountain man of fiction, Dick Summers from A. B. Guthrie, Jr.'s THE BIG SKY, summed it up best for the original mountain man. He was also speaking for today's buckskinners, each of whom has his own forested Shangri-La, his own precious version of Summers' upper Missouri:

"I seen most of it. Colter's Hell and the Seeds-kee-dee and the Tetons standin' higher'n clouds, and north and south from Nez Perce to Comanche, but God Almighty, there's nothin' richer'n the upper Missouri. Or purtier. I seen the Great Falls and traveled Maria's River, dodgin' the Blackfeet, makin' cold camps and sometimes thinkin' my time was up, and all the time livin' wonderful, loose and free's ary animal. That's some, that is!"

How to Get Started

by J. W. "Doc" Carlson

JAMES W. CARLSON, BEST KNOWN to us all as "Doc", has been tinkering with black powder guns for over thirty years. An acknowledged authority on the sport, his first love is buckskinning.

He got his first muzzleloader when he was 14. He bought it in a second hand store for $35 and couldn't afford the powder horn that was with it. The gun was a full stock Kentucky percussion and he still has it. It was the first rifle that he owned and he hunted with it until he realized that it was valuable. At the time that he got the rifle there was no help for anyone who wanted to learn. He had to go on what little he could find reading. There were no catalogs of suppliers and, of course, he had never heard of the National Muzzle Loading Rifle Association.

Doc is a gunsmith, manufacturer and dealer in the black powder trade and practices veterinary medicine to a limited degree. He is the Technical Editor for MUZZLE-LOADER Magazine and Product Review man for the NMLRA magazine, MUZZLE BLASTS.

A Life member of both the National Rifle Association and the NMLRA, he serves both organizations on their Board of Directors. He is also a member of the American Mountain Men and the National Association of Primitive Riflemen.

For a man so completely involved in the gun sports, Doc and his wife, Dee, still find the time to attend various buckskinning events around the country.

THE ONE THING THAT all buckskinners have in common is this . . . we all had to start. No one is born buckskinning — although there are probably some that will argue with that point of view. It is something that grows within a person, either through a deep love of early American history or muzzleloading, or both. Usually, both the desire and the knowledge required are acquired over a long period of time. To get into buckskinning or rendezvousing you'll need to understand just what it is and isn't. It is about as fine a way to spend a family vacation as I can think of. It isn't merely a chance to get away and ''play Indian'' for a time. While the living is early American, the soul of the buckskinner goes much deeper than the surface trappings. You must 'feel' buckskinning. It is a very hard thing to explain to those who have never felt it. There is a kinship with those that lived this type of life years ago, a kinship with the old values of our country and its greatness. The sight of ''Old Glory'' means more at a rendezvous than other places, although the feller with the big lump in his throat at the ball game when they're singing the Star Spangled Banner is, like as not, a buckskinner, or could be one. You'll be hard put to find a wild-eyed liberal at a rendezvous. Those people pride themselves on not only their outfits but their self-sufficiency. Granted, true self-sufficiency is hard to come by these days with all our interdependence, but 'skinners come close.

Buckskinning is not a chance to drop all the civilized morals and taboos. It's not a chance to go back to nature and live, for a time, with no regard for others. The modern rendezvous is a recreation of the ''Trappers' Fair'', the annual get-together of the far flung

14

The primitive camp at the National Matches held twice yearly at the National Muzzle Loading Rifle Association properties out of Friendship, Indiana. This is an excellent place for the aspiring buckskinner to receive much help and assistance in his selection of clothing and equipment.

trappers and brigades, to trade, resupply, discuss geography and trapping opportunities and just exchange gossip. That's pretty much what it is today. Traders are there in abundance, to tickle your fancy with various "gee-gaws" and items of practical nature. There is plenty of chance to imbibe in your favorite spirits or not, as the mood strikes you. There is little irresponsible 'hell-raising'. There was at one time, but the rendezvous has become more family oriented and, therefore, more mannerly. Serious 'hell-raising' is dealt with much the same as it is anywhere else. There is fun a-plenty, and sometimes a lot of hootin' & hollerin', but the rights of all people in the camp are considered. The old adage "your right to swing your fist ends one inch from the tip of my nose" is adhered to. You are free to have fun in your own way, as long as it doesn't bother or hassle someone else.

There may be some who think that the rendezvous is just a short jump from a full-fledged 'motorcycle gang' meeting but such is not the case. I'm convinced that the original rendezvous wasn't either. I find it hard to believe that independent men who fought the elements, animals and Indians for eleven months out of the year went to a rendezvous and fought each other. They darn sure cut loose and had a good time but I think they were probably very careful of the rights of others, just as they

expected their own rights to be respected. Most of the wild accounts of such gatherings were written by missionaries and are, therefore, colored with the distaste with which such people viewed any jovial gathering of the time. I spent a lot of time, during my younger growing up days, working at various ranches in the Idaho-Montana country. Bunkhouses were shared with all types of people but they all had one thing in common, a great respect for others' rights. They were courteous almost to a painful degree. When you live in close proximity to men who are often 'short fused' this type of behavior becomes second nature. It was needed to get along during long working days and nights associated with bunkhouse living. I think the old time frontiersmen were cut from the same bolt of cloth as these highly independent, tough ranch hands.

Well, enough of philosophizing . . . let's get on with this buckskinning game.

The first step is, of course, to find out where the rendezvous are going to be held. There are several good magazines and papers that are available to those interested. MUZZLELOADER, MUZZLE BLASTS, BUCKSKIN REPORT, BLACK POWDER TIMES are some that come to mind. MUZZLE BLASTS, the official journal of the National Muzzle Loading Rifle Association, comes with your membership in that or-

15

Everyone has to start some place. Here is a young pilgrim that is on his way to becoming a full fledged buckskinner. Note the fine rifle and shooting bag. This is unusual in that most acquire their clothing prior to getting such a fine rifle.

Catalogs are a good source of ideas. The publications mentioned before will have many advertisements of firms offering catalogs. I'm an avid catalog collector because I can get innumerable ideas from them. Ideas as to dress, camp gear, etc. are easily found in the various suppliers' books.

Well, if you have gotten this far, you're almost ready to get your feet wet and go to an honest-to-bygolly rendezvous. Pick one that is fairly close to home. Write the "Booshway" or Rendezvous Chief and ask what he (or she) would advise. Tell him that you are a first time pilgrim and would like to visit, with an eye to getting into the game. Most of these people will bend over backwards to help the newcomer. As I said at the start of this diatribe, we all started. We were all "greenhorned pilgrims" at one time.

A very good "first" camp is the National Matches in either the spring or fall at Friendship, Indiana. These are put on by the National Muzzle Loading Rifle Ass'n and have both a large modern camp and a 'primitive' camp site. This is one of the few primitive camps where visitors can prowl through the camp with no restrictions on dress. At most other gatherings, even visitors are required to be dressed in period costume within the camp area.

The first time visitor should make some attempt to wear clothing that will blend with the scene. This doesn't have to be elaborate. A pair of tan pants and a brown, loose fitting shirt will suffice for men and women. A long print dress or skirt works pretty well for women, also. Kids can be dressed in similar fashion. Blue jeans and Hawaiian flowered shirts are verboten! Shorts and the like are also out, at most of these gatherings. The aim of any rendezvous or primitive camp is to be able to shoot a picture at any time and have nothing in the picture that would look out of place for the time period of the conclave. With this in mind, it's not hard to see why some types of clothing tend to stand out like the proverbial sore thumb. In short, it doesn't have to be fancy or expensive, but it should look right. Again, writing to the Booshway ahead of time can help you pack what will be accepted and what won't.

ganization and every muzzle loader, buckskinner or rendezvouser should belong. The addresses for these publication and organizations are listed elsewhere in this book. Subscribe to and/or join a few of these and read the literature that comes to your door. It isn't all pertaining to rendezvous activity but it's all interesting to those who have an interest in the front loading guns. In these publications you can find out where get-togethers will be held and who to write to for information as to dress, period, type of camp, etc.

Rendezvous vary a great deal in the authenticity that they require. They'll range from a fairly easy going "most anything goes" type, to the strict, absolutely nothing made after 1840 allowed . . . and about anything in between. The easiest type to fit into for the first time is the more easy going type. You can find out exactly what is required by the published information about the rendezvous, by ads or brochures, or from corresponding with the "booshway" in charge. Even the most "easy going" type of gathering will usually have enough of the "hard core" buckskinners in attendance so that one can see some pretty good, authentic outfits. Most will have a place for the first timers to camp if they come with "tin teepees" (modern camping trailers).

Observe buckskinners as to their dress, equipment and guns. Ask questions. Most will be more than happy to help you learn. This skinner is dressed as an eastern longhunter.

While at your first rendezvous, you'll have time to look over other people's outfits, look at what the traders have for sale or trade, and see what time period interests you most, if you haven't already picked one. The period of the rendezvous gatherings is from roughly the mid-1700's to 1840 when the Western fur trade died out. This covers the active Eastern and Western Fur Trade eras pretty much. The area of the county where you'll be doing most of your activity will, to some extent, dictate the style of dress and the period that you'll get into. The Western camps tend to be 1800 to 1840 while the Eastern gatherings are usually of the earlier period. The area of the country will also be of consideration in the type of shelter that you will want. Tipis are great on the plains but don't work as well in the high humidity and all day horizontal rains of the eastern forests.

Look closely at clothing that the people are wearing. Most are very happy to show you how it's made and give you tips on where to get patterns and supplies. Much of your outfit can be purchased right on the grounds of the camp. But, go slow. Maybe a shirt or part of an outfit, but it is easy to go overboard and get things that you won't need after you learn a little more about the sport. I would advise most people to not buy anything in the way of an outfit at the first camp you attend. Get the addresses of several of the traders and go home, think about it, and then buy some of the outfit/gear by mail after you have had a chance to digest all that you have seen. A camera is of great help in capturing details that you may have missed when you first looked, so by all means, take a camera.

17

Keep one thing firmly in mind, however. The camp, while looking almost like a movie set, is the home of the buckskinners in attendance. Conduct yourself as if you were a guest in someone's home. You are! 'Fer cat's sake, don't lift the door to a lodge and stick your head in. Don't let your kids do it either! Either rap on the poles, or ask "Is anyone home?", or "Ho, the lodge," in a voice loud enough to be heard inside. You will usually be invited in to look around. Most primitive campers take a lot of pride in their outfits and are only too happy to show visitors around. Meal time is not a good time to visit, however, anymore than it is back in the civilized cities. So, use your head and good common

sense. Keep in mind also that some people are more hospitable than others, just the same as they are anywhere else. Here again, checking with the rendezvous chief could be of help.

There are "dog soldiers" at most every gathering. Usually these people are identified by some type of arm band or the like. They serve much the same role as would volunteer police in our modern day life. They are there to help solve problems, advise first timers, answer questions and in general, help wherever they are needed. They also help to enforce the rules of the camp.

If invited into a tipi, step in carefully, always circling to the left. Don't pass between a seated person and the

Here some new buckskinners look over some plunder at a traders lean-to at the N.M.L.R.A. National Matches at Friendship, Indiana. Notice the shirts, dresses and skins. A blanket coat hangs to the right. Most traders will be very helpful in aiding you in the proper selection of clothing and equipment.

fire if there is room to go behind. Don't bumble-foot around and kick over pots and pans or step on the personal effects of the occupants. Very few buckskinners are cannibalistic, but they might make an exception with your child if you let him raise havoc in someone's lodge and tip the dinner into the fire. If you think that you will have any interest in tipis, I would recommend the book, "The Indian Tipi", by the Laubins. It can be purchased from many suppliers and gives a lot of correct tipi etiquette. It is recognized as the "bible" of tipi living.

Basically the same etiquette holds true with wall tents or lean-tos. Don't walk upwind of someone and kick up dust — especially if they are eating! I, myself, have considered several forms of mayhem and torture for those "pork eaters" who have done this to me. By the way, a "pork eater" is a boor, lout, oaf, or unmannerly person, while a "pilgrim" is merely a first timer and is expected to be somewhat ignorant of camp etiquette. Most buckskinners will go out of their way to help a "pilgrim" but will do darn little for a confirmed "pork eater".

Once you have decided upon the time period that you wish to recreate, books are probably your best friend. Read everything that you can find on the subject time period. That will be an impossible task, but it will keep you entertained for a life time! Contemporary journals are a very good source of the every day life of the period. Many of the little things are very hard to find. Mostly they just didn't write down the daily, mundane happenings of life. Museums are another very fine source of help and if you really want to get 'in depth' information, your state historical society can be invaluable. You will have noticed probably, that there are things that are accepted in primitive camps that probably weren't in use during the time period. There is a line to draw between what is accepted and what is authentic. I would advise the new buckskinner to go with what is accepted at first and, as more is learned about the era, then branch out with your own ideas. For instance, lean-tos are very much accepted at present. They are relatively cheap and do a credible job of keeping you and your outfit dry and out of the weather. One of the lean-tos seen a lot is the Whelen style which was in-

The lean-to is a popular shelter for one or two people. It is particularly practical for short camps and hunting camps. Easy to erect and take down, it is a very adaptable shelter.

vented by Col. Townsend Whelen in the 1920's. No, that's not a misprint — 1920's is correct. However, by use, it has been accepted. The wall tent or the inverted "V" type of tent, on the other hand, haven't been much in evidence. They don't have the romance connected with them but they were probably the most common shelter of the trapper and trader when he carried a shelter. You'll see few of them in primitive camps, however. It boils down to what is popular and what isn't. So, go to a camp and look and learn. Go home and read. Get all the catalogs you can lay your hands on and then you can begin to make some 'educated' decisions about what to acquire for your own outfit.

Probably the first step in outfitting yourself will be in the clothing line. This is a logical first step, but again, don't jump off the deep end until you are sure what you want. You can outfit yourself for a relatively small outlay of money to begin with and then add to it as you go along. A cotton shirt will cost $15 to $20 and a pair of buckskin pants in kit form will cost from $85 to $100. Moccasins will vary from $20 to $100 depending on the quality of leather, hand made versus machine made,

The tipi is undoubtably the most comfortable shelter ever devised. Warm in winter, cool in summer, it is ideal for the family in buckskinning. For rendezvous and week long camps it offers ample room and comfort for several people dependent on its size.

More and more wall type tents are being seen in the primitive camps. They are more authentic for the period than the lean-to and afford more room and protection from the elements than the lean-to.

Two typical eastern hunting frocks. The one at right is made from heavy cloth material. The originals were made from linen or other homespun materials. They are very comfortable and allow freedom of movement. The frock pictured to the left is made of buckskin and would certainly offer more warmth in cooler weather. This type coat was generally made in wrap around style and held closed with a wide belt.

amount of beads and beadwork, and etc. Be careful when buying your moccasins. First, you need a heavy enough sole to protect soft, "city" feet but you also want them to look right. Look at Indian designs of the period and locality you are interested in. Beware of most commercial made "tourist" moccasins. They tend to look "hokey" with a good buckskin outfit. Now as for myself, I have two pair . . . one beaded 'Sunday-go-to-meetin' pair and one plain pair for wearing in the mud, dew, dust, etc. My fancy pair are Blackfoot made and fully beaded in a plains style. I bought them for $20.00, more years ago than I care to remember, at the western store in my home town in Idaho. One recent spring at the national shoot at Friendship, Indiana, I was walking in ankle deep water/mud during a rainstorm. As I passed another couple, the woman looked down at my moccasins, poked her husband in the ribs and said, "Look at that fool wading water with a pair of $125.00 moccasins on!" I had never thought too much about it before, but shortly thereafter I bought my plain pair of "mudders".

Sometimes the most acceptable first step into buckskinning is to get the clothing together and camp in the "tin tipi village" with the family to sort of break yourself and the little woman into the primitive way of life. Quite often it is surprising how fast the women get involved in the ways of primitive camping and camp gear. Often the wife and kids will end up more 'into' the primitive living than the "Lord and Master".

While you will see a lot of buckskin clothing around most rendezvous, there will be much cloth in evidence also. The high cost of leather has dictated part of this, as has comfort. For those unaccustomed to wearing it, buckskin will seem hot for most summer temperatures. It's worn more in the evenings during "dress up and go visiting" times. A simple, drop sleeve cotton shirt is very "right". You'll see most of them with a calico type print, although to be absolutely authentic, probably solid colors or at most, 2 color prints, were more commonly used during the era represented. (Calico in the 1800's was in fact what we would call unbleached muslin today.) This style of shirt is easily made by anyone

Typical inexpensive shirt and dress made from calico material. This is Whitey and Shari Wannemacher at their lean-to during the Mid-America Rendezvous.

This buckskinner is dressed as a western mountain man. Note the fine quill work on the strips and rosette which have been added to the shirt.

with a little sewing experience and patterns are available from several sources. Generally pants are buckskin but cloth pants are just as authentic but seem to be less popular. Again, patterns are readily available. The easiest way to go is to take a pair of old pants that fit you well, cut them apart on the seams and use it for a pattern. The other possibility is to use one of the kits that are on the market. But, a word of advice — most of the available kits have lacing included so that the shirt or pants can be laced together. This is an easy way to do the job, granted, but it looks 'pilgrimish' to my way of thinking. I'm sure that there were very few buckskins ever laced together in the era that we are talking about. Maybe, if some "hivernant" got caught and lost all of his gear and had to make do, he might have merely laced something together to cover his hide but, I'm sure that he changed for some well made 'skins when he could. By "well made", I mean stitching them with thread. The best is to hand sew them. This is more accepted and will get you by at the strictest rendezvous but, if you are the impatient sort, the skins can be sewn on most any

A good example of a capote or blanket coat that is very popular with today's buckskinners. These coats are very warm and practical.

home sewing machine. Be sure to use a leather needle rather than a regular lightweight needle for cloth, and go slow and most machines will stitch leather. Having sewn leather by all the methods, I still recommend hand sewing. By gluing the edges with a good leather adhesive and using a hand sewing awl, you can really do the best job.

Leggings and breech cloth are being used more and more and are probably very authentic, as I'm sure they were worn by those who had Indian wives and lived "Indian". Believe it or not, corduroy was available during the fur trade era and I'm sure was probably worn a lot by trappers. I've never seen it at a rendezvous however, and I'm sure it would create a lot of stir if it was worn. Whoever was wearing it should probably be pretty well armed with evidence to support its use by trappers.

The "rifleman's coat" or hunting jacket is popular as a coat, at least in the eastern gatherings. It is accepted at western rendezvous also, but not as common. The pattern for this style is available from several suppliers. This is the wrap-around, loose fitting smock style jacket with a large, cape-type collar that was worn by many during the Revolutionary War period. It was popular well into the 1800's. The colors are generally brown, off-white or sage green, with brown and off-white being the most popular. They are fairly easy to construct, the toughest part being the finding of a suitable coarse type of cloth that will resemble hand woven linsey-woolsey, which was a cloth made of wool, woven on a linen warp. The same style coat can also be made using buckskin and it looks good.

Head gear runs the gamut from the kitted voyageur type stocking cap through the flat-crowned, wide brimmed felt hats, including all sorts of fur caps. Beaver fur hats and caps (muskrat, fox, skunk and, of course, coon) are all seen and one is about as "right" as another. Some merely wear a bandanna headband, while a goodly number just go bareheaded. To start out with, bare-headed is the cheapest. Again, don't jump in and spend a lot of money for headgear until you know what you want. If you decide to go the route of the western trapper, then the wide brimmed, flat-crown beaver felt hat is vogue, however it will look odd with an eastern "boshloper" outfit.

Capotes are very popular and practical. This is a mid-calf length coat made from Hudson Bay blankets. They are very "correct" as are those made of the Witney blankets. They were used in both the east and west so are interchangeable for most any era. They are 100% wool blankets and are very warm on cool nights found frequently in rendezvous camps. Blankets other than 100% wool can be used but the man-made fibers are not usually as warm as wool, but the price is generally less. Patterns are also available for capotes.

One of the major sources for outfit ideas are from paintings done by the early artists. Remember however, that a painting, at least later ones, weren't done from life and often represent someone's idea of what was worn during that time. It may or may not be right, so a person has to be careful. Bodmer, Catlin and the other contemporary painters were there and their work probably reflects what was worn at the time. Russell

Four types of headgear worn by buckskinners. Clockwise beginning below: Balmoral Bonnet, Voyageur or Liberty Cap, Fur Hat and Bridger Hat.

Jim Bridger, one of the most famous of the mountain men, is pictured here in later life. Bridger was one of the truly great pathfinders in our early west.

knew many of the old mountain men and, I think, his work is pretty authentic. Remington tended to romanticize a lot so his work must be weighed against what we know. He also painted from life after the fur trade era was long over and the mountain men, Indians, trappers and the like had changed considerably. Many of the modern painters are doing mountain men and trapper-trader subjects. Most of these painters are researchers and are striving for authenticity. However, many of their scenes come from modern rendezvous so mistakes in history tend to be picked up and perpetuated. So, don't take everything you see as "gospel"!

Beards are the subject of a lot of controversy. You'll see many around the camps. The truth of the matter is this — the early French traders probably wore beards in the east. It was popular at this time and fashionable. The eastern Indians were not as prejudiced against beards as the western tribes. However, at the time of the western fur trade era, beards were not in fashion in the civilized areas of the country and the western Indians did not like beards. One of the strongest insults in the Blackfoot language is "Dog Face" meaning hairy face like a dog and therefore, an S.O.B. If you were trying to live amongst the Indians in the west and get along with them, you were clean shaven. Also, you came from a culture where the beard wasn't popular. For these reasons, I'm sure most of the mountain men were clean shaven. We have many accounts in journals and diaries of shaving soap being used. Remember, the mountain man of the 1806 to 1840 era had a pack string with him and he carried many more "luxuries" than did his eastern fore-runner. The west was too big to take off

with only a horn of powder and a little salt and make it. A man that lost his horses and outfit was in deep trouble indeed.

Beadwork and quillwork are both something that you can add as you go along. It's not something that is purchased right away. Good beadwork is expensive, as is quill work. If you do it yourself, as many do, it takes a lot of time and you'll want to be sure what you're getting into before spending the time and the money involved. As an aside, the small seed beads didn't come into use until the 1870's which was well after the fur trade era. The beads that were traded to the Indians during the times we're talking about were of the "pony bead" size — almost twice as large as the seed bead. While the pony bead doesn't make as fine a design, it is more authentic and also easier to work. Most modern Indian beadwork, and for that matter, most rendezvous beadwork is of the seed bead variety. Again, use has made it accepted, although not "right".

Remember, when getting geared up to go to your first rendezvous, that the "hillbilly-hippy" look is not what you are trying to portray. Merely looking dirty and seedy isn't what buckskinning is. The things worn all have a reason because what you are trying to do is recreate the look of another time. The biggest and most common mistake made by the beginning buckskinner is to try to look very trail worn. By and large, the clothes worn to the original rendezvous were the "Sunday-go-to-meetin' " clothes that they had. The fancy, beaded buckskins and the like were kept for special occasions and weren't worn every day. So, you don't have to be dirty and patched to fit in.

25

Your camp outfit, when you get to it, will contain a lot of cast iron gear. A cast iron pot, skillet and dutch oven are basic necessities. That is, if you intend to cook as they did then. Plates and cups were of the tin variety. You'll see a lot of granite-ware around and it is more practical and looks OK, however, granite-ware didn't come in until the 1870's. You'll also want a set of iron utensils for your fire. You can get along quite nicely using rocks to set kettles and skillets on, but an iron grate and a set of forged stakes with cross piece to hang pots on makes the chore much easier. An ice chest is a necessity. There weren't too many plastic coolers at the original rendezvous, I'm sure, but jerky and fresh meat to shoot are in short supply in most camps, so we must have some way to keep meat and perishables cold. It is a good idea to make a rough board chest to contain your ice chest, although if a blanket or buffalo skin is thrown over it so it doesn't show, that will pass "inspection", and that's all that's required. Pour your beer or soda pop into a tin cup and don't carry the can around. And, take off your wrist watch. All of these things take away from the "look". Nothing looks worse than a picture of a rendezvous with all the lean-tos and tipis and right in the middle is a feller in full buckskins sitting on a plastic cooler with a can of refreshment in his hand! Modern day items really take away from the "mood" that is intended to be set.

An ice cooler is hidden in this rough wooden chest. This certainly helps to keep the primitive look to a camp.

A good camp fire set up. Fire irons and iron ware can usually be purchased from one of the blacksmiths in attendance at rendezvous.

Just a little bead work can spruce up an outfit as illustrated by this beaded belt bag.

You can sometimes pick up a lot of cooking gear by checking around second hand stores. Old skillets and pots can be picked up at a reasonable price often times. A set of starter camp gear can be collected for under $100 if you poke around a little. Most people have some cooking pots that will suffice right in their kitchen. One spin off that I've noticed is that many modern housewives get started cooking with cast iron skillets and the like at primitive camps and find that they are a very good cooking utensil and windup cooking in them at home. The reason that cast iron cook ware went out of use is that detergents came in! The detergents cut the grease out of the pores of cast iron allowing rust, which results in a metallic taste to whatever is cooked in it. If you use soap only, and be sparing with it, you'll find that nothing will cook as well as cast iron. You just can't fry chicken and other meats any better than in cast iron.

What kind of rifle should you take? Well, it's nice if you have a fine Kentucky or a custom made Hawken but there are several guns on the market as reproductions that will fit in nicely and are priced fairly reasonably. Connecticut Valley Arms produces several. Their Mountain rifle and Frontier rifle are both good. The Western Arms Co. Hawken, the Lyman Products Company Great Plains rifle, Browning's Mountain rifle, to mention a few, are all good firearms. Others worth mentioning are Hatfield's Squirrel rifle, Navy Arms Co. Hawken rifle, Dixie Gun Works' Southern rifle & Ozark Mountain Arms' Hawken rifle. These all are priced in the $200 to $500 price range which is the average price range as muzzle loading firearms go. You

A group of well dressed buckskinners as seen here on the set at the filming of "The Mountain Men".

don't have to have a rifle to enjoy your first rendezvous, however. Shooting is very informal at most camps, usually consisting of blanket shoots. In this form of match a blanket is laid out, the target is agreed upon, and each shooter puts a prize on the blanket as his entry fee. These prizes are usually handmade items with a probable value of $5 to $10. First place gets first pick of a prize from the blanket and so on until even last place gets something. It's kind of a fun way to add a new item to your outfit.

In summary — get yourself a very simple set of clothing so you won't stand out like a sore thumb, then go to a rendezvous. Look and listen. Talk to the participants and ask their advice. Look at various forms of shelters and camp gear. See how different people cook and do the many camp chores. Check over the many types of clothing and costumes that you'll see. Then, and only then, give some thought to buying or making your own outfit. Pick an era or type of character you want to recreate and then do a lot of reading and research. You'll never complete an outfit. You'll always be trading, discarding and adding to your entire outfit. It seems to be a never ending process. Something that you have been satisfied with for a long time will become obsolete in light of new information that you'll discover. That's what keeps it fun and interesting. It's like muzzle loading in general — there is no end to the tinkering, building, upgrading, improving and learning that you can do.

Come on in, pilgrim, the water's fine!

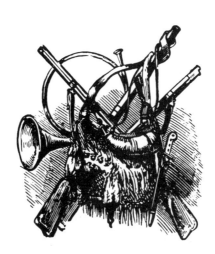

Rendezvous & Shoots

by Mike Nesbitt

MIKE NESBITT HAS BEEN shooting black powder since the late 50's and he has always had a very strong interest in the history of the fur trade. That interest naturally extended into buckskinning and Mike is a member of the Cascade Mountain Men, the National Association of Primitive Riflemen, and the National Muzzle Loading Rifle Association. His articles on black powder shooting appear in several publications and now he is also the Black Powder Editor of *GUNS* Magazine. Mike lives in Vancouver, Washington and is employed by the Washington State Department of Transportation.

HISTORIANS WILL TELL YOU that the first rendezvous took place in 1825 and it was held on or near Henry's Fork located in Southwestern Wyoming. With it was born a trend that would remain the hey-day of the mountains for the next decade and a half. The object of the rendezvous, for the businessmen, was fur, beaver fur specifically. For the trappers it was something else again. At the rendezvous the trappers took the lid off of the anxieties that had been building up inside of them like a pressure cooker for a full year and they had so much fun that every now and then a couple of them wouldn't survive it. The sky was the limit, fortunes that took a year to earn were sometimes spent in a day. Beaver was the standard of currency and the trader's prices were high, an exaggerated result of "shipping and handling". The rendezvous were real, very real, and in their way they helped set the course of history. When the trends of fashion changed, the value of beaver dropped until the fur trade was virtually dead and the rendezvous also died.

But they only died if you elect to observe the strict definition of the Western Fur Trade Rendezvous. Likewise, there were actually several gatherings prior to the Western fur trade. These, however, were not fur trade rendezvous. Furs were probably traded, since they were a recognized standard for barter, but the main factor that drew people to these earlier gatherings was guns. That's the same thing that draws us together today at our own gatherings so even though our camps might be modeled after the mountain men's, our rendezvous are in many ways more like the very early shooting matches.

Just how early these shooting matches began is really hard to tell. We could speculate that they were, in a way, a carry-over from the archery meets of an earlier era. They really got underway in this country before our independence and in "*The Kentucky Rifle*" by Captain Dillion, there is a pretty vivid description of one of these shoots complete with a reproduction of a printed announcement which is dated 1727.

The printed announcement is pretty interesting itself. It urges all who might read it to spread the word and it was distributed enough in advance that shooters would have time to travel considerable distances to attend the match. It also indicated that the prize for the first day of shooting was an ox and for the second day a new snap-haunce gun would be awarded. There were to be several lesser awards as well, which would include traps, skins, robes, and knives. Entry fees for the more important matches were two shillings per shot, closest shot to center would win, and the matches shot for the lesser prizes had reduced entries. The way the entries were regulated was that each shooter simply bought his target. Wooden slabs served as targets with an "X" scribed on the side with charcoal. Distance for the shooting was specified as fifteen rods for offhand shooting.

It also gave information that visiting riflemen could be boarded at a nearby place at a rate of one shilling per day and that horses could be kept at the livery for a half a shilling per day. A shilling is equal to about 16⅔ cents and those sounded like pretty good prices. Another thing the announcement printed out was the lead, powder, and flints would be for sale and bear and wolf traps as well.

That announcement didn't sound too much different than the invitations we see today for rendezvous and matches. The dates are obviously as different as the

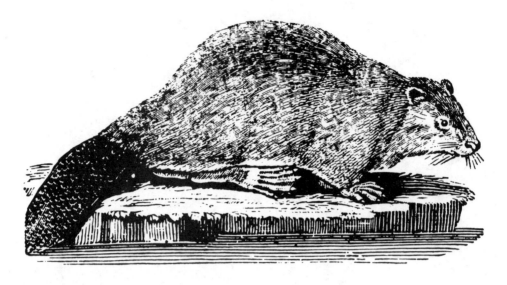

The beaver was largely responsible for the exploration
of America by white hunters and trappers.

prices, but almost everything else is the same. It told who the sponsor was, where the doin's would take place, and it gave a rundown on the events. How about the horses and the livery? Well, we have the same thing for the trend of the times because some of the match or rendezvous announcements of today brag that they will have "adequate parking" available.

At today's rendezvous there are many things traded for and dealers and traders will come from far and wide to display the items they have on their trade blankets. From the trading point of view the rendezvous of today

This ad which appeared in 1822 in the St. Louis
MISSOURI GAZETT attracted such men as Jim
Bridger and Jedediah Smith both of whom,
became famous mountain men.

are quite a bit like the rendezvous of the Western fur trade because the time spent in camp can turn into a big beautiful shopping spree. There is no better place to find the equipment and accessories needed and used by the buckskinner than at a rendezvous. Several individuals hand-craft items which they will trade for other things that they want and, of course, cash is always acceptable either for full payment or when a trade needs a little "boot" before both parties are pleased.

This is probably a good time to point out that there is more than one kind of rendezvous and what a rendezvous really is. When I compared our present day rendezvous with the shooting matches of over two centuries ago, it was only to point out the common ground that draws us together, and that is the muzzleloading guns that we use. At a rendezvous there usually are no scheduled shooting matches. Where matches are scheduled the function should properly be called a "shoot" and the matches that do take place at the rendezvous are generally done on a very informal basis. There is also more than one kind of rendezvous. Several clubs have one or more rendezvous per year and on top of that, a club or just an individual might organize a "primitive" rendezvous where dress and equipment is much more regulated to a particular period of time.

Within a year after I got a muzzleloading rifle of my own I joined the Cascade Mountain Men. Several of my friends were already members and a couple of them gave me some advice that I'll pass on to others who are considering joining a muzzleloading club. That advice is, if you are going to participate in the club's activities, by all means participate. Be active within the club. Setting up a shoot or rendezvous requires some helping hands and all too often these details are left to a minor few.

On the weekend prior to the first rendezvous I ever attended, there was a work party to prepare the grounds. Since I was a member of the sponsoring club I went to the work party and that was honestly just as much fun as the rendezvous. There was a lot of work to be done, clearing some brush, digging holes for the outhouses, and designating areas for camps and parking. That only took about two hours and the rest of the day was spent shooting on the camp's range area. Working with your fellow club members is probably the best way to get introduced.

A week later I found myself at my first rendezvous and since I had attended other club functions, including the work party, I wasn't a complete stranger to the rest of the folks. This was the Cascade Mountain Men's spring rendezvous and it is not a primitive rendezvous. At that time I didn't have a set of 'skins and only a few that were there wore them. My gear was actually pretty skimpy. A couple of experienced buckskinners took me under their wing and that night I made my bed in a tepee for the first time and the bug hit me immediately. Being able to see the things these buckskinners did, and the way they did them, impressed me to the point that I knew I would join their ranks rather quickly.

There was only one shooting match at that rendezvous. The weather had turned sour and the match was held during a lull in the rain. It was a primitive type of match but a primitive costume was not required. The target was a metal triangle which represented a turkey head and it was mounted on a hinge. The turkey head would flop over each time it was hit and it could be pulled back to an upright position with a string that was attached. Shooters fired at the target one at a time on the "miss and out" basis. Each time the line of shooters went through a relay, those who had hit the target stepped back a couple of paces and did it all over again. Every time, the number of "hitters" was reduced quite a bit.

One reason that I remember this match so well might be because this was my first match at a rendezvous. Another reason could be because I was the winner. That old Green River Rifle Works Hawken I was using still performs well and every .54 caliber ball I fired at the turkey head was a hit. Since then, I haven't always been so lucky.

At that same rendezvous I met some people who have remained my closest friends and one of them is a 'skinner who I have camped and hunted with many times since then. This is "No-Feather" Walker. Of all my very good friends among the buckskinners, it was "No-Feather" who taught me the most, mainly by example, about buckskinning and the primitive ways. When you're learning it's a big help to have a friend like that and one of the first things I learned was one of etiquette, namely not to light my pipe with a match while a guest in "No-Feather's" lodge.

A rendezvous, or a shoot, like the one I've just described, should be considered essential for a beginner because it allows the newcomer to see what is going on and what buckskinning is all about. This includes everything from the authenticity of the rifles to the authen-

NOTICE

SECOND ANNUAL

Tennessee Longhunters Muzzleloading Rifle Frolic

Saturday & Sunday May 6 & 7, 1978

AT CHARLIE HAFFNER'S OWL HOLLOW RANGE 8 MILES SOUTH OF FRANKLIN, TENN. ON HIGHWAY 431. LOOK FOR SIGNS.

MEDALS & MERCHANDISE AWARDS
23 MATCHES • 5 AGGREGATES

FLINTLOCK, PERCUSSION, MUSKET, PISTOL, LADIES & JUNIOR MATCHES

- NOVELTY SHOOTS *INCLUDING RENOWNED MOVING DEER TARGET*
- BRING YOUR TRADE GOODS
- PRIMITIVE CAMPING AVAILABLE. BRING YOUR OWN WATER

This is an example of a modern day muzzle loading club's rifle frolic announcement. Note that to some degree it carries the same flavor as the 1727 announcement as described on page 30.

An early morning mist rises in the valley of South Sylamore Creek, site of the Mid-America Rendezvous. This rendezvous was sponsored by MUZZLELOADER Magazine and was near Mountain View, Arkansas. Note some of the lodges are painted while others are not. Those that are so decorated have special meaning to their owners.

ticity of the dress. Authenticity is the key word with almost everything and it's also a frame of mind that must be developed to really appreciate it. Many times a newcomer, or greenhorn, will want to become a buckskinner and try to copy the dress with non-authentic materials. Such people are usually disappointed because the buckskinners don't feel they are being met on common ground. Things like plastic bear claws are looked upon in the same light as rubber tomahawks.

These informal rendezvous are a good place to start for other reasons. No one can be expected to be fully equipped on his first time out and luxuries such as flashlight or a gas camp stove won't be looked down on. If the beginner is going to become a primitive buckskinner, the gas stove will soon be left at home and fire irons will take their place for cooking over an open fire. The flashlight will be replaced with a candle lantern. Other pieces of authentic gear will work its way into the primitive plunder and nobody can expect this to happen overnight.

Most all rendezvous have various "areas". There is usually a primitive area for the tepees and lean-tos and sometimes the camp rules state that campers in the primitive area must have primitive dress. This does not mean that new-comers cannot visit the primitive camp. Tents, trailers, and campers are usually located in another area but still part of the main camp. This is referred to as the "tin tepee camp" and there are no restrictions for dress unless specified by the rendezvous sponsor.

Areas like these are important because any large rendezvous will have a wide spectrum of people in attendance. This also allows a buckskinner to include the rest of the family when the primitive bug has not yet bitten the other family members. The primitive areas are naturally very popular because several buckskinners spend their time in the camping area doing beadwork and displaying the many skills involved in this type of recreation. Visitors are very welcome but they should bear in mind that several people will drop by the primitive area to take photographs and a person in modern dress can spoil the effect of those pictures.

In all areas of the rendezvous, safety should always be observed. Every now and then a visitor will arrive in camp without the realization that the things to be seen are real and not a setting to show what things used to look like. The firearms are just as real as they were in 1835 and there is no reason to have a loaded gun in camp. The axes, knives, and tomahawks are just as real and they are usually well sharpened. An area for throwing these knives and 'hawks will be carefully set and that is the only place where the edged tools should be thrown. At other times they should be stored when not in use and handled with the respect they deserve at all times. There is nothing more real in camp than the campfire and this must be treated with a great deal of respect as well. It's a little surprising but some of the newcomers to our camps have very little experience around an open fire. None of the things mentioned here are particularly dangerous but they are the types of

The camp chief (Booshway) presides over the camp. In this camp meeting he may be explaining the camp rules. Rules are important for a safe and happy camp.

things that demand respect.

Within a month after my first rendezvous, I went to another one that was sponsored by another club and the rendezvous site was in the Cascade Mountains near Wenatchee in Washington State. This was the trip where I had to let myself be singled out for not remembering anything to sleep in, no bedroll or blankets. Ed Grems, my partner on that one, happened to look in the back of the pick-up after we were about 100 miles away from home and brought the fact to my attention by asking, "Hey, what are you going to sleep in?" This experience taught me more about the great deal of fellowship that is in the atmosphere at rendezvous. In no time at all, I was invited to share space in a tepee and an extra sleeping bag was made available for me.

This rendezvous did have some scheduled shooting events and Ed and I both had some prizes when we made the return trip two nights later. Ed took first place in a 100 yard offhand match and I was lucky enough to place first in a ricochet match. The object of that was to shoot at a piece of boiler plate and break a clay target that was a couple of feet away. I got lucky, like I said, but I had watched several shooters before me fire and miss and that gave me a fair idea on where to hit the boiler plate. Just like the turkey head, this was a "miss and out" match.

That rendezvous was also my introduction to team shoots and I was able to enter two of them and in one case, I was on the winning team. The first team match required a team of two shooters and the targets were

Primitive living in a buckskinners camp is a relaxing way to spend a week. You can tell from this picture that this man and his son are making memories.

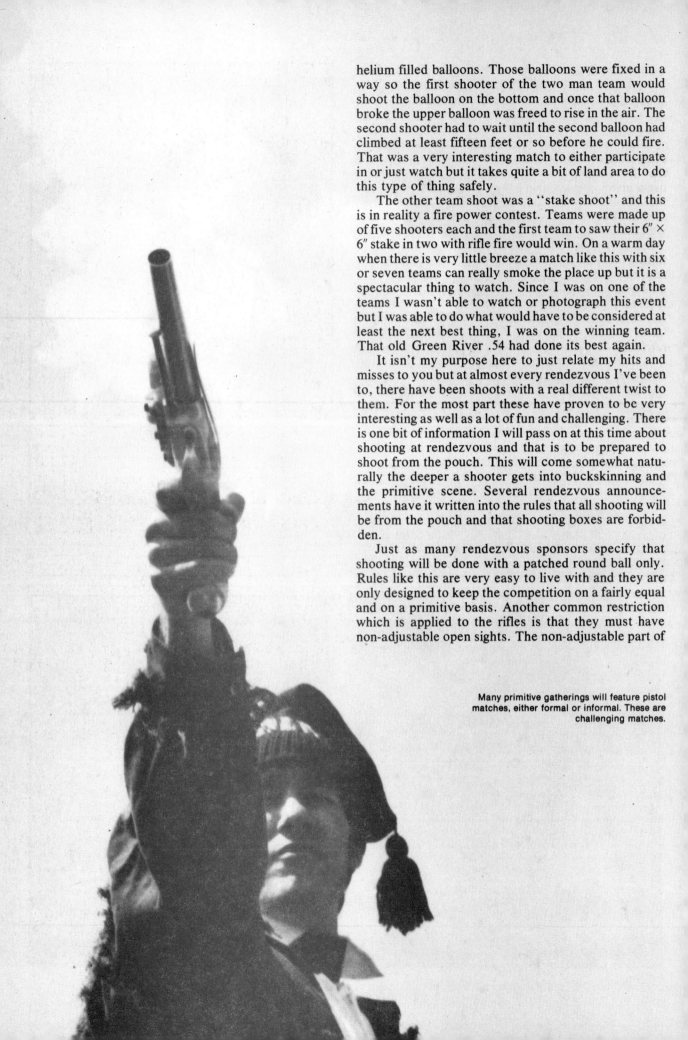

helium filled balloons. Those balloons were fixed in a way so the first shooter of the two man team would shoot the balloon on the bottom and once that balloon broke the upper balloon was freed to rise in the air. The second shooter had to wait until the second balloon had climbed at least fifteen feet or so before he could fire. That was a very interesting match to either participate in or just watch but it takes quite a bit of land area to do this type of thing safely.

The other team shoot was a "stake shoot" and this is in reality a fire power contest. Teams were made up of five shooters each and the first team to saw their 6″ × 6″ stake in two with rifle fire would win. On a warm day when there is very little breeze a match like this with six or seven teams can really smoke the place up but it is a spectacular thing to watch. Since I was on one of the teams I wasn't able to watch or photograph this event but I was able to do what would have to be considered at least the next best thing, I was on the winning team. That old Green River .54 had done its best again.

It isn't my purpose here to just relate my hits and misses to you but at almost every rendezvous I've been to, there have been shoots with a real different twist to them. For the most part these have proven to be very interesting as well as a lot of fun and challenging. There is one bit of information I will pass on at this time about shooting at rendezvous and that is to be prepared to shoot from the pouch. This will come somewhat naturally the deeper a shooter gets into buckskinning and the primitive scene. Several rendezvous announcements have it written into the rules that all shooting will be from the pouch and that shooting boxes are forbidden.

Just as many rendezvous sponsors specify that shooting will be done with a patched round ball only. Rules like this are very easy to live with and they are only designed to keep the competition on a fairly equal and on a primitive basis. Another common restriction which is applied to the rifles is that they must have non-adjustable open sights. The non-adjustable part of

Many primitive gatherings will feature pistol matches, either formal or informal. These are challenging matches.

that is quite often relaxed but the open sight rule is fairly standard. At any rate, a 'skinner who shoots round ball ammunition in a rifle with non-adjustable open sights will find his equipment acceptable for almost any rifle match.

Many of the matches at rendezvous are shot with a combination of guns. There are numerous versions of the "Seneca Run" where each shooter might need to use a pistol, tomahawk, and a knife in addition to his rifle. Even though no two Seneca Runs are the same, they are usually run against the clock and the shooter with the fastest time through the course is the winner. When time is the only factor, it usually means that all targets must be hit. If a target is missed the shooter is required to remain at that station and keep shooting until a hit has been made. In other cases a time penalty is set for missed shots. Just like the shots made with the rifle, a tomahawk or knife throw doesn't count unless it sticks and time can really add up when you have to retrieve your 'hawk or knife just to throw it again.

One of the most interesting twists of the Seneca Run I've ever seen was at the Spring rendezvous of the Spokane Falls Muzzleloaders and the thing that made this so special was that it was run in canoes. Equipment needed by each shooter was a rifle, with horn and pouch, and a pistol. With this he would sit in the bow of a canoe while another skinner paddled the canoe through the course. The creek that this was done in is notorious for having muddy water so only one rifle shot was fired from the canoe. Since reloading a rifle can be very awkward in a confined space, the possibility of dropping a rifle into the creek seemed high enough to warrant loading the long guns only while both feet were on solid ground. This meant that only one shot would be fired from the boat with the rifle and that shot was the first one of the course.

Three or four shots were to be fired with a handgun and percussion revolvers were used for the most part. I had a .50 caliber single shot which I decided not to use and borrowed a .36 caliber Navy Model when I took my

Tomahawk throwing contests are a part of most primitive gatherings. Here a skinner is throwing his hawk to make it stick handle up in the block.

38

trip down the stream. The rifle I used was my favorite .40 caliber Beaver Lodge Rifle built by Ted Fellowes and it did very well even though the two rifle shots were both at rather long range.

Like I said, this was one case when the shooter didn't have to paddle his own canoe. I might have been better off if I did, though, because the 'skinner who ran me through the course was my old pal, Blasphemous Bill Falk. Bill had a peculiar glint in his eye as he began to paddle the canoe down the creek. When we got to where the first target was visible I found out why. The target was a cardboard "Indian" about 110 yards up the hill and Bill turned the canoe so there was no way I could comfortably aim my rifle at it. In order to overcome this, I used my .40 left-handed and that fooled ol' Bill. After the shot, which was a hit, he just sat in the back of the canoe like his ears weren't even ringing.

On down the stream there were three or four closer targets for the pistols. These were cardboard faces of either Indians or river pirates. The rules said the shoot-

er was to fire at these as soon as he saw them and by shooting too quickly, I missed one.

After the pistol part of the course, the canoe was beached where the shooter got out and reloaded the rifle for one more long range shot at an old circular saw blade. That target was also well beyond 100 yards and the ringing noise made by the striking ball was a very rewarding sound.

Shortly after I finished the course, it was my turn to take Bill through it. Did I get even, you ask? You bet! Quite a while ago, I had put a hex on Bill's rifle so that it just would not fire whenever I was near. That never worked any better than at that moment. Bill finally gave up trying to get his .50 caliber Hawken to shoot and took a shot at the first target with his pistol. He over compensated for the distance, though, and aimed too high which resulted in a miss. This all happened a couple of years ago, and at this time I don't remember if he even shot the last target which was also a rifle shot.

Once all those who wanted to enter the match had been able to go through the course, it was determined that no one had been able to hit all the targets but there were eight shooters all tied with one miss each. This meant a shoot-off would be in order and the sponsor of the match posted a single target where each shooter was to get one shot and the closest to center would be the winner. The shooters were backed up to about seventy yards and these shots were taken offhand.

A buckskinner primes the pan in preparation for firing. Primitive style rifle matches are both fun and challenging.

39

A buckskinner on the Seneca Run
course. This match is a part of many
primitive shoots and is very
challenging to the contestants.

Dave Cooper took the first shot. The judge stepped up to the target to mark the hole and he called out that Dave's shot had scored a 10-X. My shot was the second one. Again the judge stepped forward to mark the target. This time he looked at the target for several moments and then called two more men over to look at the target. Then they walked around to look at the back of the target and a little while later returned to the front side to look at it some more. Finally satisfied, the judge marked the shot and called out, "10-X" again. My .40 caliber ball had just barely brushed the side of the hole made by Dave's .50 caliber ball. I was lucky to hit so close to center but if I'd been any luckier the shot would have been judged a miss. As things turned out, Dave won first place, I got second, and Bob Banta, from Idaho, took the third place prize.

Shooting matches are not the only thing that hap-pens at a rendezvous but they can be very spectacular and it takes very little to get the folks out shooting. Usually the prizes are items that were handmade by the sponsor. In the match I just described, the three prizes were a possibles bag, a liberty cap, and a Green River Knife. The first place winner, Dave Cooper, selected the prize he wanted from those three items. As the second place winner, I picked the knife which I made a sheath for and I still carry it as my belt knife. The third place winner gets what's left, if you want to put it that way, but the prize is still very much worth having.

Sometimes a match is called where there aren't any real prizes at all and that certainly doesn't stop anyone from joining in on the shooting. One such match was a spur of the moment thing a couple of years ago at a winter rendezvous. Pappy Mancke found a broken and worthless pocket watch in his possibles and hung it from a tree limb. Then he called for the shooters and there was quite a number of both guys and gals standing out in the snow just waiting for their turn to shoot at that watch. Pappy explained the "rules" just before the shooting started. Each shooter got one chance and whoever was the first to hit the watch also won it.

There are some rendezvous that don't need any organization and maybe they shouldn't really be called a rendezvous but they amount to nearly the same thing. A primitive hunting season is a good example of this. In Washington State, the muzzleloading season for deer comes after the regular hunting season and several members of many clubs gather at one or more main camps. Just walking into one of these camps can bring a sight really worth seeing. The tepees are covered with snow to a line even with the top of the liner on the inside. Above the liner the tepee is not insulated and the snow melts just like on the surface of a heated tent. In the camp area people are busy cutting wood and doing camp chores and the smoke coming out of the tepee's smoke flaps lets you know that it is cozy and warm inside. There are few sights more inviting than a warm tepee on a cold, snowy day.

A winter hunting camp is quite common among buckskinners. At left two hunters preparing to leave for the day's hunt. Below, one lucky hunter has made meat by downing a fine buck.

Just like a rendezvous, these hunting camps are by no means for men only. Many families take part even when the wife does not actually hunt. Far more father and son teams take part and there are many things to do in camp in addition to the things that must be done. One of the best things to do is just visit with other buckskinners but camping in the winter can open up several new ways to do things, even if it only amounts to how to keep your feet warm.

Sometimes our hunts fall over the Thanksgiving holidays and that Thanksgiving feast in camp is a real highlight. With enough contributing members that can turn into a potluck that is something grand. If the camp has been a lucky one, some fresh game will be on the menu and since it is a hunting camp that is really the object of the whole thing. Seeing fresh game in the camp adds a great deal of realism since the rendezvous of old always had hunters to provide meat and this is something that usually can't be done at a spring or summer rendezvous.

To break the monotony of tramping the frozen ground when game is scarce, the hunters will often turn to other doin's rather than just giving up and going home. A rifle's ramrod can quickly become a fishing pole and a very good breakfast can be caught by jigging through the ice on the lake that is next to the camp. That can take more patience than hunting and after a while, a warm lodge is even more inviting.

The very best part of a winter camp during a hunt is still the victory dinner of fresh deer liver cooked over the tepee fire. Somehow that does taste best when it's your deer but it sure doesn't ruin the meal just because the meat might have been brought in by another hunter. That is just as true when the evening's fare is small game too. The times like this that I've been able to attend have been the best part of buckskinning and the fellowship among the hunters seems to be the greatest of all.

In the summer, there can also be some hunts and in a lot of ways these can be better than the big game hunts in the fall. The weather, of course, is better with mild temperatures during the night and primitive camping is naturally more comfortable. During the day your feet don't get cold and those moccasins are all you need on them, if that. In addition to those things, the game being hunted usually offers more shots and lots of fast action.

Many times in the past, No-Feather Walker and I have met in the rabbit woods for some fine primitive hunting with our small bore rifles. As often as not, No-Feather is accompanied by his wife, Betty, and his daughter, Trish, who is becoming a topnotch rabbit hunter. Trish has a .40 caliber Bedford County style rifle that her dad built and before she got that rifle she used a .32 caliber original percussion. There's no reason these hunts can't include the whole family just like any rendezvous.

No-Feather and I like to get a little competitive on our rabbit hunts, either to see who can get the most rabbits, (I've never beaten him), or to see who can make the best blunder, (we're tied). In the area where we hunt, there is a particular trail that makes a good circuit to follow. Leave the camp and the trail will lead you through some good hunting and then lead you right

Trish Walker returns to camp with a nice big rabbit bagged with her .40 caliber Bedford.

"No Feather" Walker with his favorite small game rifle, a .40 caliber flintlock.

back to camp without covering any of the area twice. No-Feather went out on that trail once and I heard him fire four times but he only came back with three rabbits. I decided to follow the same trail to get the rabbit he missed and, in a way, I did just that.

Soon after starting out, I saw a rabbit within range and my shot was good enough to collect it. I reloaded and continued along the circuit. My next sighting was one of the gray rabbits sitting on a grassy mound right out in the open. This was almost too good to be true and I took the shot. The rabbit didn't move, fall down, or show any sign of being hit or even shot at. I stepped a little closer and it didn't look like a rabbit anymore. On close examination it proved to be a gray granite stone and right next to the lead smear where my bullet had hit it was the smear where No-Feather's ball had hit. That night we had a good time laughing at each other.

On another hunt in the same area Betty was carrying No-Feather's smoothbore trade gun while he toted his .40 caliber flinter. She was really just carrying the trade gun in case he needed a second shot. He never needed it. We arrived back in camp about the same time and decided that No-Feather and I would hunt an open field together with trade guns, so I grabbed mine and loaded it with a one ounce dose of number five's.

We were paralleling each other when a rabbit flushed from cover and went my way. The trade gun was to my shoulder in a snap but even though I got spark, the flinter didn't fire. Before the rabbit got out of range, I had the hammer back, ready for a second try. At that pull of the trigger my only reward was a real dull thud as the hammer fell. I had forgotten to close the frizzen and No-Feather had the heartiest laugh I've ever heard.

The day wasn't over yet, though, and in a minute or two another rabbit tore out of the grass and headed his way. With all the ease of the experienced hunter that he is, No-Feather raised his trade gun and sighted just ahead of the running rabbit. All he got was a flash in the pan. That can happen to any flintlock shooter. No-Feather re-primed the piece and made sure the touch hole was clear and we went on our way. The next rabbit went his way too and this resulted in another flash in the pan. Now he took a closer look at his gun and it was soon determined that he had never loaded it. Did I laugh at him for that? You bet!

Maybe I shouldn't fill this chapter up with hunting tales but that's the very place that a lot of rendezvous campfire stories get started. Besides that, these all take place at a type of rendezvous and if I'm trying to express what goes on, I certainly should include them. With that in mind, I'll tell you one more.

This also involves No-Feather and it took place in the snow near the deer hunting camp at Lyman Lake. No-Feather, an excellent deer hunter with scores for the last thirteen or fourteen years, was on the track of a whitetail buck and he had followed it for at least a couple of hours. As the buck meandered through the pines, it came a little too close to Crazy Lindsey, another hunter whose tepee was set up right next to No-Feather's in the same camp. Crazy dropped the buck with one shot from his .50 caliber flinter and had the deer gutted out before heading for camp to get help dragging it out. No-Feather, still on the trail, came across the dead and gutted deer, read the story that was in the snow, and went another direction to hunt somewhere else.

Not very much later No-Feather came back into camp just as Crazy was coming in with the deer and No-Feather recognized it right away. This resulted in a friendly verbal match on who was the better mountain man. No-Feather was a good tracker, that was sure true, but as Crazy was quick to point out, it was he who had made meat and brought it into camp. No-Feather agreed but added that a real mountain man always enjoyed a good meal of raw liver after a kill. With that, Crazy picked up a piece of the liver and took a good wholesome bite without even brushing off some of the loose deer hairs that had fallen on it. That settled the question, if a question existed, and it's just one of the things that earned Crazy his name.

Rendezvous do come in all sizes, all times of the year, and in all parts of the country. If I had to be pinned down and say what I think the best rendezvous are, I would have to admit that I like the primitive ones the best. Primitive rendezvous, just like rendezvous in general, can take place any time of year and the only real stipulation is that those in attendance will not have any equipment that wasn't in use during a certain time period, usually 1850 or before. This will, in a way, eliminate newcomers because it can take about two years for a new buckskinner to acquire the gear that will be needed in a primitive camp.

It can also take a couple of years of experience before a buckskinner will even want to go to a primitive rendezvous since it is an attitude that must grow a bit. With a little help, and there's plenty of that, it isn't hard for a newcomer to be at his first rendezvous which is also a primitive doin'. These folks are usually pretty well aware of what they're going to see, though, and friends have seen to it that they have enough gear to get by.

What will they see? Plenty, for sure. They'll see wooden boxes built only to hide a modern camp cooler. These things are "legal" in a primitive camp as long as they are out of sight and no restrictions by the rendezvous sponsor has been made against them. In the same vein, they'll see many a hot and tired buckskinner take a cold beer from a cooler, open the can, and pour the contents into an old style cup. The cans are not of a primitive nature and therefore are kept out of sight as much as possible. They'll see smokers with either pipes or hand-rolled cigarettes which are lit either with flint and steel or a twig from a fire. Bedrolls are made up with wool blankets or sleeping bags are disguised with canvas covers. Everything is done with the time era in mind and this is often referred to as "living history".

It's a little hard to generalize the things at a primitive rendezvous because each one is so different. They, of

This rendezvous was a small one, as you can tell from the size of the camp, but a lot of times those are the best.

course, can be big or small, winter or summer, in the high mountains or in the desert. Some sponsors will even stipulate many interesting angles such as how you will arrive and what you will have with you.

One primitive rendezvous that comes to mind as an example, is one I did not go on, but I've heard so much about it that I can pass on several of the highlights. First, this was a walk-in doin's and the camp was a little over a mile from the area where the cars were parked. Second, it was a primitive camp where nothing dated past 1850 was allowed. There are always exceptions to these rules concerning the dates; cameras are usually allowed with grace, as well as some of the things we consider the necessities of life. Since it was a walk-in, I doubt there were very many tepees, if any, and lean-tos were used the most. The hike to the camp was just as primitive as the camp and this short trip was to be made while wearing 'skins; even the backpacks had to be authentic.

There was one twist about this rendezvous that I liked because it reproduced a big part of the mountain man's life. No more than five rifle balls could be carried in the pouch while hiking to the camp and all other balls were to be cast while in the camp. This meant that there would be a lot of lead pots being heated over the campfire coals and every rifleman carried his bullet mould with him. This added a lot to the atmosphere of the camp life.

A lot of primitive shooters are lucky enough to have an original bullet mould that's still in good condition for casting bullets and I don't know if the moulds used on that walk-in rendezvous had to be authentically styled or not. It would make sense that they should be.

Casting balls over an open fire with a new aluminum mould would sure get the job done but it wouldn't look very realistic. There is a source for some good primitive styled moulds that have worked very well for me and that source is Dixie Gun Works. They call it their "Kentucky Mould" and it's available in just about any diameter you want at a very reasonable price. When I say those moulds have worked well for me, I mean just that and I have taken three deer with balls from the Dixie mould I use for my .52 caliber rifles.

Another primitive rendezvous that stands out in my mind is one that I did go to and it was a real good one. This one was not sponsored by any particular club and

This mountain man is casting (running) balls as it was done in bygone days. Many buckskinners emulate as nearly as possible the old ways.

This group of skinners are preparing to start the "combat course". These courses offer a real challenge to your all around ability as a buckskinner.

you could drive to the camp. Vehicles were allowed inside the camp area only for loading and unloading so most of the folks had tepees and there were several families involved. The only thing that put a bit of a damper on the whole thing was the weather but even in all of the fog and rain, most of the people were fairly comfortable.

The one feature that stands out the best about this rendezvous was the match put on by the Lamping brothers, that can be best described as a mountain man's combat course. It wasn't really a combat course, although a little combat was involved. The real gist of the course was that it was run by teams of four men each and each shooter was to arrive at the starting point with everything he would need, except food, for a three or four day outing. Once the course was started the team would encounter several varied situations and they were to handle these situations as the mountain men would have. Survival was one of the keys and the teams were told to be ready for just about anything. Since the element of surprise was part of more than a couple of these situations, nobody who was familiar with the course was allowed to compete in the contest.

At the starting point the four man team was assembled and the first situation was for each team member to shoot one shot at a gong. Hits gave the team points and misses counted zero. This was just to give the team members a little confidence for what was to come and I believe all members hit the gong when I followed them through the course.

After each had taken their shot, the team was led to a small clearing and they were told to control their team just like a small brigade. They chose a leader and another man was to be the hunter. Also, at this point the gear they had was inspected and the team received more points for the items of equipment they had brought. Blankets to sleep in added points and if one of the four had an axe, more points were added. Tools in the shooting pouches also added points as long as they were primitive.

At the same time, points were taken away from the team if one of the members was found to have anything that wasn't primitive. "Square Barrel" Ackley was nipped for a couple of points because he had a plastic bottle of bore cleaner and one of the other team members got "gigged" for a plastic handled screwdriver.

46

Then the team would proceed down the trail as indicated by the judges who went along to do the scoring. Just down that trail there was a full sized cardboard deer. C. T. Henry, the hunter for this group, shot at the deer with his heavy barreled .50. The judges said that he should then go "take care of the meat". Here the team made a mistake, they let Henry go check the meat alone. Henry also made a mistake by not reloading his rifle. Just before getting to the deer target, Henry tripped a hidden wire and he was charged by a cardboard grizzly bear. Since he had an empty rifle the bear bagged him and the team was reduced by one man. As far as the course was concerned, Henry was dead and the other team members took what they thought they might need from his plunder before moving on.

Down the trail several small game animals, rabbits and grouse, were on either side of the trail. Everybody got at least a couple of shots at these and every hit added more points for the team. This was also intended to deplete the team member's supply of ammo and it did just that for Square Barrel. He knew his horn was getting lighter, so he reduced the powder charge for his .50 to sixty grains per shot. At one point in the trail there were four cardboard grouse sitting together in one tree.

The "Indians" have just been pulled on their pulleys to the middle of the creek. These skinners are both preparing to defend themselves.

Since this was to be done as realistically as possible, the team lined up and all three rifles spoke at the same time. The judges awarded them several points for this, because if only one man had shot, the remaining grouse would have flown away.

Around the next bend in the trail there were several things posted as targets and one of the judges announced that the three man team was surrounded by 100 Crow Indians. Any team member that raised his rifle was pronounced dead but no one in this team tried that. For them it was time to trade and parley. The trading was done with the judges acting as the Indians and the more trading that could be done brought a reward in the form of more points. The rifle that belonged to the man who had been killed by the bear would have brought several points if it had been carried along. Extra knives, traps, and blankets were traded off and the team left the friendly Indians to continue on the course.

Just ahead was a creek and here's where our team of trappers each made a beaver set. Doug Prine was the one who added points to the team's score here because he was the only one who entered the water down stream from where he put the trap. After each man had made a

set, they pulled the traps and moved on once more.

On the other side of that creek there was an Indian waiting in ambush and none of the team members saw him. This meant that the Indian would have gotten one of the three. To decide which one, the judges had them draw straws and the holder of the short straw turned out to be Doug Prine. Now the team was down to two men, Square Barrel Ackley and Bob Davis. Once more the dead man's plunder was gone over and necessary items were taken. Square Barrel, being low on powder, made sure he got Doug's powder horn and it came in handy.

The next situation was just a couple of paper plates and the two remaining team members were told to hit the plates as many times as they could in the three or four minutes the judges had set as a time limit. This had a bit of a catch to it. The only place the plates could be seen from was while standing in the stream and of course, that's where the reloading took place also. Standing knee-deep in water can really slow things down when you can't put the rifle's butt on the ground while you're ramming a load home. Points were given for each hit and the more shots the team could get meant more points awarded.

They did pretty well on the plates but the next

The primitive life can be enjoyable for all the family. Here a family relaxes by their lodge and makes some music.

Here's the big kids in an even bigger tug-o-war. Shooting events are not the only kind of competition at rendezvous.

Yours C Carson —

situation is where they really excelled. There was a cardboard elk across the creek and Bob Davies shot it. Once more they had to check the meat. They both decided to do this, since the last time one man checked meat, they'd lost him. The creek was deep, though, so they didn't take their pouches or horns but both men did have loaded rifles. Bob Davies showed us how deep that stream really was and he's been known as "Deep River" Davies ever since.

It was a good thing that they both went to check the meat because while "Deep River" was noting where his ball had gone, Square Barrel noticed the cardboard Indian that was waiting in ambush. His shot was a good one and the judges gave them several points for getting their meat and saving their bacon as well.

By this time the team had a pretty fair number of points and the two remaining members were trying their best to be sure they completed the course. At the last situation the judges instructed them to set traps again on the far side of the creek. Back into the water they went. When they were halfway across the stream two cardboard hostiles hung on an overhead wire came out

An airborn view of the camp in the Bitterroot Valley. This was the first joint N.A.P.R. — N.M.L.R.A. rendezvous held in 1976.

in attack. Square Barrel fired, taking one of them out, but Deep River's rifle misfired. That meant that Deep River went under and since Square Barrel didn't have a pistol for another shot he would have to fight the remaining Indian hand-to-hand. This was settled by a cut of the cards and Square Barrel came in second. The team had been wiped out.

Maybe calling that match a combat course isn't too far from the truth. Actually, it was a super trail walk with a mixture of a Seneca Run and quite a bit of thinking thrown in. Very challenging to say the least and the teams that finished with at least one "surviving" member were in the running for some very worthy prizes.

Every rendezvous is different and there is no easy way to describe all of the things that happen, even if this whole chapter was devoted to just one buckskin rendezvous. The N.A.P.R./N.M.L.R.A. joint rendezvous of 1976 stands out in my memory and there were many more contests than just shooting and tomahawk

You are never too young or too old to enjoy the primitive life. Here a young mother and her child show by their expressions that they do.

throwing. That was a large camp and on a couple of evenings it seemed that the whole passel of folks turned out for tug-of-war. There were events like this for the kids as well as for the bigger kids. At this rendezvous, held near Darby, Montana, there was also horse racing and a canoe race down the West Fork of the Bitterroot.

The shoots and other competitive activities held at that rendezvous don't make the Darby rendezvous stand out in my memory nearly as much as the people do. Since it was such a large rendezvous, I was able to meet many more people there than I could ever remember. My camp was made in a lean-to borrowed from No-Feather and I set it next to Larry and Yvonne Janoff's lodge. Larry had a trade blanket featuring his art work and it became a sort of gathering place for a group of 'skinners like "Black Bear" Lange and many more that I might not have met otherwise.

Things were not scheduled real close together at Darby so there was a lot of time to enjoy the camp or the surrounding area which was very beautiful. Larry Janoff and I went shooting several times and one afternoon Larry, Yvonne, and I went out on a squirrel hunt. That was the very first rendezvous for Mike Branson and Mike joined us on that squirrel hunt. A hunt it might have been but most of the time was spent sitting in the

shade exchanging things on history. Our bag for the day was one squirrel and even if we hadn't got that one it would have still been a perfect day and a very enjoyable hunt.

The year after Darby, the N.A.P.R. rendezvous was held just a little way out of Big Timber, Montana and the setting was entirely different. Darby was like a big mountain meadow, which it was, and the Big Timber camp was on an "out on the prairie" landscape. There was still game around, though, as I saw a rabbit and some folks killed a couple of rattlesnakes. No one who was there would ever forget the grasshoppers. I don't think that was the best camp I've stayed in but it was good and the fellowship of buckskinners in general, not to mention my very close friends, made that rendezvous a good and memorable one.

For those that might not recognize the letters, N.A.P.R., they stand for the "National Association of Primitive Riflemen" an organization founded by John Baird and the functions of that organization are open to all subscribers of *The Buckskin Report Magazine*. The letters, N.M.L.R.A., of course, stand for the "National Muzzle Loading Rifle Association" whose monthly publication is *Muzzle Blasts* and this organization also sponsors buckskin rendezvous.

Three buckskinning publishers meet: L. to R. is Fred Holder from *Black Powder Times*, Oran Scurlock from *Muzzleloader*, and John Baird from *The Buckskin Report*.

While those N.A.P.R. rendezvous are quite large, I just recently went to a rather small one that sported about eight lodges. This was the Lower Tapteal Rendezvous, a primitive doin's that is expected to become an annual event. The booshway was Roger Lahti, an old friend that I met several years ago at another rendezvous and he had a good camp set up. This was in desert-like country near the Yakima River. There were so many things to do, including varmint hunting, that everyone had a real good time and no one should ever pass up a rendezvous just because it is a small one. A lot of times those small ones will be remembered as the best.

The last rendezvous I've had the chance to go to, as this chapter is being written, was the first Mid-America Rendezvous sponsored by *Muzzleloader Magazine* and it showed that buckskinning is certainly not a recreation enjoyed only in the West. Other organizations hold Eastern rendezvous but this was the first primitive doin's I've been able to get back to and it was held near Mountain View, Arkansas. I did get back to Friendship, Indiana, one year for the N.M.L.R.A. Spring Shoots and while they do have a primitive camp at Friendship, that is not really a rendezvous. The doin's at Friendship are huge and they should be seen but those activities are actually shoots.

Rendezvous are always good. I've never been to a bad one but it is true that some are better than others. The rendezvous can be called a lot of things, yet they are all gathering places for buckskinners. Even without all the shooting matches and trade blankets a rendezvous would still be something to see because most buckskinners have put a lot of time and effort into their 'skins and plunder. Shooting is a great sport and black powder shooting is one of the best parts of that sport. Black powder shooting itself can be broken down into sections too, like bench rest and skirmishing. In my way of thinking, none of them are as much fun as buckskinning, primitive shooting, and the rendezvous.

The Lodge

by George Glenn

GEORGE D. GLENN HAS BEEN collecting, making and shooting muzzleloaders for 30 years, and has considered himself a buckskinner for over twelve years. He started writing for *Muzzleloader* in 1975, and has been a member of *Muzzleloader's* editorial staff since 1976. In 1974 Glenn developed and taught the first college-level course in muzzleloading at the University of Northern Iowa, Cedar Falls, where he is an Associate Professor of Theatre in the Department of Speech. Glenn's professional academic specialties include theatre history and stage fight arranging: the latter gives him the opportunity to combine his knowledge of the theatre with his interest in firearms and edged weapons. He has worked professionally in theatre, film, radio and television as actor, director and fight arranger. Besides writing for *Muzzleloader* and other firearms magazines, his publications include the recently-published *Super 8 Handbook* (Indianapolis: Howard W. Sams, 2nd edition, 1980).

Glenn has long advocated considering muzzleloading, and, in particular, buckskinning, to be "pragmatic history." He states that "one of the best ways to really come to grips with the past, and understand it, is to occasionally relive it in as much detail as possible." Glenn feels that he is fortunate that his interest in buckskinning is shared and supported by his wife, Sandra; their three children, Stephanie, Laura and David; and their 19-year-old buckskinning cat, Willie, who loves a rendezvous as much as the rest of the family.

I'LL ALWAYS REMEMBER an evening a few years ago during the Fall Nationals at Friendship: it was late at night, and I was very tired as I made my way to the Primitive camping area. I'd been at my booth in Commercial Row all day; it had been hot and dusty, and I was looking forward to returning "home" — my tipi pitched in the Primitive area.

Passing through the gate, my way led me through the lower part of the camp. On either side of me were tipis, lean-tos and early-style wall tents. Campfires flickered, and the smoke mingled with the low-lying mist that hugged the hillside. Here and there a tipi showed a gentle golden glow from within, visually punctuating the playing and singing coming from a camp-fire circle farther up the camp. I knew I had reached my "neighborhood" when I came upon Jerry Book's blacksmith wagon and his brother Dave's wall tent. My tipi was next door, right where I'd left it.

I pulled the door flap back and crept in. Striking a light, I lighted a candle lantern. Its light revealed the inside of the lodge: in the center was the fire-pit, with my buffalo-robe bed directly behind it. Flanking my bed were two willow-rod back rests, or "lazy-backs;" there was my hump-backed wooden chest for my personal effects, and another flat-topped wooden chest for food and cooking utensils; my ice chest was covered with a painted canvas cover; hanging from the lodge poles were my rifles, my shooting bags, and some painted canvas "saddle" bags for clothing and personal effects. Extra clothing hung from the liner rope; neatly folded Hudson's Bay and Witney blankets added spots of color to the interior. All was as I had left it that morning, and it was good to be home.

As I rolled into my bed and blew out the light, I glanced up at the smoke-flap opening above me. There, perfectly framed in the opening was a full moon. It seemed more beautiful in that setting than any full moon I could remember. I lay looking at it, watching the occasional small cloud drift past, until I fell asleep. It is an image that has remained with me, and has come to symbolize for me the quality and contentment of living in a tipi.

Over the years the tipi has come to be the epitome of the buckskinner's dwelling. Just as the mountain men of the past borrowed and adapted many of the aspects of the life-style of the Native Americans, so has the modern-day buckskinner adopted the Indian tipi. It is doubtful if many of the old-time mountain men actually lived for any length of time in a tipi, unless they were visiting an Indian village or wintering with a tribe. The tipi is actually more suited to the modern buckskinner's needs than it was to the trapper's — which is to say that in some ways the modern buckskinner and the plains Indian share similar requirements for a place to live. The Indian tended to be as nomadic as the buckskinner,

who may travel to many rendezvous in the course of the year. It is as necessary for the 'skinner, as it was for the Indian, to have a comfortable home that is also easily portable. The tipi answers that need.

The tipi is a conical tent, supported by a dozen or more long, thin poles tied together near the tips. There is a single, oval door opening, usually covered by a flap-type door. The one-piece cover wraps around the poles and is pinned up the front with wooden "lacing" pins, and is staked down around the base. Inside, reaching up the wall about five feet is an inside liner, or dew cloth, which extends completely around the interior. Above the door, near the apex of the cone but in the front, the tipi opens up into two smoke flaps, which can be adjusted like lapels on a coat to suit the requirements of wind and weather.

Cover, liner, door, smoke-flaps: the listing of just the parts of a tipi make it sound just like an oddly-shaped tent, but it is more than that. There is a symmetry, a blending of form and function, which makes the tipi one of the most efficient and most beautiful dwellings in the world. It is no more "just a tent" than a Hawken is "just a rifle."

No one knows where, when or by whom the tipi was invented or perfected. When the white man first became aware of it, it had already reached the form it has today. Originally, of course, it was made of brain-tanned buffalo hide, and usually averaged about 14 feet in diameter at the base. It probably started out as a buffalo hide thrown over a simple framework of poles as a temporary shelter. Gradually, the tipi got bigger and more complex as some enterprising Indian stitched two or more skins together and wrapped them around a taller set of poles. But until the development of the liner, the tipi was just another tent.

The liner, or dew cloth, as has been mentioned, extends all the way around the inside of the tipi, and is about five feet high. It is traditionally made in three sections which overlap. It is tied to the poles at top and bottom, and at the bottom there is a portion of it which turns in and seals off the inside of the tipi. The poles are sandwiched between the liner on the inside and the cover on the outside. The air space thus created tends to draw air in from the outside, and convection currents carry the air out at the smoke flaps above. When a fire is lighted in a tipi, it is this air current that carries the smoke up and out. There is always fresh air in a tipi with a liner; yet, conversely, the liner cuts down on drafts. It helps prevent the condensation of moisture on the inside, which is where it gets its other name, "dew cloth." The liner also adds extra protection in rainy weather, helping to keep the tipi dry. A final advantage, in these days of canvas tipis, is that the liner acts as a "modesty" screen, and prevents shadows cast on the cover from being seen from the outside.

Nothing beats the sight of a group of tipis set against a pretty backdrop. A primitive camp offers an opportunity to see tipis of various sizes and to help you determine the size which will suit your needs.

56

Shelters at rendezvous vary, but tepees are the most popular. Here's one that is made of leather using several hides.

An extension, called an ozan, can be added to the liner.[1] The ozan forms a sort of low ceiling inside the tipi, and is useful for helping keep the occupants dry in very wet weather, or to concentrate the heat of the fire in cold weather. The Laubins give directions for the construction and use of the ozan: as far as we know, it is not available commercially.

In the old days, the liner was made of buffalo hide like the cover. Now, of course, both are made of canvas duck. Canvas began being used for tipis around the middle of the last century as it became available from the traders and the Army moving west. Canvas was supplied to Reservation Indians who could no longer hunt buffalo for the hides — and it wasn't long before there were virtually no more buffalo anyway. The day of the canvas tipi had arrived.

The canvas tipi had some advantages over the old hide lodge: it was lighter (both in weight and in how much light it let in); you didn't have to hunt it; and, because it was lighter, it could be made bigger. One disadvantage was that you couldn't make moccasins out of the well-smoked hide at the top of the lodge. Today's tipis usually are made with a cover of 10-12 ounce white cotton duck canvas, with the liner and the door being made of lighter-weight 8-10 oz. duck. Both cover and liner are usually waterproofed by the maker, although this feature is optional.

---

[1]Reginald and Gladys Laubin, *The Indian Tipi, Its History, Construction, and Use* (New York: Ballantine Books, 1971), pp. 69-70. This book is one of the basic references for this chapter; further references will be in the body of the text.

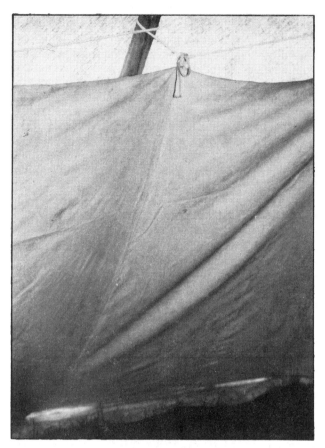

The liner tied in place. Notice the relationship between the cover, pole and liner. You can also see how the liner overlaps at the bottom.

To take advantage of the breeze in hot weather, the cover can be folded up like this.

There are a lot of advantages to the tipi. In the first place, the tipi is large and roomy. You can stand upright in it, unlike all but the largest cabin tent. What's more, you have enough room overhead to clean a rifle without worrying about poking holes in your roof with your ramrod.

The tipi was designed so that it's easy to have a fire inside; in fact, the tipi has been described as a chimney you can live in. A fire inside is nice when it's cold; it's nice when it's raining and you have to cook dinner, and it's especially nice when you sit around it with family and friends after supper, smoking and maybe sipping something.

In the summer you do as much cooking outside as possible, of course, but when the weather turns cool the tipi is relatively easy to heat with the inside fire. You do have to keep an eye out for sparks, and you can't have too big a fire; however, even in the coldest weather you can survive inside a tipi with an open fire. Some people have modified their tipis to handle a small wood stove. The stove pipe is extended up to or through the smoke hole, and it is claimed that a tipi equipped with such a stove gets and stays warmer than one with just an open fire. Of course it's hardly authentic, and there is a transportation problem, but it works.

Just as a tipi is relatively warm, so is it usually cool in the summer. If the lodge is pitched so that the cover doesn't quite reach the ground, there's always a current of air moving under the cover and up and out the smoke hole. When it gets really hot, one can pull a few stakes and roll or fold up a section of the cover to let more air waft through the lodge.

If the breezes become more than gentle, don't worry: the unique cone-shape of the tipi makes it almost impossible to blow it down. There's nothing for the wind to grab hold of; it just slides around and over the cover, and if the tipi is well-pegged down around the base, and if the anchor rope is solidly attached inside, the tipi isn't going anywhere. It is said that tipis have stood through tornadoes and hurricanes. Mine has stood through a storm with winds so high that the rain was blown horizontally through the canvas, and every wall-tent in camp was blown down. Not a tipi went down. The only wind damage to a tipi I've ever seen was when a friend was taking his tipi down: he had the cover half-off when a sudden, unexpected strong gust of wind caught it, and it ripped up the back.

Buckskinning is a family activity, and the tipi is admirably suited to families. There's plenty of room for all the extra food, bedding and gear that camping with a family entails. Of course, a lot depends on the size of the tipi involved, and the size of the family. A 12' or 14' tipi is considered adequate for a couple, with perhaps one or two small children. As the kids or the family

The smoke flaps adjusted so that there is a minimal opening at the top, for when bad weather is expected, or for when you have to be absent from your lodge for some time.

sized cabin tent from Sears and have enough left over for a propane stove. Although a tipi can be set up and taken down easily and quickly, transportation can be a problem, especially when it comes to carrying the poles. A tipi is not altogether maintenance-free. Despite your best care, repairs will have to be made: small rips sewn up, tie-tapes replaced when they pull loose, ropes replaced, lodge poles replaced when they break, etc. These things do not happen very often, nor will they prevent you from getting your tipi pitched. It is surprising how resilient a tipi can be: mine still shows the tire track across the door where some yahoo backed into it with a pick-up truck. Our tipi is now over four years old and has seen some heavy use and a lot of travel. It has had rips repaired around the door and up at the smoke-flaps; it has had liner tie-tapes replaced; it needs some repair at the bottom of the door where the dog's chain caught and tore the canvas. It has mildew stains from the time at Friendship when it was raining as we were packing up, and we had to stow it wet and drive 500 miles in hot sun before we could get home to dry it out. The scars are honorable; it's good for many more seasons.

On the whole, I think the advantages outweigh the disadvantages. For the nomadic life of the buckskinner, going from rendezvous to rendezvous, the tipi is the best choice. Now: how do you get one? There are only two ways: make it or buy it.

I have known some people who objected to what they perceived as the high cost of a ready-made tipi, and decided to cut costs by making their own. They ran into problems. It's not difficult to find or adapt a pattern; the Laubins' book lays it all out for you. To make your own 18-foot tipi, you'll need 68 yards of 36"-wide canvas for the cover, and another 35 yards for the lining. As of this writing, the price-per-yard locally for 10-oz duck is $3.10 a yard. That figures to about $320.00 just for canvas. Next you'll have to beg, borrow or rent a heavy-duty sewing machine, and find a place to work where you can spread out the material as you sew. Once you have it stitched together, and have hand-stitched the reinforcing around a lot of lacing-pin holes, you can waterproof it with a dry, non-waxy waterproofing. How long has all that taken you? How much have you spent? Have you saved any money when you can buy a ready-made, brand-new tipi, with liner, door and cover waterproofed, for around $350.00 or so? Buy it, don't made it.

If you have decided to buy a tipi, the next decision, after deciding what size you need, is whether to get a new one or a used one. If you decide to purchase a new one (see the end of this book for some sources), don't forget that what you get is only the cover, door and liner. You still have to come up with all the rope, poles, pegs and lacing pins. Let's look at some of these necessities in more detail.

1. Poles. The poles are usually of some species of pine, since pine poles are usually straight and light-weight. Lodgepole pine was used extensively by the Indians, and its name is obviously derived from its function. It is still the preferred species if you can get it.

grow larger, the 16′ or 18′ lodges seem more practical. A 20′ lodge is really large; there are a few 24′ lodges around that seem like mansions. (One owner of a 24′ lodge told me that they had once slept 35 people, and could seat 75 for a meeting.) Our tipi is an 18-footer, and it's quite adequate for my wife and myself, our three adult-size children, and the dog and the cat. (Cats seem to take to a tipi instinctively, but we have yet to convince our dog that the tipi isn't a tree or a fire hydrant.) We *have* slept the whole family, including cat, dog and a friend of my daughter's, in a 12-foot lodge with a fire going in the center, but it was very cozy.

Since nothing's perfect, there are some disadvantages to a tipi. Tipis are relatively expensive. For what you spend on a tipi and poles, you could buy a good-

Other species have been used, and are quite satisfactory. If you don't live in an area where you have access to a stand of young trees, you'll do best by purchasing from one of the dealers advertised in the various muzzleloading magazines. Try to get poles that have been winter-cut, since they don't take as long to dry out, or season.

For an 18-foot tipi, you'll need 15 poles about 23-24' long for the main structure, plus two shorter poles for the smoke-flaps. The lodge poles should be about 3-4" thick at the base, and an inch to two inches thick at the point where they cross. A 12-14' lodge can get by with 12 main poles, plus two smoke-flap poles, while a 20' or larger lodge will need as many as 18-21 main poles. The length will vary according to the size of the lodge, too. 24' will do for the 18-footers, and correspondently shorter or longer for the other sizes, up to 40' long for the 24' lodges. As they get longer, of course, transportation becomes a major problem.

The poles should be de-barked and smoothed. A smooth pole won't poke holes in your cover, and won't drip water all over the inside of your lodge when it rains. You may wish to apply a wood preservative to your poles, especially if you store them outside over the winter.

2. Ropes. You'll need a variety of ropes and cords, for everything from pitching the lodge to pegging it down, to hanging the liner. The main rope for tying the poles needs to be about 45' long, and should be at least ⅜" hemp (Manila). Some authorities advocate ½" Manila for this, but for an 18' or smaller lodge this rope needn't be that heavy.

To tie the liner up, you'll need about 40' of 3/16" or ¼" cotton line; clothesline will do. This same kind of line will also be used for the ties at the tips of the smoke flaps: you'll need two lengths about 15-20' long.

You'll need about 25 one-foot lengths of ⅛" or 3/16" line to use as peg loops. It is these cords that are used instead of sewn-on loops or ties around the base of the cover. To attach them, you'll also need 25 or so ½"-¾" smooth pebbles, glass marbles or musket balls. We'll describe exactly how these are used later. Incidentally, it is only in the case of this cord that I have gone to a "non-natural" material: I've used Nylon cord for its superior strength and wear-ability. After a season it ages so that it doesn't look out of place with the other lines.

3. Pegs and Pins. To stake the tipi down, you'll need 25 pegs, each about 18" long and ¾" to an inch in diameter. Chokecherry or ash are traditional, but any hardwood will do. Point them and peel the bark from all but the last six inches or so at the top (the un-peeled part will help keep the peg loops from slipping). In addition to the stakes for the perimeter of the lodge, you'll need one or two stouter stakes to use as anchor pegs inside the lodge.

To fasten the tipi up the front, you'll need a dozen or so pointed sticks, or lacing pins, 12-14" long, and about ⅜" in diameter. Hardwood dowel will do, but doesn't look authentic. The pins should be peeled of bark, except for two or three inches at the un-pointed ends. Decorative rings or designs can be carved in the bark.

The graceful beauty of the tipi fits well in any wilderness setting as illustrated by this two lodge camp.

You'll need two short poles about 3' long and an inch or two in diameter to insert in the tubes sewn at the top and bottom of the door flap. These serve to keep the door extended at top and bottom.

A pole 6-8' tall or taller is used to place in the ground in front of the lodge to attach the lines from the smoke flaps. Some people also use this as a flag-pole or trophy pole.

Some other things to consider when buying a new lodge are: (1) make sure that all lacing-pin holes are reinforced with "buttonhole" stitching; you don't want any metal grommets in your lodge; (2) the bottom edge of the tipi need not be hemmed, since the canvas is (or should be) cut on the bias, and will not ravel; (3) you don't want ties or grommets along the bottom edge of the tipi — we'll mention a better way of tying it down later; and (4), the pole pockets should be separate pockets sewn in place, not just a single thickness of canvas sewn to the smoke flap.

Used lodges are often available, usually from people who have outgrown a smaller lodge, or who are moving into a smaller lodge from a bigger one. Occasionally you will find a tipi that is being sold because the owner has become disenchanted with buckskinning (rare), or is trying an alternate style of dwelling, such as a wall tent or a Revolutionary War officer's marquee. Some good bargains can be found in used tipis. They usually come on the market at the bigger rendezvous, or at the national meets at Friendship. Wander around and you may spot a "for sale" sign; better yet, ask around if anybody knows of a used lodge for sale — somebody probably will.

Be sure you examine your prospective purchase carefully, preferably while it is set up. The age or extent of use of the tipi can be roughly indicated by the darkness of the smoke-staining at the top. See if there are any obvious signs of repair, and if so, were the repairs neatly and efficiently done? Usually, a tipi will be sold with the poles, ropes and other accessories as part of the package. Check on their condition. Are any of the poles cracked? (Don't worry about cracks and checks running lengthwise on the poles — these are a natural consequence of the drying process.) Are the ropes in good shape? In short, check it over as carefully as you would any house you are planning to buy. About the only thing you don't have to worry about is whether the basement leaks.

How much should you expect to pay for a used lodge? Obviously there is no simple answer; so much depends on the size, age and condition. A good rule of thumb might be to total how much everything might cost you new, say $500-$550 for a new 18' tipi with everything, and for a used lodge in good condition offer about half that. If you can get it for less, do so; if it costs you more, don't fret — it's still cheaper than everything new. You won't necessarily have been taken, since so many variables go into determining price, including the relative bargaining skills of you and the seller.

Cover, liner, door; ropes and lines; pegs, pins and poles — now all you have to do is to put it all together and you have a tipi. Let's assume that you're starting with all new materials. Your first job is to spread the

Marking the Door pole (on top) and the North and South poles where they cross.

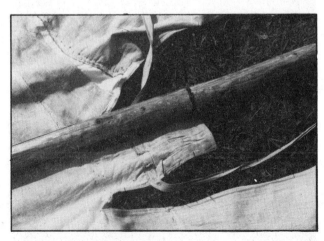

Marking the lift pole where the cover tie flap will be tied to the pole.

A trial set-up in the back yard begins by marking the tri-pod poles for tying. Lay the tipi out flat on the ground, with the North and South poles laid out in the middle of the cover, and the Door pole laid out along the edge. The poles are marked where they cross at the top of the smoke flaps.

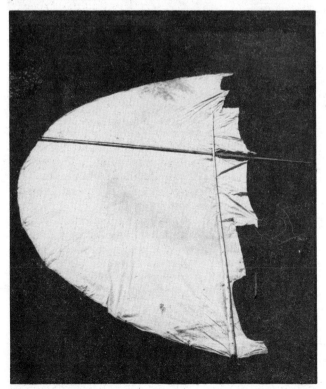

cover out flat on the ground. Since the tipi is traditionally pitched with its door to the east, we'll follow the Laubins' lead and refer to the various compass points in giving our directions. So spread the cover out with the curved bottom edge to the south (the straight front edges will be running east/west).

Choose your four stoutest poles: three of these will make up the basic tri-pod which is the foundation for the rest of the construction, while the fourth — the "lift" pole — will be used to lift the cover into its final position. The three tri-pod poles we will name "door", "north" and "south." Lay the three poles (the door pole on top of the north and south poles) so that they meet and cross at the top of the cover. With a permanent marker of some type, make a mark on each pole where they cross.

At this time you might as well mark the lift pole as well. Lay it on the cover and mark it at the end of the tie-flap.

We have always marked the poles with their ends even with the bottom of the cover, but for hot weather, when you might want the cover off the ground a bit, you can mark the poles with their ends extended past the edge of the cover a couple of inches or so. We've never done this, preferring to have only one set of marks so we won't get confused.

With your tri-pod poles marked, lay them on the ground, the door pole on top, and lying in the same directions as when you marked them. With your rope, make a clove hitch around the poles where they cross, take a few more turns, and finish up with a couple of half-hitches. This should leave you with the bulk of your rope extended away from the juncture of the poles. This is your anchor rope.

Above: Tying the tri-pod poles; the first knot is a clove hitch and then followed by one more wrap with a half hitch as shown at left.

62

Setting up the tri-pod; the North pole is being swung in the direction of the arrow.

Stand at the apex, facing the butts of the N and S poles (facing south, in other words). Pick the poles up, grasping them where they are tied, and start to walk them up. It helps to have someone hold the long end of the rope, and pull on it as you raise the poles. You can do the whole operation by yourself, but it's tricky, particularly with the long poles of a large tipi. As the tri-pod goes up, grasp the pole to your right, which should be the north pole, and swing it around to the north. This opens the tri-pod up so it will stand by-itself: as the Laubins point out, this "locks" the tri-pod so it won't slip or fall down.

You now have your basic tri-pod set up. The door pole will be to the east; the south and north poles will be farther from the door pole than they are from each other, with the south pole a little farther away than the north.

Now you're ready to start laying the remaining poles in place in the crotches formed by the tri-pod poles. (Be careful with the tips of seasoned poles as you lift them in place, for it's easy to snap them off). Starting at the door pole, you'll lay poles 1-4 in the front crotch, working your way towards the north pole; the door

Poles 1-4 laid in the front notch formed by the Door and North poles.

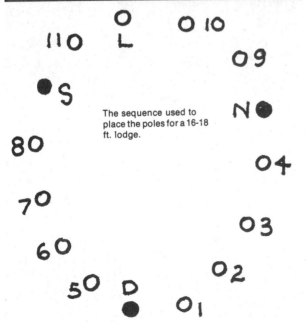

The sequence used to place the poles for a 16-18 ft. lodge.

63

pole, and the first of this set of four will frame the door opening. The next four poles, numbered 5-8, are laid in the same front crotch, but in order from the door pole to the south pole. Thus, of the 15 total poles, nine of them, including the door pole, are in the front crotch. This is necessary so that the cover will fit properly.

The remaining three poles, excluding the lift pole for the moment, are laid in order between the north and the south pole in this order, from north to south: #9, #10, gap (for the lift pole), and finally, #11. The gap which will eventually be filled by the lift pole will be opposite the door opening, as defined by the door pole and pole #1.

The next step is an important one. Take the anchor rope, which until now has been dangling down, and bring it out by the south pole. Walking around the poles clockwise — or "with the sun", as the Indians would put it — wrap the rope four times around the poles at their apex. As you go around, you can snap the rope up into place, pulling it tight. After four turns (four turns are safe, as well as being symbolic of the four compass points), bring the rope back in to the center of the lodge by way of the north pole.

Poles 9-11 in place in the back notch formed by the North and South poles. Notice the gap between pole #10 and pole #11; the lift pole with cover attached will fit in here.

Poles 5-8 laid in the front notch between the Door and the South poles.

After wrapping the rope four times David brings it back into the center of the lodge by the North pole.

The rope can now be tied off to an anchor peg driven in near the center of the lodge (or you can wait until the cover is on if there's no wind).

If your cover is still laid out on the ground, you can now fold it into a pizza-wedge shaped bundle (you will have laid it out with the outside up, the inside towards the ground). Start with the door edge, (either one) and

With one-half of the lodge cover folded into its triangular shape, Laura starts to fold the other half, by pulling the door edge around to the middle of the cover.

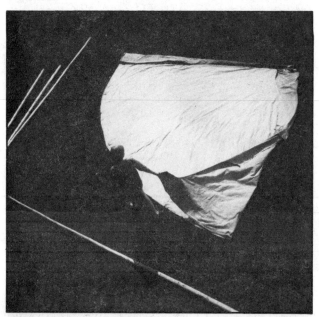

The lift pole laid on folded cover ready to be tied in place.

The cover tied by its flap to the lift pole where it was previously marked. It must be tied fairly tightly so it won't slip down off the mark when it's lifted into position.

bring that edge to the center of the cover. Continue this for two or three times, working from the edge to the center, until you have a long, triangular bundle. Place your lift pole alongside (or on) the bundle, and tie the flap to the pole where you have previously marked it. Be sure you tie it so that the pole is on the inside of the cover. Fasten it by wrapping the tapes criss-cross around the pole, and tie it tight so that the cover won't slip when it is raised into position.

It helps to have someone "foot" the pole as you position the butt end in the gap you left in the poles in the back crotch. Walk it up and drop it into position, giving it a twist as it falls into place so that the cover is on top. Unwrap the cover and pull each side around to the front. Make sure the cover is snug, and not too high or low at the top. At the base of the smoke flaps you will find tie tapes, which you can now tie together. The cover is now ready to be laced up the front.

Overlapping the south side over the north, insert a lacing pin into each pair of lacing pin holes. Start at the top, where you tied the tapes, and work your way down, keeping the south side overlapping the north. You'll also find a couple of lacing holes below the door opening.

Dropping the lift pole and attached cover into its position between poles #10 and 11. It's easier if there is someone who can "foot" the pole, but it can be done alone.

65

Once the lift pole is in position, the cover is unfolded and pulled around to the front of the tipi.

Next, take your last two poles, which are your smallest and shortest. If you are working with new poles, you'll have to cut these to an exact length, but if your poles came with your lodge they're probably already the right length. These are your smoke-flap poles. Their function is to fit into the pockets at the upper tip of the smoke flaps; they are used to manipulate the smoke flaps; open and close them, and adjust them for the direction of the wind. Their length will depend on the size of your lodge, and its style. Traditionally, a Cheyenne-style lodge, with narrow smoke-flaps, has the smoke-flap poles cut to a length that, with the smoke-flaps fully extended, will meet but not cross at the center of the back of the tipi. Sioux-style tipis, with wider smoke-flaps, have longer smoke-flap poles, and they cross in the back. Our smoke-flap poles for our Cheyenne-style tipi are 19' 6½" long, but measure your own to be sure. It doesn't matter if they're too long, but you will have a problem if you cut them too short. Be sure, too, that their tips are rounded so that you won't poke holes through the canvas of the pole pockets.

Overlapping the left side of the cover over the right (or south over north) so that the pairs of holes match, pin the cover down the front.

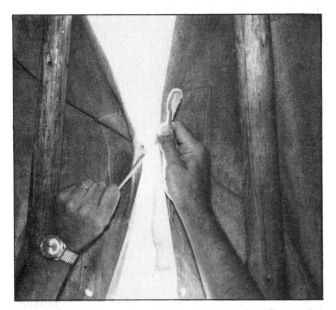

The cover meets in front between the Door pole and pole #1 (here on the left, since we're on the inside looking out). Tie the cover together with the tapes at the base of the smoke-flaps (above the lacing pin holes).

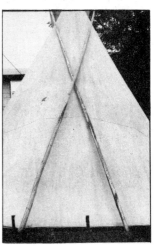

Smoke flap poles as seen on Cheyenne style (left) and Sioux style (right).

66

After you have the cover pinned up in front, insert the smoke flaps into their pockets and extend the smoke-flaps. This can be a frustrating operation, especially if there's a wind to blow the smoke-flap away from you just as you're about to get the thing in the pocket. When you've done it, open the smoke-flaps up, but don't put a lot of tension on them until you've staked the tipi down. That's your next chore after making the final adjustments to the poles.

When you set the poles into the tri-pod, they should have been set in a smaller circumference than their final one, since it's easier to get the cover in place that way. Now that the cover is on and pinned in place, go inside and push the poles out against the cover, spacing the poles evenly. You may have to twist and yank with some force to move them. The final configuration of poles, if you were looking straight down on the tipi, will not be a circle but an egg shape, with the small end of the egg being the door.

You may find out at this time that one or more of the tri-pod poles seems too long or short; the door pole, for some reason, is susceptible to being mis-measured. You can adjust your mark the next time, but be certain that it was due to mis-measuring and not to uneven ground.

Now, starting with the front and back, you can peg

Stephanie carefully maneuvers the smoke-flap pole into its pocket at the tip of the smoke flap.

A closer look at the smoke-flap pole being inserted in the smoke-flap pole pocket.

down the tipi. This is where you need your one-foot lengths of cord and your marbles. Place a marble about 6″ up from the bottom of the cover, and on the inside. From the outside, tie a piece of cord around it with a square knot or clove hitch. Tie the free ends together with a square knot. There you have your peg loop. Insert a stake in the loop, and twist until the loop is twisted close around the stake, like a tourniquet. Now hammer the stake into the ground. In hard or rocky ground you might want to use an iron rod to make a pilot hole first, and save your stakes from excessive hammering. You'll find that you can set the peg with just a tap or two, and it'll hold perfectly well. Also, you needn't angle the pegs: they can be driven in straight up and down, and be easier to pull while holding just as well. They look nicer, too.

We recommend the use of a large mallet or small sledge hammer for driving stakes — not the back of an axe, unless you're not worried about scalping yourself on the upswing.

Peg down the front first, with a stake to either side of the door, and perhaps one in the center of the door opening. Next stake down the center of the back. Now work your way around the tipi, staking down the sides. You should have at least one stake for every pole — more won't hurt.

The stake is inserted in the loop and twisted, tourniquet-style, to hold it under tension.

Fastening a peg loop to the base of the cover by tying it around a large marble or pebble.

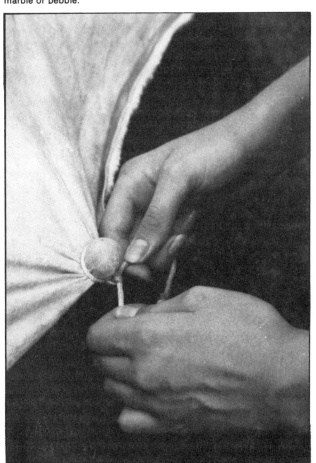

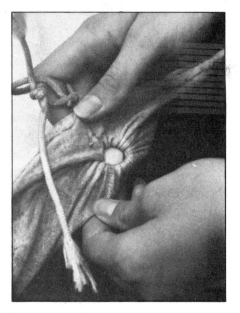

The underside of the cover, showing the marble tied in place.

Now you can go back inside and make any adjustments you need to the poles. Go back outside and fasten the door flap in place. It will have a flap that has a pair of holes in it which will match the lacing pin holes in the cover. Pull the lacing pin in the second or third set of holes up from the door opening, and pin the door flap in place.

Now step back and view your creation. Adjust the smoke flaps. Swear in dismay as you see that your magnificent structure is wrinkled at the top, sags in the middle, and is lop-sided to boot. It doesn't look like it does in the pictures or in your imagination. Don't worry: nobody's going to laugh at you for not getting it right on the first try.

Stephanie pins the door into place, matching its lacing-pin holes with holes in the cover.

The door pinned into place.

The first time my wife and I set up our brand-new R. K. Lodges tipi was at a rendezvous at Fort Snelling in Minnesota. We'd followed all the directions; we'd even practiced setting it up a few times in the back yard at home. This time was a disaster. We simply couldn't get it right. Finally, a blond, bearded fellow came over to offer help. He turned out to be Dick Kopp, owner of R. K. Lodges, and he'd made the tipi we were making such a botch of. He was helpful, encouraging, and didn't snicker behind his hand. "Hell," he said, "if you could set this up on a perfectly even and level gymnasium floor, it'd come out perfect every time. But you always have to deal with the slope and irregularities of the land you're on, and it's never going to be perfectly level. Don't worry about it." So we never have.

With the cover in place and staked down, you're only half-done. You still have to put up the liner. Start by taking your 40' of clothesline, and tying one end off about 5' up on the lift pole. You start with the lift pole in case you should ever have to take just the cover down for repairs: all you'll have to do is untie the rope at the lift pole.

So, one end of your rope is tied off at the lift pole. Now go from pole to pole, wrapping the line around each pole, from the front and around the back of each pole, so the line is on the side of the pole opposite the cover. Go all the way around, ending up at the lift pole again. You'll probably find that even after you've performed this operation a few times, that you'll still have to make adjustments in the height of the rope.

The next step is to tie your liner to the rope at the top and to the butts of the poles at the bottom. You'll have noticed that your liner comes in three sections, each made up of trapezoidal pieces of canvas sewn together, so that the bottom of each section is longer than the top. This is so that the liner will fit the different circumferences at the base of the tipi and at five feet up the sides. The tie tapes at the top edge of the liner are sewn on right along the edge, but the ties at the bottom are sewn in 6-8" up from the bottom edge. The liner thus overlaps on the inside of the lodge.

You can install the liner by tying it first to the rope and then tying it off at the bottom, but we've found it easier to tie the bottom tapes to the poles first, and then tie the top. This has the advantage of helping you make a final adjustment to the spacing of the poles, since you'll have to move some one way or another so that the ties will reach.

The three sections of lining will be made up of a different number of pieces each: for an 18' tipi you'll probably have 4-, 5- and 6-piece sections. Start with the 5-piece section, and start tying it off to the south side of the door, working clockwise around towards the back. The first piece of this 5-piece section can be used as an inner door flap, so start your tying with the second tie. The next section to go in is the 6-piece section, and it will overlap the first section. Finish up by tying on the 4-piece section, and so working your way around to the door again. Hopefully, everything will fit just right, and you'll end up at the door where you should. The liner should be drawn up fairly tightly, with little or no sag to it.

69

The liner rope wrapped around a pole so that it is to the outside with the pole between it and the cover.

Some iconoclasts we have met have defied tradition and sewn the three sections of their liner into one long strip, and for the life of us we can't see why this wouldn't work, but we've never tried it so can't recommend it.

If you think it might rain, it's a good idea to put two little sticks under the rope where it crosses on each pole to form a channel for rain water running down the pole to continue following the pole down behind the liner instead of dripping on your head.

At this point, if you haven't done it earlier, you should tie off your anchor rope to a stout, long peg driven into the ground near the center of the lodge. You may drive in two stakes at an angle to one another for a more secure anchor. It is this anchor rope that will prevent your tipi from taking off should strong winds hit.

We must mention here that one should never use metal stakes to tie the anchor rope to, or have any metal on the poles themselves. The Indian may have lived in his chimney, but he didn't live inside a lightning rod.

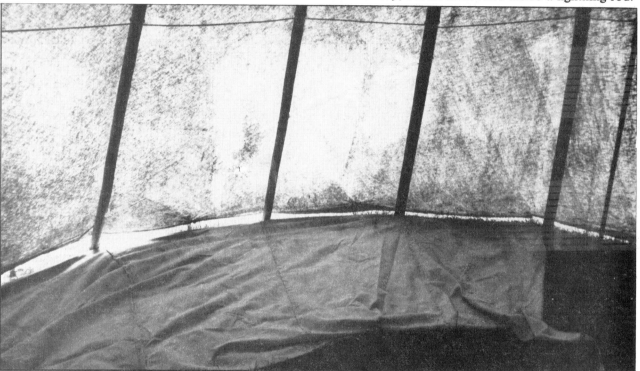

A section of liner tied off to the base of the poles before being tied to the liner rope. Doing this helps in the final positioning of the poles, assuming that the ties on the liner are positioned correctly.

Rain sticks in place under the liner rope. Water will run down the channel thus formed and go behind the liner.

70

Taking the tipi down isn't as complicated or as time-consuming as putting it up, but there are a few points that need consideration. Essentially, you simply reverse the setting-up process. Start by taking down the liner and the liner rope. Go outside and remove the smoke-flap poles and un-tie the flap lines from the pole that sits in front of the lodge.

Go around the tipi and pull all the stakes, but you can leave the peg-loops attached. It's not necessary to untie the cords from the marbles, and it'll save a lot of time the next time you pitch your lodge to leave them attached.

Pull the pin that holds the door flap in place, and un-pin and untie the front. Grasp one of the front edges of the cover and carry it around to the lift pole in back. Continue folding for two or three times, then repeat the process with the other side of the tipi. You'll end up with your pizza-wedge shaped bundle lying on the lift pole.

Again, it helps to have someone foot the lift pole as you lower it to the ground. Untie the cover from the lift pole, and fold it into a bundle (when you unfold the bundle the next time you set up, it'll be ready to tie to the lift pole). Try not to fold the cover up if it's wet or even damp; if you must pack up when the lodge is wet, be sure you spread it out to dry the first chance you get.

Unfasten the anchor rope from the anchor pegs, and unwrap the poles. Take them down in reverse order from the way you put them up: again be careful that you don't snap off the tips by dropping them. Having someone hold on to the anchor rope, swing the north pole around towards the south pole, and lower the tri-pod. Untie the anchor rope, gather everything up and pack it away, and you're done. Don't forget to kill your fire, fill in your fire pit and replace the sod. One unvarying characteristic of the buckskinner is that he always leaves the area looking better than when he set up camp.

Once you have your lodge pitched, you're ready to move in. We've seen lodges decorated and furnished in a variety of ways, from "pure" Indian to modern camp. It's up to you, but we recommend that you consider the traditional Indian arrangement for the inside of your lodge, since it's an arrangement that's been years in the developing.

Opposite the door, in the center of the lodge, is the space for the fire. This is the only place for it, really, since you want the fire directly under the smoke-flap opening. We usually dig a shallow fire-pit, and line the pit with dry rocks if possible. (Don't take rocks from a stream bed, since there may be moisture in them, and they can explode in the heat of the fire.) Indians reserved the space immediately behind the fire for the family altar. That's a good place to save the sod from the fire pit if you don't go in for altars.

Immediately inside the door, either to the right or left, is the place to store your firewood and water, and your food and cooking gear. We also keep our ice chest just inside the door, covered with a fitted canvas cover to help disguise its non-authenticity.

Beds are arranged around the back perimeter of the lodge. Traditionally these were of furs, primarily buffalo, and that's the best way to go still if you can afford the furs. We made do with blankets and a couple of hair-on deer hides until we were able to get a good brain-tanned buffalo robe. We have made a couple of concessions to modernity and "progress;" we use plastic ground cloths under our beds, and we bought a couple of pieces of 3"-thick foam rubber to put under the skins. They don't show, and they sure make a difference as far as comfort is concerned. We recommend the ground-cloths even if you don't opt for the foam rubber, simply to preserve your blankets and valuable skins from the damp ground.

Whatever you use for a bed-cover or rug, whether it's buffalo, deer, or an old hair-on horse hide or cow hide (and both are practical and attractive), or whether it's blankets, be sure you use only natural materials and all-wool blankets. The modern fake-fur substitutes and acrylic blankets are just too dangerous to use anywhere near a fire. We remember a few years ago at Friendship when a couple of fellows lost their lodge and nearly their lives when a spark from their fire jumped to the fake-fur rugs they were using. They were asleep at the time, and their lodge was half-burned when someone went in to pull them out. While a spark may smoulder and burn a hole in a real fur rug or all-wool blanket, it won't flame up.

Some people advocate the use of a ground cloth that covers the entire interior of the tipi, with a hole cut out in the middle for the fire. While this may seem like an attractive idea, there is a major disadvantage: you have to sweep it. You never have to worry about keeping crumbs, ashes or dirt off the grass.

Other furnishings in the lodge can consist of trunks, food lockers, ice-chests, seats, storage bags, lanterns and lamps, etc. Seats can be a problem. You can sit cross-legged on your robes or blankets, of course, but sometimes it's nice to be able to lean back and stretch your legs. Regular chairs don't work too well because they put you up too high. You have to get a fair distance away from the sloping walls to clear your head, and this can put you too close to the center of the lodge. It can also get your head up in the smoke. The lower down you are the farther back against the wall you can get, and the more room there will be for everyone else.

The Indians solved the problem by constructing lazy-backs out of thin willow rods strung together in a mat, which is hung from one end from a tri-pod. These back-rests, traditionally always made in pairs, are very decorative and practical for use either inside or outside the lodge. When not in use they can be easily rolled up and stowed out of the way.

Lately we've seen some back-rests constructed like a small hammock, with a rod at each end of a strip of canvas. They resemble a smaller version of the old canvas deck chair, except that they're suspended at one end from a tri-pod. They're cheap and effective and look pretty good.

Another effective seat is the small "canoe" or "snowshoe" chair. These small, very low, folding chairs are made of bent wood and rawhide webbing like a snowshoe. They're practical, don't take up a lot of room, and they look authentic. They are expensive, though.

Many of your choices on tipi furnishings depend, of

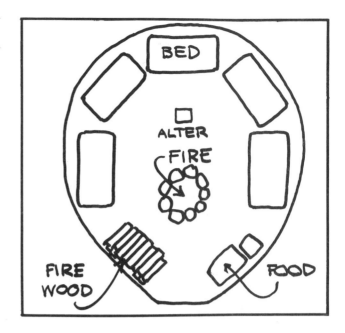

The proper arrangement of the lodge is illustrated by the drawing above.

Tipi living is quite comfortable, especially when you make use of such items as this willow back rest. Accessories such as this can be made by most anyone and add a great deal to looks as well as comfort.

72

A tipi ready to be lived in. Notice that the slope in the front is less steep than the slope in the back.

The interior of a well-furnished tipi showing placement of beds, backrests and fire pit.

course, on how authentic you want to be, or even how "Indian" you want to make your lodge look. If you're just camping, then you won't feel awkward about using modern camping equipment, or feel that it's out of place. When you're at a rendezvous, however, people will look askance at you if you display anything that doesn't fit in the 18th or 19th centuries. Instead of a Coleman lamp, you'll use candle lanterns (even kerosene lanterns may be considered too modern). A campfire with a wrought-iron grill, tri-pod or cross-bar set will replace your propane camp stove. An ice chest is necessary in these hygienic times, but you will camouflage it in some way, either by covering it or by enclosing it in a wooden box so that it looks like a storage chest.

Cooking and eating gear can be cast iron, blue-speckled enamel-ware, tinware (no aluminum), pewter, brass or copper. You can eat out of tin or pewter plates, drink out of tin cups, and keep your beer and pop cans out of sight. Store your water in a wooden keg or wooden bucket. (A wooden bucket full of water is a good thing to keep handy anyway, in case of fire.)

Wooden trunks, similar or identical to the old trad-

ers' "cassettes," are available commercially or can be made. We use one for storing clothes and gear and another for dry and canned foods and cooking gear. Woven oak or hickory split pack baskets or laundry-style baskets can also be used to tote and store a lot of stuff, and don't take up a lot of room. One advantage to the wooden boxes is that you can use them as "end tables," or to sit on.

Some people make up canvas copies of Indian buckskin saddle bags, paint them with appropriate designs, and hang them from the poles inside. They hold a lot and are decorative. Of course, you can make them out of buckskin, and do the designs in beads or quills. You can get or make some rawhide and build your own parfleches or rawhide boxes. Checking a standard reference like the Laubins' book, or *Mystic Warriors of the Plains* [2] will give you a lot of ideas on what is authentic and will look right. Don't forget to check your local museum, too.

[2] Thomas E. Mails, *The Mystic Warriors of the Plains*, (Garden City: Doubleday & Co., 1972).

74

All this won't come at once. You'll gradually work your way into the kind of decorations and furnishings that will suit you and your particular life-style, in the same way that you furnish your permanent home. In effect, you will be setting up a second home, and you'll find that no matter where you set up, once you have your things arranged around you in your lodge, you'll be as "at home" as you are in your mortgaged split-level.

You may feel impelled to paint your lodge after you have seen some painted tipis at a rendezvous. Both the cover and the inside liner can be painted (see Laubin for examples of authentic designs). In the old days, painted Indian tipis were relatively rare, and were accounted "medicine" lodges; that is, lodges which were painted with designs which had come to their owners in visions. They had great religious and mystical significance and were not for everyone. It may be for this reason that we have not painted our lodge, never having received the

appropriate inspiration. But it's a matter for your own decision.

The liner can be painted in abstract designs, however, and can add a great deal to the decorative nature of the lodge.

If you paint your tipi cover, it's a good idea to keep away from very dark colors at the top, since they can cut out a lot of the light that comes in. The Laubins have suggestions as to the kind of paint to use, but we have taken a clue from our friends who are theatre scene designers who have painted a lot of canvas over the years. You might want to experiment with the following on some scrap canvas first.

Get some exterior latex house paint in the colors you want, and dilute it. If it's top quality paint you can dilute it 50%; if it's bargain basement stuff, don't dilute it more than 25%. The reason you dilute it is so you won't add weight and stiffness to your cover. Remember that the paint will be much runnier than it is in

Looking through the door of this lodge you will note the cover raised in the rear. This allows better air circulation during warm weather.

its undiluted state. If your tipi has been waterproofed, or has seen a season or so of use, you shouldn't have to worry too much about shrinkage as the paint dries, but if it's new canvas and is untreated, then keep it stretched taut as the water-based latex dries.

Living in a tipi is somewhat different from living in a regular house, or even in a modern tent. For one thing, "tourists" and "flatlanders" often have a hard time comprehending that that pretty and interesting thing is your home, and not a display. Almost everybody who's been rendezvousing for a while can tell you stories of being interrupted in some activity or other by people who didn't realize that they were walking into somebody's home without knocking. There are some standards of tipi "etiquette" that have evolved over the years which can ease the strains of living in such close quarters. Following are some of the "rules" which are followed by most buckskinners, whether they do it consciously or not.

A tipi is considered "locked" if a pair of crossed sticks is laid over the closed door flap. Some of these crossed-stick locks are rather elaborate, with feathers and other decorations, but fancy or plain they mean that nobody's home and the door is locked.

If somebody's home, whether the door is open or not, it's a good idea to "knock" before entering, although the Indian often entered without ceremony. You can do this with a hail: a "Hello, the lodge!" or "Anybody home?" will do, or, you can actually knock if you can hit a lodge pole under the cover.

Although it isn't really a matter of etiquette, you might do well to remember that canvas walls are thin and transmit sound readily. People inside can hear very well what's going on outside; and conversely, people outside can hear what's going on inside. We are conditioned by the thick walls in our houses to think that once you're inside you can't be heard from the outside, but when you go inside a tipi, remember that you can be heard outside, and don't say anything you wouldn't want anyone to hear.

If you are invited to eat in someone's lodge, it's considered the correct thing to bring your own eating utensils. You can't expect your host to supply plate, cup, knife, etc.

Although not observed as rigidly today, traditionally men sat on the north side of the tipi and women on the south. When entering the lodge, men turn to the right as they go in, while women turn to the left. The owner of a lodge has his seat at the back of the lodge, with a seat of honor for guests to his left. Other guests also sit to his left, or the "heart side" as the Laubins point out.

When you enter a lodge, try to pass behind other people already seated around the fire. If you must pass between someone and the fire, always do so with an apology.

Many buckskinners like to add a special touch to their tipis by hand painting them. This lodge is nicely done.

76

If you should find yourself in a pipe-smoking ceremony, the pipe will be lighted by the host at the rear of the lodge, and then passed to his left. Each person to his left will take a puff or two, and continue passing the pipe to the left until it reaches the door. The stem of the pipe always points to the left while it is being passed. After the pipe reaches the door, it will be passed back without smoking until it reaches the person seated by the door on the other side, whence it will be smoked and passed to the left again. The pipe is never smoked unless it is being passed to the left, and it never passes the door. In Indian society, when the host cleaned his pipe (depositing the ashes on the altar), the guests were expected to leave.

If you're unsure how you should behave in a tipi, let common courtesy be your guide, and you won't go far wrong. It's better to err on the safe side and be too polite than to show yourself up as a boor. If you're a host, conduct yourself towards your guests as you would wish to be treated, and conversely.

One of the drawbacks to camping or living in a tipi is that it can be difficult to transport. The cover, liner,

etc., pack up into compact enough bundles, but it's really difficult to fold up your poles.

A variety of methods for hauling the poles is available, but more ingenuity may be required as the trend to smaller cars and trucks continues. We have an old ex-phone company van with the ladder racks still attached, and our poles tie nicely to the top of the van. They extend quite a ways in back, so we have to be aware of warning flag and light requirements. If we're also pulling a trailer we don't have to worry, because the tips of the poles don't extend past the trailer.

Before we got the van, we had a rack that extended the length of the car and fit into sockets bolted to the front and rear bumpers. It was braced so that it was fairly sturdy. A growing number of people are modifying boat trailers or making their own long, light-weight trailers to carry their poles. We've also seen poles carried across the top of a car on a half-inflated large inner tube to serve as a cushion. The poles were bundled and tied down to the front and rear bumpers.

How you will decide to carry your poles will depend, to some extent, on how many you have and how

long they are. We've always thought that long poles extending way up above the top of the lodge, with long, red streamers attached to their tips, are aesthetically more pleasing than short, stubby poles, but there's no denying that the latter are easier to transport. We are sure, however, that anyone who's smart enough to choose to live in a tipi has enough ingenuity to figure out a way to travel with his lodge.

Tipis are, of course, not the only style of "primitive" dwelling available to the buckskinner. As with any form of human endeavor, buckskinning has its fads — remember when everybody *had* to have a Hawken rifle? In the last couple of years there has been a growing interest in traditionally-styled wall-tents, the best being styled after the officers' marquees of Revolutionary times. For some sections of the country these may be more appropriate than the tipi. The tipi, after all, is a Western dwelling, and for those 'skinners who are Eastern oriented, the wall tent may be what they want. A nice feature of a wall tent is that with an asbestos-lined hole in the roof, a sheet-metal stove can be used. Also, because of the straight walls of the tent, cots can be used.

For the single buckskinner, or for one who is travelling without his family and with a minimum of gear, the lean-to may be the answer. There are several styles commercially available (the "Baker" and the "Whe-len"), but in its simplest and most primitive form, a lean-to is nothing more than a piece of canvas stretched over a cross-bar, providing a sloping back to the ground and an open front. The fire is usually set directly in front of the opening, so that, in effect, you are living in a reflector oven. Most lean-tos are designed so that there is a flap of canvas that can be dropped to cover the front opening, and most also have sides, so that the interior can be closed off pretty effectively. For one or two persons the lean-to can be adequate except perhaps in the roughest weather, and it has the advantages of being very portable and comparatively inexpensive. If you can't afford a tipi or a wall tent — and they will cost about the same — consider the lean-to to get you started.

Well, we've given you some suggestions on primitive living quarters, and hopefully have given you enough information so that you will feel confident about obtaining and living in the queen of dwellings, the tipi.

Bibliography:

Laubin, Reginald and Gladys. *The Indian Tipi; Its History, Construction, and Use.* New York: Ballentine Books, 1971.
Mails, Thomas E. *The Mystic Warriors of the Plains.* Garden City, NY: Doubleday & Co., 1972.

The Guns

by Charles Hanson, Jr.

A NATIVE NEBRASKAN, Hanson has had an active life as an engineer, historian and museum director. He has directed numerous major research projects and has written three popular books: THE NORTHWEST GUN, THE PLAINS RIFLE, and THE HAWKEN RIFLE: ITS PLACE IN HISTORY.

He has traveled extensively in the continental United States, Alaska, Canada and Europe, doing detailed research work, and is a recognized authority on the materials and methods of the fur trade. A life member of the National Muzzle-Loading Rifle Association, he began shooting muzzleloaders forty years ago.

Hanson has been director of the Museum of the Fur Trade in Chadron, Nebraska for eleven years and has edited that institution's quarterly magazine for sixteen years. He has made many contributions to the "buckskinner" movement and is a member of the American Mountain Men.

He has three sons. Charles III, of Chadron, Nebraska, is a gunsmith and author of two sketchbooks on trade guns and trade rifles. William, in Anchorage, Alaska, is an engineer and big-game hunter and James, in Washington, D.C., is a Smithsonian Institution staff member and author of four buckskinner sketchbooks and a buckskinner cookbook.

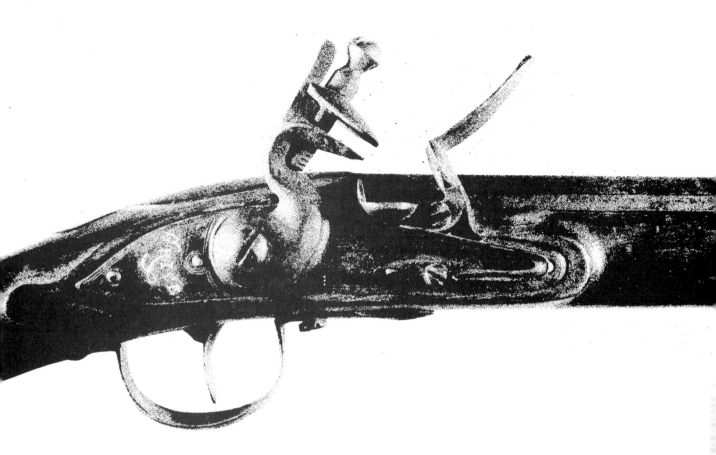

EVERY MAN WHO LEFT the earliest Colonial settlements and ventured into the wilderness carried the best gun he could find. It was his companion, his protector and his commissary. If it ever failed him, he might not come back.

These early guns were marked by strong national characteristics but they shared some common features. They were relatively long, plain, sturdy, lighter in caliber than the contemporary muskets and they were all flint locks.

The Dutch brought long light fowlers with heavy butt stocks and slender barrels of .50 to .65 caliber, and 50 to 55 inches long. An open rear sight and round bead front sight were standard equipment. The locks were light and crude but adapted to frontier use. These Dutch guns were some of the best available in the seventeenth century and were used not only by Dutch traders and thousands of Iroquois hunters but also by other tribes in Pennsylvania and New England.

The French "hunting gun" for "coureurs de bois," voyageurs, and friendly Indians in the eighteenth century were iron-mounted with 28-gauge barrels about 44 inches long and plain full stocks deeply curved at the butt. Front sight was a large blade set several inches back of the muzzle; there was no rear sight. These French guns were serviceable, light and easy to handle in the woods.[1]

Spaniards in Florida, New Mexico, and later in California, carried short light full-stocked miguelet shotguns of typically Spanish Catalonian pattern. The barrels averaged about 38 inches long and of 16 gauge, fitted with iron semi-circular iron front sights only and spur guards. Early British and American writers often

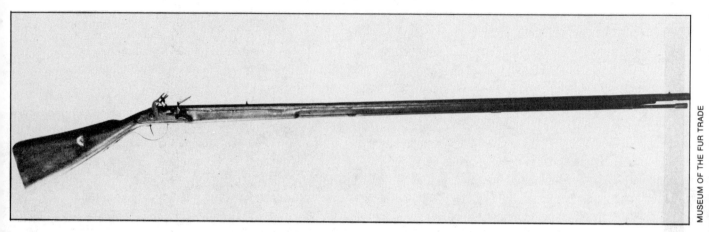

Original Dutch trade musket ca. 1650, 53 inch barrel of .65 caliber.

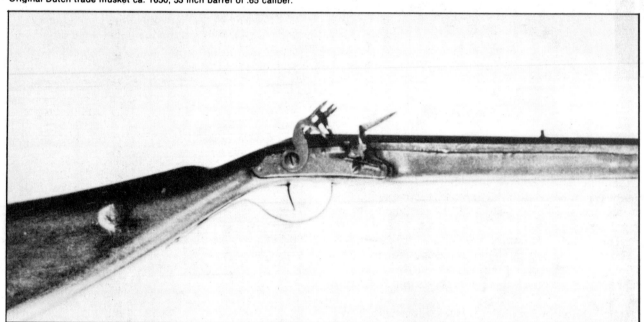

viewed them with contempt due to their antiquated appearance but they were probably the most rugged and durable guns of their time. The miguelet lock had heavy springs and could even draw sparks from roughly shaped pieces of New Mexican quartz. These guns were often referred to in literature as "escopetas," which is simply the Spanish word for "shotguns."

Swedish and Finnish traders in Delaware and New Jersey brought some of the most exotic weapons to the new continent. The parts of at least one western Russian style hunting gun have been found in Delaware. These early guns had relatively short octagon barrels of small bore, usually rifled, flaring buttstocks and snaphaunce locks with straight hammers fitted with a finger loop on the top jaw.[2]

The first standard musket of the English colonies was a match lock but these guns were of little use for long travels in the woods. Light slender flintlock fowling pieces soon appeared in quantity and by 1680 the prototype of the famous Northwest gun was already being sold in Hudson's Bay. It had a part octagon barrel

81

French hunting gun found in Ontario. Made at Tulle about 1740. Iron-mounted, 45-inch barrel of .63 caliber.

at least four feet long of about 20 gauge, fluted rod pipes, flat nailed-on butt plate, an ornamental serpentine brass sideplate, a conventional flintlock and an iron guard with thin finials and a wide bow.[3] Similar light fowlers, many of them more finely made and with brass mounts, were carried all over the English frontier for the next hundred years.

Most of the fowlers were imported from England but the colonists themselves began in the eighteenth century to produce the American rifle. In all its succeeding variations this was the gun of the American frontier — one of the tools of American destiny. Popularly known as the "Kentucky rifle" after 1800, it was a modification of the short, large-bore hunting rifles brought from Europe by early German settlers in Pennsylvania. By the middle of the eighteenth century the pattern was fairly well set, with the rifled octagonal barrel, heavy buttstock with cheek-piece and patch box of the German rifle combined with the graceful lines and lighter bore of the English fowler.

The extent of the rifle's use on the frontier before the Revolution is amazing. They were in general use not only in Pennsylvania but in Georgia, Kentucky, Virginia, the Carolinas, the Ohio valley and Michigan. Many rifles in the period still used the Germanic sliding-wood patch box; others had rather plain and simple brass patchboxes — another American innovation. Many of them had plainer wood than later guns, and single triggers were very common. They were made for frontier service and calibers were usually in the range of .45 to .52. Some sophisticated Indian tribes like the Delaware and Shawnee had adopted the rifle by the time of the Revolution.[4]

In the last quarter of the eighteenth century there were two significant developments in the Kentucky rifle story. The Pennsylvania rifles blossomed forth in a new quality of craftsmanship and ornamentation that produced "The Golden Age" of rifles, and in the southern highlands a new breed of rifle-makers began to produce a distinctive "Southern" Kentucky, much plainer but still long and heavy.

Early southern rifles were of heavy caliber for bear hunting and Indian fighting, unlike those of later years intended for deer, 'coon and squirrels. Iron mountings were common and some of them were crude. Dozens of these rifles began their careers killing bears in canebreaks for hams and oil and ended their existence in the wilds of the Rocky Mountains.

The early riflemen who crossed the Appalachians already had distinctive equipment. They were tomahawk men and the hand-forged hunters' tomahawks of that period make a fascinating field for collectors. Many of them had a hammer poll opposite the blade, others carried spikes or spear-like points, but few of them had the pipe bowl of the tomahawk intended for the Indian trade. Early hunting bags tended to be of a deep rectangular shape. Horns were large and often carved. Some horns and pouches were carried military fashion on separate decorated shoulder straps. Other accessories included hand-made hunting knives, bullet molds, carved bone or antler chargers, tinder boxes and clasp knives.[5]

The shooting skill of the experienced frontier rifle-

Seventeenth century Spanish civilian shotgun or "escopeta." Carried to California by Colonists from Mexico.

The American Longrifle made in Pennsylvania was a favorite of pioneers on the eastern frontier.

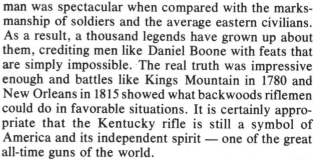

Lancaster-type rifle by Pennsylvania gunsmith Jacob Dickert. Top flat of barrel bears maker's name and crossed arrow and tomahawk in an oval stamp. This .50 cal. barrel is 43¾ inches long.

MUSEUM OF THE FUR TRADE

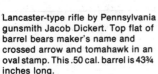

man was spectacular when compared with the marksmanship of soldiers and the average eastern civilians. As a result, a thousand legends have grown up about them, crediting men like Daniel Boone with feats that are simply impossible. The real truth was impressive enough and battles like Kings Mountain in 1780 and New Orleans in 1815 showed what backwoods riflemen could do in favorable situations. It is certainly appropriate that the Kentucky rifle is still a symbol of America and its independent spirit — one of the great all-time guns of the world.

Some observations of Colonel George Hanger who served as captain of a Hessian jager corps of the Revolutionary War, may be of interest:

No small shot gun, during my residence of seven years of war in America, was ever kept in the house of a backwoodsman. You will often see a boy not over ten years of age driving the cattle home, but not without a rifle on his shoulder; they never stir out on any business, or on a journey without their rifles. Practice from their infancy, teaches them all distances . . .

I never in my life saw better rifles (or men who shot better) than those made in America. They are chiefly made in Lancaster, and two or three neighboring towns in that vicinity in Pennsylvania. The barrels weigh about six pounds two or three ounces and carry a ball no larger than thirty-six to the pound; at least I never saw one of a larger caliber, and I have seen many hundreds and hundreds.[6]

83

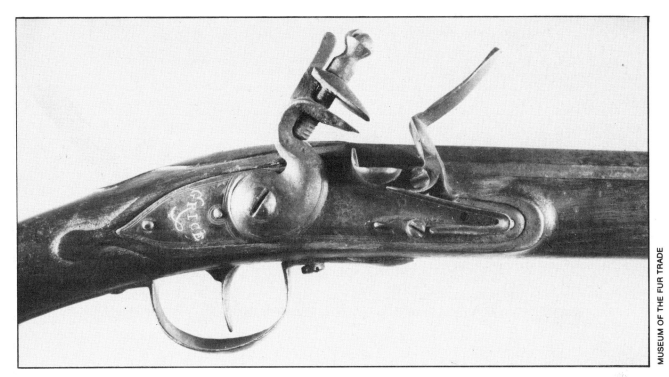

Very early Northwest gun by Grice with three screw lock and unbridled pan.

Most people today are most interested in early Kentuckies for their artistic and historical attributes. Fortunately, we do have left to us the specifications of a few "long hunter" rifles.

The famous Edward Marshall rifle, an early transitional Jager-Kentucky, had a 37½ inch barrel of ⅝ inch bore with six grooves and weighed 9¾ pounds.[7] A rifle made by Mills of Harrodsburg, Kentucky, about 1806 had a 45-inch, wide barrel of 36 gauge and weighed 9¼ pounds. It was full-stocked, steel mounted, fitted with double set triggers and a fine English lock by Egg.[8] A rifle made by Michael Humble of Louisville, Kentucky, in 1782 and believed to have been carried by Daniel Boone, was described by Horace Kephart:

> The total length of the weapon is 63½ inches.
> The barrel is 48¾ inches long, of 1 inch exterior
> diameter, and 7/16 inch caliber (.44 taking 54
> round balls to the pound). The front sight is of
> silver, set very low on the barrel, 1⅞ inches from
> the muzzle. The rear sight is iron, set 35 inches
> from the muzzle and about 17 inches from the
> eye. The barrel was made from a bar of wrought
> iron, hammered to an octagonal form, and
> though quite smooth, shows the marks of the
> hammer. The flintlock and double set triggers
> are of the customary backwoods pattern. The
> stock is of maple . . . The rifle weighs eleven
> pounds . . .[9]

During all this period of development for the American rifle, the light, efficient, smooth bore Northwest gun reached its final stage of standardization as the gun of the fur trade. It was being regularly turned out by English gunmakers in barrel lengths of 36, 42 and 48 inches of 24 gauge, normally using a 28 gauge ball. The long slender barrels were part-octagon, the rounded locks had gooseneck cocks, replaceable pans and unbridled frizzens and tumblers. Though a light, cheap gun the locks were dependable and the barrels were government proved to be as safe as any other civilian weapon. No rear sight was provided at the factory but a tall iron semicircular front sight about 3/16 inch high was brazed on a few inches from the muzzle. Ornamental tear drops were carved at the tail of the lock plate and around the barrel tang. The walnut stock had a deeply curved butt with deep grooves on each side of the comb. The buttplate was a flat piece of sheet brass with a short rounded tang, fastened on with small square nails. The rod guides were ribbed brass and the guard was flush mounted iron with rounded end finials, held with two or three screws. The distinctive side plate was a cast brass sea serpent in a design which remained a trademark for at least 150 years. This light musket performed well with either shot or ball and it was a universal favorite of Indians from Louisiana to Hudson Bay, along with thousands of voyageurs and mixed-blood hunters and trappers. In fact, the Northwest gun was almost the universal shot gun of the fur trade frontier for everything from duck shooting to running buffalo on horseback and serving as a garrison gun in trading post guardrooms.

After we became a world nation, the frontier moved on rapidly. In the Northwest territory the frontiersmen

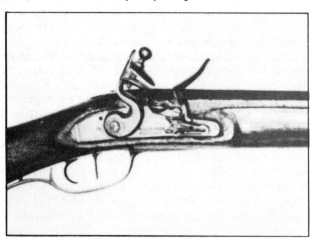

Flintlock Indian trade rifle, by Henry Deringer ca. 1820, 44-inch barrel .54 caliber. Note "eaglehead" patchbox finial.

still forged ahead with their long flint lock rifles but some of them were now marked by makers in Ohio and Kentucky.

Muskets were seldom used by long hunters but some backwoodsmen did use them for bear hunting and general shooting for the pot. The third model Brown Bess was readily available in the United States and Canada and was seen in frontier use occasionally. The Museum of the Fur Trade has an 1806 example which was carried by an Iroquois Indian voyageur and another obtained from Indiana Indians in 1828. Third models carried by Manuel Lisa and Solomon Juneau were pictured by Dillin in *The Kentucky Rifle*.

The Indians still preferred the Northwest gun but more and more of them were using commercial-grade Pennsylvania rifles of the regular Kentucky pattern. A great many of the early Indian rifles came from the Henrys of Pennsylvania. Hundreds of others came from England by way of British traders and peace commissioners. In the late 1790's the U.S. Office of Indian Trade was selling rifles by Jacob Dickert and Henry De Huff. A few years later that office tried Frederick Geotz and George Kreps as suppliers and finally switched to Henry Deringer in 1809.[10]

These trade rifles were intended primarily for sale to Indians but they were available to anyone visiting a United States Office of Indian Trade "Factory" (trading post). The earlier American rifles were conventional "Kentuckies" of plain grade, with brass patch boxes and fittings. Deringer, on the other hand, developed a rather distinctive style of trade rifle with a

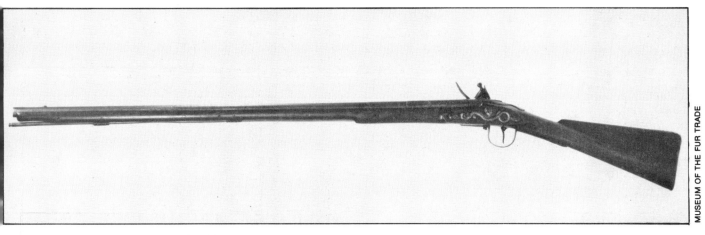

Northwest gun by Pritchett, 1819. Lock and barrel stamped with tombstone fox mark.

slightly roman-nosed stock, a sturdy Deringer-made lock with flat gooseneck hammer and a cast brass patchbox with a top finial in the shape of an eagle's head.

The English trade and gift rifles were even more distinctive. Some of the earliest models by Grice were almost exact duplicates of Lancaster rifles, including patchboxes with daisy finials and early Kentucky butt plates, side plates and guards of cast brass. The stocks of all English rifles were walnut. By 1780 or 1790 the English trade rifles were using the simple Baker type patchbox and the stocks had lines somewhat suggestive of contemporary English muskets. In 1820 the American Fur Company was selling English rifles around the Great Lakes, gradually shifting to American suppliers like Henry during the 1820's. English trade rifles were also sold to the southern Indians by English trading firms based in Florida and Spanish Louisiana. By 1820 most southern Indians were using American rifles.

By this time the Northwest gun had been slightly modernized. The old three-screw lockplate gave way to a pattern using only two side screws. Gradually the antiquated tang screw coming up from the bottom of the stock gave way to one going downward through the tang to engage a half trigger plate. Bridles were placed on the pan and the tumbler of the lock. Shorter thirty-inch barrels were introduced for those who wished them. Butt plates fastened with two screws began to supplant

the old nailed-on variety but were not adopted by the Hudson's Bay Company until about 1850.

By 1810 a few Northwest guns were being made in Belgium and the first American Northwest guns were produced by Deringer in 1816.

Almost as soon as Louisiana was purchased in 1803 and the old Spanish restrictions on trade and intercourse by foreigners was lifted, American settlers moved into Missouri and Arkansas and American traders and trappers started up the Missouri toward the Rockies. They brought rifles from Pennsylvania and Kentucky with a generous sprinkling of rifles from Ohio, Indiana, Virginia and Tennessee.

To meet the demands for new guns and replacements on the frontier, John Joseph Henry and a score of lesser makers began the organized shop production of good plain American flint lock rifles. Skilled labor and expensive machinery was scarce on the frontier and those smiths who did establish themselves in places like St. Louis could not compete either in price or quantity with the established Pennsylvania gunmakers.

For this reason, the large trapping brigades organized by entrepreneurs like William Ashley and Astor's American Fur Company were generally supplied with rifles made in Pennsylvania. Most popular model was the Henry "Lancaster" pattern, a cheap version of the Pennsylvania-Kentucky rifle with full maple stock, checkered wrist, long patchbox, 5-inch flint lock, 42 to

Late Hudson's Bay Company Northwest gun by Parker Field & Co., 1868.

Belgian Northwest gun
stamped "Burnett 1844,"
original flintlock, 36-inch
barrel.

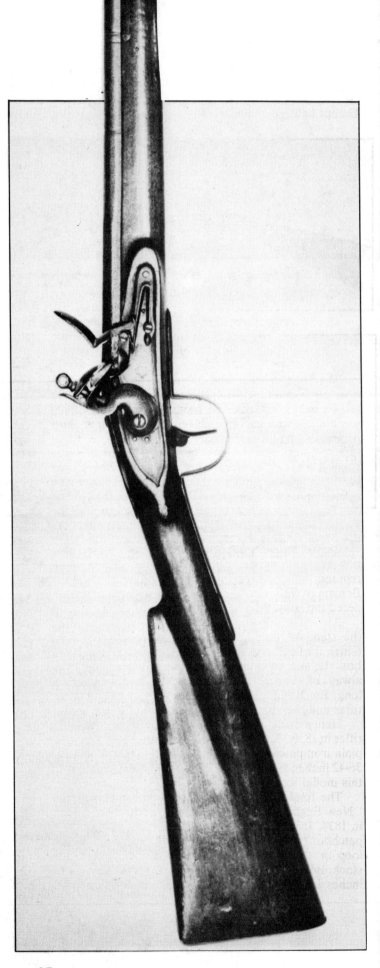

44 inch barrel varying from 28 to 45 gauge and single or double triggers. Similar guns were supplied in smaller quantities by Henry Gibbs, Joseph Brandt, J. Moore of New York, Jacob Gumpf, John Dreppard, Christopher Gumpf and Jacob Fordney.

"Lancaster Pattern" flintlock trade rifle by J. Henry, Boulton, Pa.

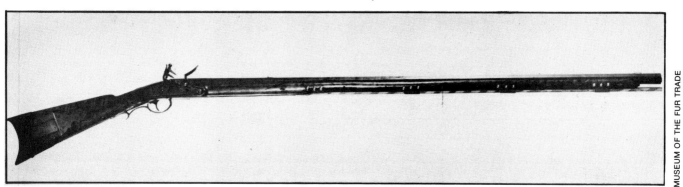

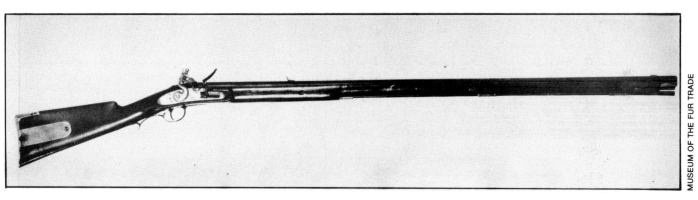

Flintlock trade rifle in "English Pattern" by J. Henry, Boulton, Pa.

This Lancaster rifle was used by the Rocky Mountain Fur Company in its later years. Kit Carson is reputed to have carried a rifle of this type made by Benjamin Gill. The American Fur Company first ordered this style for its "Mountain Outfit" in 1826.

Also first ordered in 1826 was Henry's imitation of the standard English trade rifle with walnut stock, 6-inch flintlock and British military-style brass patchbox. It was known as the "English" rifle and was always of 32 gauge with octagon barrels 42 to 44 inches long. Jim Bridger is known to have used one of these rifles and they were popular in the mountains.

Henry made a few special steel-mounted trappers' rifles in 1830-33. They had a steel Kentucky guard, long plain iron patchbox, rainproof flintlock and barrels of 36-42 inches long with bores of 28 to 40 gauge. Most of this model were sent to Fort Union.

The final model of the Henry trade rifle was the "New English" or "Scroll Guard" pattern developed in 1834. It was ordinarily fitted with the English style patchbox (with the Lancaster patchbox as an option), a loop or "scroll" guard, 5-inch flint lock and maple stock. Bores varied from 32 to 35. Barrels were 40 to 44 inches long. This style was popular with traders and

J. Henry flintlock trade rifle in "New English" or "Scroll Guard" pattern.

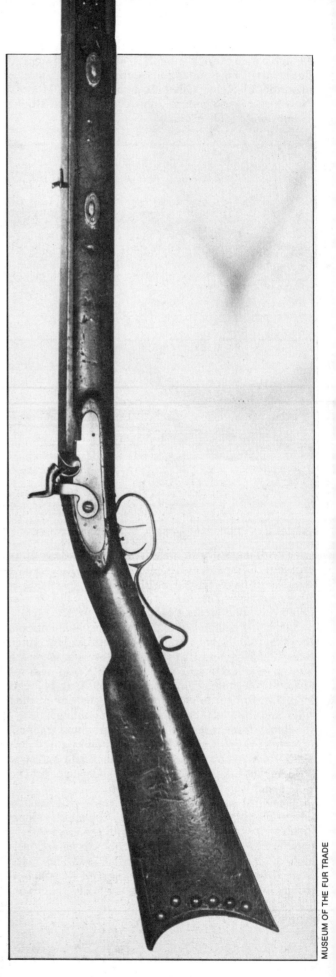

trappers in the 1835 to 1840 period. After 1840 both the New English and the Lancaster styles were also made in percussion, primarily for the Indian trade.

Western trappers who brought their own rifles used a variety of Kentucky and Southern rifles. One of the most famous western riflemaking firms in St. Louis was J & S Hawken, a partnership formed in 1825 by two brothers, Jacob and Samuel Hawken of Hagerstown, Maryland. Their production was small, probably a hundred rifles per year or less, but they developed a distinctive rifle which showed some southern influences. It was of heavy bore, .45 to .54 caliber, iron mounted with scroll guard and wide butt, nearly always in percussion with barrels usually under 40 inches. Stocks were made generally of maple in both full and half stock styles.

Hawken percussion rifles were being carried by mountain brigade leaders as early as 1831 and they were popular with American Fur Company employees. Legend has long credited the Hawken rifle with being the universal gun for the mountain men but this simply is not so. They were expensive and uncommon in the mountain man period but they were available in percussion very early and were of fine quality. Men like Lucien Fontenelle, Andrew Drips and Peter Sarpy carried them in the 1830's while the trappers who stayed in the mountains generally preferred flintlocks.

Hawkens were popular in the 1840's on the Santa Fe Trail and continued to be good rifles for scouts, explorers and traders until the Civil War period. Jacob Hawken died in 1849 and Samuel Hawken continued the business alone until 1854. His son W. S. Hawken took over the shop but it failed in 1857 and passed to William Watt, who sold it to John P. Gemmer about 1865. For a very detailed history of the Hawken rifle and its contemporaries see *The Hawken Rifle: Its Place in History* by Charles E. Hanson, Jr. (Chadron, NE. 1979).

The gold rushes in 1849 and 1859 brought many new gun shops into being in St. Louis and the plains rifle burst into full flower. Rifles of the Hawken type, generally half-stocked, usually iron mounted, with heavy barrels of .54 caliber were made by dozens of St. Louis makers like H. E. Dimick, Reno Beauvais, Tristam Campbell, T. Albright, Frederick Schwarz and Meyer Friede. In the same period similar guns were being made by S. O'Dell in Natchez, Mississippi, Carlos Gove in Council Bluffs and William Rotton in Nebraska City.

The old Henry firm in Boulton, Pennsylvania was still producing heavy half-stocks in both brass and iron mountings during the Civil War and some of them were captured from hostile Indians in the 1870's.

Tryon of Philadelphia produced flintlock trade rifles from 1830-1855 but the most prolific supplier in later trade days was Henry Leman. He made flintlock trade rifles as early as 1837 and supplied them at least as late as 1855. He also produced large numbers of short full-stocked "Indian rifles" with percussion locks, plain brass mounts, heavy barrels of .45 to .60 caliber and artificially-striped maple stocks with distinctive cap boxes having a finial of fleur-de-lis design.

The muzzle-loading plains rifle held on until after the Civil War in the face of increasing competition from Sharps percussion and early cartridge hunting rifles and finally from the Henry brass-framed .44 rimfire repeaters.

In the mid-19th century a few improvements were made in Northwest guns. The late 1850's saw the introduction of some percussion models by American suppliers, notably by Henry Leman. The Hudson's Bay Company adopted double-throat hammers and five-screw buttplates about 1850 and introduced percussion

guns with Enfield-type locks in 1861. By 1865 Henry, Tryon and Leman were no longer making Northwest guns due to the limited market and the few still being sold were imported from Belgium. Importations from that country continued until at least 1877.

Double barreled shotguns played an important role on the frontier in the nineteenth century. The Hudson's Bay Company sold double flint shotguns at least as late as 1860. It introduced light percussion doubles in the 1840's and continued to sell them until World War I. Pierre Chouteau Jr. & Co. sold both flint and percussion doubles made by W. Chance & Son of Birmingham in the 1850's and other traders sold ordinary doubles from firms like Tryon of Philadelphia and Robert Hyslop of New York.

Double shotguns formed part of the equipment for trapper brigades and they were mentioned by Jim Beckworth, Bill Hamilton, Josiah Gregg on the Santa Fe Trail, Fremont in 1842 and Frederick Kurz at Fort Union in 1857. At the time of his death Kit Carson still owned a light double shotgun made by Frederick Hellinghaus who worked successively at St. Louis, San Francisco and The Dalles, Oregon. In the 1850's H. E. Dimick advertised heavy shotguns for buffalo running. An example of this type in the Museum of the Fur Trade has short heavy 30-inch barrels of 13 gauge with heavy breeches, thick butt stock and double barrel keys.

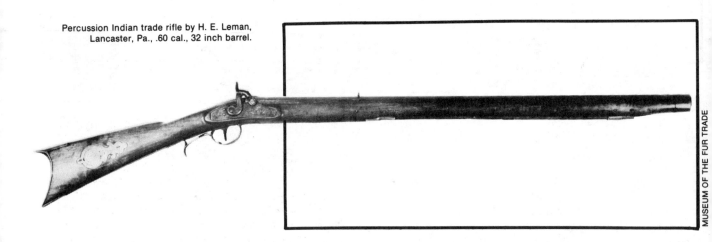

Percussion Indian trade rifle by H. E. Leman, Lancaster, Pa., .60 cal., 32 inch barrel.

MUSEUM OF THE FUR TRADE

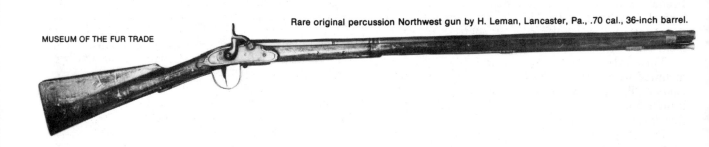

Rare original percussion Northwest gun by H. Leman, Lancaster, Pa., .70 cal., 36-inch barrel.

MUSEUM OF THE FUR TRADE

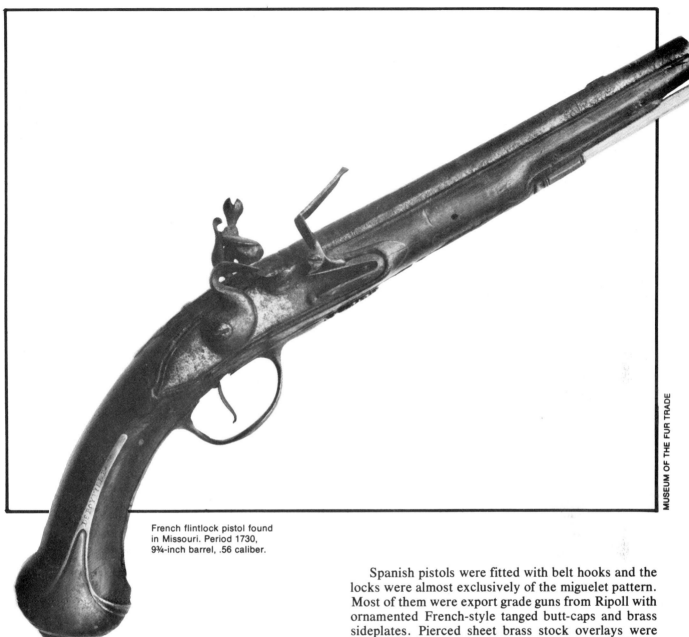

French flintlock pistol found
in Missouri. Period 1730,
9¾-inch barrel, .56 caliber.

So far we haven't talked about pistols but they were important. It was the only way a man could have a second quick shot in the days of muzzle-loaders.

In the century preceding the Revolution, the Dutch, French, Spanish and English long hunters all carried typical semi-military holster pistols of their own national patterns. Barrel lengths ran from seven to twelve inches and calibers varied from 0.50 to 0.75.

The early Dutch pistols were generally iron-mounted with sloping stocks and thin barrels of small caliber. The typical trigger guard, whether brass or iron, had a fork at the front end of the bow — a distinctive early characteristic.

French pistols were usually brass mounted, had part-octagon barrels and graceful stocks with oval butt-caps having long tangs up each side of the grip. Many of even the plainer grades showed cast or engraved ornamentation on the brass fittings.

Spanish pistols were fitted with belt hooks and the locks were almost exclusively of the miguelet pattern. Most of them were export grade guns from Ripoll with ornamented French-style tanged butt-caps and brass sideplates. Pierced sheet brass stock overlays were common. Calibers varied from .60 to .70. These pistols were common in Florida, Louisiana, Missouri, New Mexico and California.

English pistols of the seventeenth century had slender barrels as long as fourteen inches. Until about 1680 most of them had iron mountings and the cheaper grades had surface-mounted guards like trade guns. During the eighteenth century the common English "horse" or "holster" pistol was brass-mounted, full-stocked and fitted with barrels 8 to 12 inches long, generally round and fitted with front sight only. Bores averaged 22 to 18 to the pound. Such pistols were purchased in pairs and were common in the colonies. In the 1800-1830 period most of the English and Belgian export pistols were flintlocks with brass or iron barrels 8 or 9 inches long, usually round but some of the brass barrels were full-octagon. These later flintlocks were brass-mounted and made with round butt caps without the long tangs of the older "pirate pistol" styles.[11]

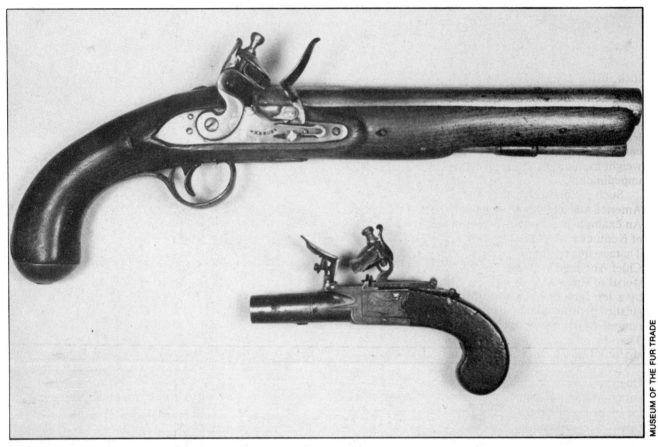

Top: .68 caliber Wheeler belt pistol with 9-inch iron barrel. Bottom: Wheeler pocket pistol with "secret trigger" and 1½-inch barrel.

These flint horse pistols were common all over the frontier and there are numerous references to traders all the way from northwestern Canada to the posts for the Chickasaws carrying "braces" (pairs) of pistols. Hunters, trappers and a few Indians also used them.[12] The Hudson's Bay Company regularly purchased "pistols for trade" in Colonial times but no identified specimen has come down to us for study.

These flintlock smoothbore pistols were not made in calibers to match trade guns, rifles or even muskets carried by the owner. They were generally of .60 to .69 caliber designed to carry a multi-ball load as heavy as was practical to fire easily with one hand. Their one purpose was personal defense at short range. As an example, in the early 1800's the Hudson's Bay Company purchased some pistols, to arm its personnel, which were short, light, of big bore and fitted with belt hooks.

The plain horse pistol was a standard item on the frontier for a long time. Osborne Russell had a large "German (Belgian) horse pistol" at the battle of Pierre's Hole. Parkman saw the horse guard at Fort Laramie with a dragoon pistol thrust in his belt. Peters claimed that Carson shot the bully Shunar with a dragoon pistol at the Rendezvous of 1835. Washington Irving described his first buffalo hunt at Fort Gibson in 1832:

I was provided with a brace of veteran brass-barreled pistols, which I had borrowed at Fort Gibson, and which had evidently seen some service. Pistols are very effective in buffalo hunting, as the hunter can ride up close to the animal, and fire at it while at full speed; whereas the long heavy rifles used on the frontier, cannot be easily managed, nor discharged with accurate aim from horseback. My object, therefore, was to get within pistol shot of the buffalo.[13]

Some of the "horse pistols" were probably obsolete English or American army pistols but military guns were generally unpopular due to their excessive size and weight.

In the flintlock period the true rifleman had another choice in the way of pistols. American smith-made pistols appeared well before the Revolution. Most of the early pistols showed French, German or English design features, had round or part-octagon barrels in brass or iron and were stocked in walnut. Bores varied from .40 to .70 caliber. By the time of the Revolutionary War rifled octagon barrels and curly maple stocks had come into fashion. These newer pistols were light, graceful and attractive. Most of them had a plain brass butt cap and showed many features of the Kentucky rifle. Until the War of 1812, Kentucky pistols were generally made for civilian riflemen. From that period on, the majority of the Kentucky pistols were made for gentlemen and military officers. Some were fancy and some were very plain.[14]

The vast majority of Kentucky pistols were flint-lock, using Germanic or English locks. The style did persist into the 1840's and a few were made in original percussion. While officers liked the pistols in pairs, some hunters preferred a single pistol carried in a leather belt holster. A pair of them, could of course, be carried the same way if the owner could stand their weight in addition to his knife, horn, pouch and other impediments.

Such pistols were the first really accurate pistol in America and a few men became proficient in their use. An example in point was Colonel Richard M. Johnson of Kentucky who led his militiamen at the Battle of the Thames during the War of 1812. His encounter with Chief Tecumseh during the battle is best told in the words of Bosworth: "Let it not be forgotten that it was by a ten inch rifled pistol, in the hands of our distinguished fellow-citizen, Col. R. M. Johnson, that the famous warrior Tecumseh fell, at the battle of the Thames, and this, after the colonel's left hand had been shattered by the ball of Tecumseh's rifle." [15]

By 1830 percussion pistols were on the market and some new styles appeared. The famous Hawken brothers regularly made a few pistols and orders have been located covering the period 1826-1846. These Hawken pistols varied from short, light pistols suitable for a coat pocket to long models with swivel ramrods for use of militia officers. Peter Sarpy, Bellevue trader and partner in the firm of Sarpy and Fraeb, bought several Hawken pistols through the years.[16]

Henry Deringer finally became famous for the small pocket pistols which made his name a common noun, but in the days of the fur trade he turned out many fine pistols and they were probably the most sought-after pistols on the frontier in the 1830-1850 period. Like the Hawkens, Deringer adopted the percussion system very early. His pistols were usually half-stocked, many of them had octagon barrels, guards were usually fitted with spurs but many were the D-shaped type. Calibers varied from .36 to .54 and all the ones examined were rifled.

The famous Big-Foot Wallace said that when he came to Texas in 1837 he had a good rifle from Virginia, a pair of Deringer pistols and a Bowie-knife.[17] This was probably considered to be first class armament for a fighting man. A number of American Fur Company men carried Deringer pistols in the 1830's. Hercules Dousman did; H. H. Sibley had a pair, steel-mounted with 8-inch rifled barrels of 75 gauge and Bernard Pratte of St. Louis used a pair with 4½-inch rifled octagon barrels of 45 gauge. The company ordered a pair with steel mounts and 4-inch barrels of 60 gauge in 1839, "similar to those made for us in 1838." [18] The Museum of the Fur Trade has a good Deringer pistol, half-stocked, with steel spur guard, single-set trigger and 7-inch rifled barrel of .45 caliber.

After 1830 there were also a multitude of commercial percussion or light dueling pistols available. Jedediah Smith was carrying a pair of silver mounted

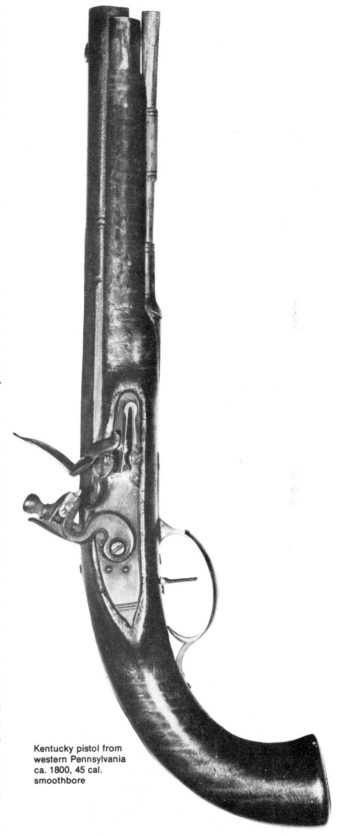

Kentucky pistol from western Pennsylvania ca. 1800, 45 cal. smoothbore

half-stocked percussion pistols when he was killed on the Cimarron in 1831. Fremont had a pair from J. Cooper, New York in 1845. Pierre Chouteau Jr. & Co. was buying 6 and 7-inch barreled half-stocked, German silver mounted chance belt pistols in 1855 and twist-barreled percussion belt pistols from Robert Hyslop as early as 1850. Guns of the same type were made by Tryon, Krider, Robinson, Constable and Robertson in Philadelphia; Marcy of Keokuk, Iowa; Hudson of Cincinnati and a host of others. By 1838 St. Louis dealers were also advertising rifled pistols with 4½ to 8-inch barrels from the Allen factory at Grafton, Massachusetts.

In 1841 Rufus Sage gave this graphic eye-witness description of a "genuine mountaineer":

His waist is encircled with a belt of leather, holding encased his butcher knife and pistols — while from his neck is suspended a bullet-pouch securely fastened to the belt in front, and beneath the right arm hangs a powder-horn transversely from his shoulder, behind which, upon the strap attached to it, are affixed his bullet-mould, ball-screw, wiper, and, etc. With a gun-stick made of some hard wood, and a good rifle placed in his hands, carrying from thirty–thirty-five balls to the pound, the reader will have before him a correct likeness of a genuine mountaineer when fully equipped.[19]

The Allen pepperbox appeared in 1837 or shortly thereafter. Through the 1840's it far outsold the Colt revolver. It was made in a variety of models — four, five and six shot, calibers from .28 to almost .40 and barrel lengths from 3 to 6 inches. The largest models were called dragoons and were popular in the West, especially with soldiers. It made a good holster gun and could belch forth six shots in a matter of seconds with a terrifying cloud of smoke and flame. A late mountain man could have had one and thousands of travelers and forty-niners did have them. In the 1840's the popular

cartoon image of the Yankee always included a big pepperbox and a Bowie knife.

The famous Colt pocket model Paterson revolvers appeared about 1837, followed by the larger belt and holster (Texas) patterns a year later. They found immediate favor in the West. Gregg carried Colts on the Santa Fe trail in 1839 and Oliver Wiggins claimed that Kit Carson and his band of scouts carried them while fighting Indians on the Sante Fe in 1841.[20] The Texas Rangers used them extensively.

After the Paterson firm failed in 1842 Colt made no revolvers until the Mexican War. The new Colt establishment which began in 1848 made dragoons and pocket revolvers and in 1850 began to make the model 1851 navy revolver which was not discontinued until 1873. The Navy was a classic western gun, a favorite of traders, and, along with a Hawken rifle and a Bowie knife, the standard equipment of scouts and old mountain men until the days of the Bozeman Trail. No other percussion revolver approached it in western popularity in the 1850's and '60's. It only faded away in the face of, first, the Smith & Wesson .44 American revolver and, then, the .45 Colt Six-Shooter.

Henry Deringer belt pistol ca. 1830. 7-inch barrel, .44 caliber, rifled.

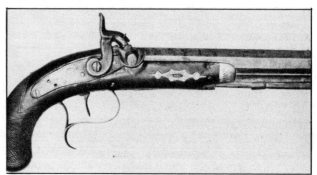

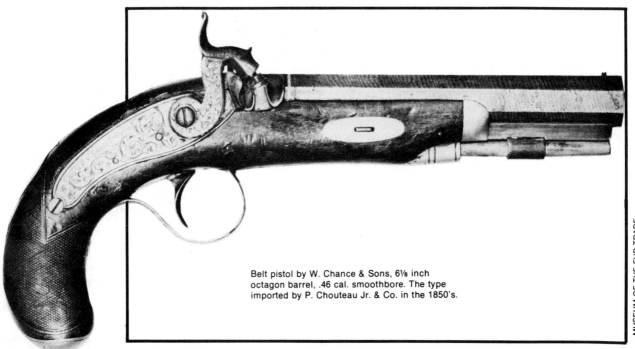

Belt pistol by W. Chance & Sons, 6⅛ inch octagon barrel, .46 cal. smoothbore. The type imported by P. Chouteau Jr. & Co. in the 1850's.

Pocket pistols, of course, went with many a longhunter. For a hundred years the little center-hammer flintlock pocket pistols with folding triggers were reassuring companions in the pocket or under a pillow. They were followed by similar little brass-framed boxlock percussion pistols in the 1830's and '40's until Henry Deringer's famous little .41 single-shot percussion guns monopolized the field. The 1860's brought the first D. Moore, National and Williamson .41 rimfire derringers, the .22 Sharps four-barrel and the little Smith and Wesson .22 up-break revolver which fascinated the famous old trader Nick Janis when he saw one at Fort Laramie in 1866. He called it a "play toy".[21]

This brief overview of longhunters' guns can do no more than give some idea of the broad range of styles and types of guns involved and of the long period of time they covered. There are excellent works available which go into great detail about the various special kinds of guns used at different times and places. Many of these guns are available to the modern buckskinner in reproduction. Most of the parts needed to build others are available but the reproduction of some types will require both skill and patience.

Above all, we can be thankful that we live in a time when we can most fully appreciate and enjoy the good parts of the past. We can devote our spare time to learning what made our predecessors brave and imaginative and at the same time self-reliant and practical. Perhaps we will find that we have more of those qualities than we thought!

Bibliography
1. Russell Bouchard, "The Trade Gun in New France, 1690-1760." *The Canadian Journal of Arms Collecting.* Vol. 15, No. 1
2. See W. W. Greener, *The Gun and Its Development,* Ninth Edition. 1910. Reprint New York. n.d. 76-77.
3. S. James Gooding, "Trading Guns of the Hudson's Bay Company 1670-1700." *The Canadian Journal of Arms Collecting,* Vol. 13, No. 3, 75-91.
4. "David Zeisberger's History of the Northern American Indians." *Ohio Archaeological and Historical Society Publications,* Vol. XIX, Columbus 1910. 85.
5. Madison Grant, *The Kentucky Rifle Hunting Pouch.* York, Pa. 1977.
6. Horace Kephart, "A British Expert on American Backwoods Rifle Shooting." *Shooting and Fishing,* February 24, 1898. 382.
7. Horace Kephart, "Reply to Captain Meyrick," *Shooting and Fishing,* December 9, 1897. 148.
8. "An Old-Time Rifle." *Shooting and Fishing.* November 25, 1897. 107.
9. Horace Kephart, "The Rifle of Daniel Boone." *Shooting and Fishing,* March 3, 1898. 403.
10. Charles Hanson, Jr., "Henry Deringer and the Indian Trade," *Museum of the Fur Trade Quarterly,* Fall 1979. 5-11.
11. See J. N. George, *English Pistols and Revolvers.* Onslow County, N.C. 1938. Chapters 1 through 5.
12. Charles Hanson, Jr., "Arming the Traders and the Clerks," *Museum of the Fur Trade Quarterly,* Summer 1975. 1-3.
13. Washington Irving, *Tour on the Prairies.* New York 1886. 110.
14. John G. W. Dillin, *The Kentucky Rifle,* York, Pa. 1959. 132-145.
15. N. Boxworth, *A Treatise on the Rifle, Musket, Pistol,* and *Fowling Piece.* New York, 1846. 104-105.
16. See Charles E. Hanson, Jr., *The Hawken Rifle: Its Place in History.* Chadron, Nebr. 1979.
17. John C. Duval, *The Adventures of Big-Foot Wallace,* Lincoln, Ne. 1966. 8.
18. Letterbooks, Volumes 7 and 8. American Fur Co. Papers. New York Historical Society.
19. Rufus B. Sage, *Rocky Mountain Life.* Dayton, n.d. 38.
20. Edward L. Sabin, *Kit Carson Days.* New York 1935. 310-11.
21. Alson B. Ostrander, *An Army Boy of the Sixties.* Chicago 1924. 102-3.

The Clothing

by Pat Tearney

PAT TEARNEY HAS BEEN BURNING black powder since about 1964, when he was invited to a Cavalry Gymkhana and Indian Wars period re-enactment. One sniff of smoke, one shot fired and he, like many others, was thoroughly hooked. Since then he has been a member of several shooting groups such as the Western States Muzzleloading Association, the National Rifle Association, the National Association of Primitive Riflemen, and the National Muzzleloading Rifle Association, of which he is currently a member of the Board of Directors. He has also been active in several local black powder clubs where he has lived.

Pat is primarily known for his fine historical garments and accessories. He has been in this field for over twenty-five years (with time out for four years in the Air Force). He was partner in an Indian craft shop in Kansas in the mid 1950's where he began his professional career as a maker of historical clothing. This was mostly Indian regalia.

After the Air Force, he entered partnership in a shop in Canoga Park, California. Here he stayed for nearly fifteen years as partner, manager, research person, tailor and pattern maker.

In 1972 Pat left "The Robe" and moved to Rawlins, Montana where he opened a new shop as senior partner. After only two years in Montana he and his wife Karalee were offered a chance to open a real 18th century trading post at Historic Fort de Chartres on the bank of the Mississippi River just an hour's drive south of St. Louis near Prairie du Rocher, Illinois.

Pat and Karalee, with their two children Heather and Conan, pulled up stakes and left the "Shining Mountains" for the "Father of Waters". Here they have settled and are once again serving buckskinners and living history buffs by making top quality historic clothing and accessories as well as offering a fine line of historic tradegoods.

IN WELL OVER TWO DECADES of professional costume making I have often been asked, "Why should I make a costume?" "Will it make me a better shot?" "Will I have a better time?"

Well, the answer to these questions can be both yes and no. It depends of course on the individual and what he or she wishes to get out of the sport. It depends on their overall interest.

To a bench shooter or a person strictly interested in competition, costume would be unnecessary. However, to the buckskinner some form of historical clothing *is* essential. It helps set the mood and background for this entire phase of the black powder sport. Without the proper clothes, it's very hard to visualize yourself back in the days of Lou Wetzel, Simon Girty, Simon Kenton, Lewis and Clark, William Ashley, Jim Bridger and all those other heroic figures from out of the era of America's Manifest Destiny. The days of the fur trade linger on, but they linger strongest when dressed in fringed shirts, buckskin pants, beaded moccasins, and carrying a fine rifle.

If that sort of thing appeals to you, if you can sit in your easy chair, close your eyes and daydream of yesteryear; if you can smell the smoke of campfires laid by generations of men and women who were bred to the wilderness; if you yearn for the days when men were more than mere cogs in the wheels of progress and women were true helpmates, I may have an idea or two for you.

So you say, "Of course, all that is true or I'd not even be reading this dang book." You probably already have your rifle and shooting gear; perhaps even an "outfit." That's great, but now let me put a few thoughts forth for your perusal.

If we accept the fact that old time clothing and gear are helpful, no, necessary, to the real atmosphere of living history, then we need to decide on what kind of clothing. Some people feel that a slouch hat, Mexican fringed jacket, and a pair of store-bought moccasins will do the trick. They are not really interested in being correct. If it's got fringe, it's old, seems to be their by word. Others feel that to be a real mountain man, you must have an outfit that's more patches, tatters and dirt than anything else. If this allows someone to enjoy and recreate himself, fine, but there is another way to go.

Let's look at the old times. Whether your thing be voyageur, courieur de bois, longhunter, military, western mountain man or whatever, there are several characteristics they all had in common. First and foremost, their clothing and gear were designed by experience, to do a job. This means it had to be in good repair. Second, they used the materials available in *THAT TIME AND PLACE!* Third, the clothing and gear were constructed using the techniques of the people (culture) from whence came the wearer. You cannot use 20th century techniques to design 18th or 19th century items. A point in question is "laced" clothing.

What Europeans thought American soldiers looked like, but didn't. This engraving from 1785 is from a drawing by a German who had fought in the War of Independence. Among other things, the caption states that "Most men run about barefoot."

Some clothing may have been *sewn* using very fine buckskin "thread" but I have not seen any example of clothing "laced" as is often done today. Punched holes weaken the material, and heavy thongs are uncomfortable on the skin. Sewing is faster and neater. In addition it is the technique of the culture in question, whether white or Indian.

When you come to the point of making your own outfit, think about patterns. If you use a pair of modern Levis for a pattern, you end up with buckskin Levis. Modern clothing is cut and sewn in a much different manner from that made in the 18th and 19th century. A little research, and a little planning ahead can make all the difference in the world. It is just as easy to do it right as it is to do it wrong.

If this is all new to you and you have not really got your teeth set yet, here are a few thoughts. Even you old timers might be interested.

If you already know what character you wish to portray, great. If not, may I suggest this? First, what kind of weapon do you carry or wish to carry? A mountain man can carry a Hawken or other mountain rifle. He can also carry a fusil, a Harpers Ferry, an early or late flinter or even a fowler. Contrariwise, a longhunter would have probably carried a rifled flinter and could not have carried a percussion weapon.

Pick a characterization that will fit what you actually want to be and do. Then find out everything you can about that type of person. What kind of clothes did he wear? Would he wear trousers, knee breeches, Indian leggings, etc.? How did he carry his gear? Was it on horseback, by canoe, or on his back? Read a few good

books about some of these men to give you a good background.

Another thought might be due at this point. Where do you live? Of course, there is nothing to stop you from being a voyaguer in Colorado or a mountain man in South Carolina. Still, have you thought about the frontiersmen around you? Every spot in this country was a frontier at one time. It is often easier and a lot of fun to adopt a personna that fits into your area "back when". Take geography and locale into account when planning your things.

If you are fortunate enough to live near some active historic site such as Bent's Fort, Fort Laramie, Fort Niagara, or my own home base, Fort de Chartres, you may have a built-in opportunity to relive history to the fullest. Here at Fort de Chartres we have a reconstruction of an original 1750's fort. We are only an hour south-east of St. Louis and easily accessible to large numbers of people. We have four active historic re-enactment groups based right here. Each group draws from all over the general area. Some come from as far away as St. Charles, MO and Vandalia, IL. One can find, within one or another of these groups, just about the full range of activities needed to sharpen the spiritual appetite of the most ardent black powder historian.

If one is interested in historic military, there are the Marines de La Francoise — The French Marines. In their blue uniforms with the white facings and white high gaiters, carrying their swords, bayonets, and Charleville muskets, they make quite a sight. They are often found camping in the guard's house, holding drill on the parade ground, or firing the ancient brass six-pounder mounted on the northwest bastion. It was the French Marines who established and held the fort when La Belle France reigned in the Illinois country.

The "French Militia of the Parish of St. Ann" is the second of four costumed units here at "The Bastion of the West." Each of the members of this group have selected a personna that represents a person or occupation that existed in the Fort de Chartres area in the 1750s — 1760s. They then research that personna in regard to his status in the community, whether wealthy or poor, the job held, etc. They then know how they would have dressed and acted. The clothing and equipment they wear reflects this research. The Captain was a man of means; he dresses very well and acts as befits a man of importance. Another dresses as a coureur de bois and looks half Indian. Others range between these two.

The Coureur de Bois de Fort de Chartres is our gun club. They are basically mountain men, voyageurs, and coureur de bois with a few Indians thrown in. Their outfits are mostly "buckskins" of various sorts. While they do not have the uniformity of dress of the others, they, too, strive to develop a basic historical background for what they do.

Last, but not the least of our Fort de Chartres units, we have the 42nd Highlanders — The "Black Watch." They have researched each plane of their historical clothing to the point that each of their uniforms is a museum reproduction, from the "bearskin" on the head to the baghose and buckle shoes on the feet. To do

The western mountain man as shown above adopted much of the clothing of the plains and mountain Indians.

PAINTING BY DAVID WRIGHT

this much research may be beyond the average person's interest, but should you consider going this far, the results are outstanding.

Having read this far, I will assume your interest in "doing it right" is quite high. It remains then to provide a trifle of help in how and where to find the answers.

I expect the first step in talking "research" is more what not to do than what should be done. Be cautious in choosing what you see at rendezvous for reference. There are some extremely fine costumes and accessories seen at rendezvous. This is especially true in recent years. It seems that every year just about everyone tries to out-do the previous year. Still, real research means knowing the whole picture about any time you wish to recreate. If it's Indian, the tribe is important but so is the era. Are the colors of beads correct? Is the item really being used as it was meant to be used? Many times we use substitute materials or techniques (such as machine sewing on many items) which is fine if we know what the substitution is and why we did it. For the above reason, it is also wise to be careful when checking with the "local pundit", even me. Be sure to check your information. The only really 100% absolutely reliable source is the original item or

source. The more references used, the better chance you will have to be correct in what you do.

At this point, some of you are saying something like: "But it's only a hobby. I want to enjoy myself, not work myself to death." That's fine. You do not have to go any further in researching things than you wish. For specific items you can just copy an original or a good reproduction. Talking to a knowledgeable person will also help a lot. Most any of the people who enjoy research will also enjoy sharing the knowledge gleaned. Just remember, we all are prone to error. Take all secondary information with a grain of salt.

Here are a few suggestions for places where you can do research. Libraries have a vast store of knowledge. Most universities or large city libraries will have books on art, stage costuming, and crafts that will help you immensely. You would also do well to read journals and novels relating to your period of interest to provide a background for you.

If you live in the vicinity of a large museum, visit it. Talk to the curator or person in charge. Tell him you are interested in researching clothing and accoutrements of a given period and type. Ask them for help and advice.

You can also talk to the people you know who are interested in making historical clothing. Share research and knowledge with them. Now is the time to really talk to the old timers too. This could lead you to a private collection that has just the things you want to see. There are some very fine private collections, but they are not usually open to the public. Should you be trusted with access to someone's collection for viewing, don't talk about it. Let the collector select his viewers. Too many private collections have been burglarized because someone carelessly talked out of turn in the wrong place or to the wrong people.

Finally check with your historical societies. Many small local groups have some very pertinent and interesting items put away which they would be delighted to share with interested persons. It goes without saying that the larger historical societies such as the Le Ames de Fort de Chartres here at Fort de Chartres can be of great service in this respect.

What do we do when we have access to an object that we wish to research? First, we measure it and draw it. Second, photograph it. Next, examine it for detail. How is it sewn? What stitch is used? What material was used? Are there any unusual construction techniques used? Remember that colors fade or darken with age, according to the material used and the finish (in the case of leather) put on them.

In researching an item you should also give some thought as to whether it is a common piece for the time and place of its construction. A good example is in the use of drop front trousers and knee breeches. By 1820 no one of fashion would have been wearing drop fronts or knee breeches except for certain English livery. However, drop fronts were still common during the middle of the 19th century in many rural areas of this country and are still to be seen occasionally even to this day.

Indian beads are another case in point. What we call seed beads were not supposedly common amongst the plains tribes until the mid 19th century. However, the

Museum of the Fur Trade, Chadron, Nebraska, has a fine display of beads from a site dated between 1790-1810. It includes a wide variety of colors and styles, including seed beads.

Please remember too, that preference on the part of people of a given area was as important as what was available to them when it came to dictating styles and fashions. The Blackfeet of northern Montana could have had seed beads in the 1850s. They seem to have preferred the slightly larger beads. Even today, most of the northern style of beadwork uses fairly large beads as averse to the fine 12/0 and 13/0 work of the southern (Oklahoma) tribes.

Comparative poverty or wealth governed much of our predecessors' actions, even as it does our own. The wealthy Pennsylvania merchant, farmer, or craftsman could afford a fine rifle, a "fancy" hunting coat and trousers, and traveled in style. He did most of his shooting in a sporting manner at the local "turkey shoot" or as recreation. If he failed to get game, he still ate well.

The average settler or frontiersman was not at all interested in being flamboyant. He wanted comfortable, durable clothes and a sturdy, reliable weapon. If he failed a shot, he might not eat; worse, he might lose his hair. He dressed to do a job. "Fancy" came with affluence.

The western mountain man often dressed like an Indian. The same was true of his eastern counterpart. The description we have of the Canadian courier de bois indicates that the majority of them such as Langlude, Tonti, Etienne Brule and many others were often impossible to differentiate by their dress from the Indians. I have even read one account (English) where the local minister wrote to the colonial governor and complained because the youth of the area came to church dressed as "savages" with naked breast and thighs, thus provoking the young ladies who, of course, paid less attention to him.

What this all boils down to is that there are a great variety of dress styles available to the black powder buff who also wishes to make an authentic costume to help him re-live his favorite era. You can be a French woods runner, a Yankee longhunter, or a member of Rogers Rangers. You can be a Militia man which gives you all sorts of possibilities. Perhaps you'd be interested in recreating a uniform for the French Regiment "La Rienne" or the fabulous 42nd Highlanders — the "Black Watch."

The ladies can become "A gentile Lady of Quality" such as Martha Washington, or one of the English ladies who resided in New York until the colonies were lost to the crown. Again, your interest could be toward the middle class. You could portray a successful burger's wife or the wife of a noted craftsman such as Mrs. Revere. Many farmers and working men's wives followed their husbands to the wars, too. You could be a camp follower such as the famous Molly Pitcher. Then too, there were many Indian women who settled down on the frontier with a "white" husband. This was always true, but, especially so during the mountain men times when, up until Mrs. Narcina Whitman came to rendezvous, there were no white women in the mountains.

CHARACTERS OF THE FUR TRADE PERIOD

Between 1750 and 1850 there were many types of people on the frontier. Descriptions of several of the more common ones will follow. These people being described are wearing "typical" garb: there were a lot of variations possible in any situation. Many items of earlier eastern style carried over into the later period of the western fur trade, so a mountain man can wear an eastern rifle shirt and still be "right".

THE LONGHUNTER

As the American Colonies grew, a new breed of men pushed the frontiers westward. Their forays into the wilderness, part trapping and part exploration, were of such duration that they became known as longhunters. Throughout the 1700s, they explored that dark and bloody ground, Kentucky, and moved into Ohio, Indiana, Tennessee and Illinois.

This longhunter appears as he would have in the 1770s; deep in the heart of unknown country. His clothing and equipment show woodswise experience and know-how. He wears a Canadian cap although a felt slouch would have been as common. Over a plain shirt of linen or homespun he wears a fringed elkskin Rifleman's Coat. These belted coats with their capes became a mark of the frontiersman. His french fly trousers are of leather, but could easily have been made of wool or heavy linen. The longhunter wears eastern style moccasins: no "tenderfoot," he wore soft moccasins to slip soundlessly through the forest. Balls and fixin's for his deadly "Kaintuck" are carried in the rifle bag at his side, while his powder horn often bore a carved map of his wanderings. In his belt he carried a sheathed butcher knife (which caused him to be called a "Long Knife") and a belt axe.

Men dressed like this not only trapped and explored; they marched with George Rogers Clark to capture Illinois and fought throughout the American Revolution.

THE SETTLERS

The longhunter, like the Indian, learned to live with the forest. To the settler, however, the forest was as much an enemy as a raiding "redskin." The settlers moved ever westward, searching for free land and free lives. They cleared the land, built cabins, planted crops and fought to defend what they had. Although he often had the skills of a woodsman, the settler was a farmer and family man. His wife could help till the fields, cook, sew and load the spare musket. This settler wears a homespun shirt, a wool waistcoat and elkskin knee breeches. He wears wool stockings and buckle shoes. The fringed linen rifle frock, often called a wamus, was a common frontier garment. Ammunition for his musket is carried in a simple flat bag. His wife's cap bespeaks her German origin. Her linen chemise, similar to a man's shirt, is worn under a heavy linen bodice. She wears a linen underdress and a wool overskirt. Like all white women of the times she wears an apron and hidden pair of pockets. Her wooden shoes are typical of those worn by German farm women.

THE COUREUR DES BOIS
AND WOODLAND INDIAN

As the French Empire spread through Canada and along the rivers of the Midwest, young Frenchmen began to discover an exciting new life. These adventurous Frenchmen became known as coureurs des bois —

the woods runners. Acting as both trappers and traders, usually without the sanction of a royal license, the coureur des bois became more Indian than the Indian. The woods runner spent most of the year living with the Indians, returning to "civilization" only to sell his furs, get new trade goods and carouse. This coureur des bois reflects his Indian attitudes in his clothes. The woolen band holding his hair is trimmed with trade silver. He wears a good linen shirt, a trade wool breech clout and leather leggings. At his belt, the coureur des bois wears a trade knife and tomahawk. His shooting bag and powder horn strap are made from blanket wool in a common Indian style. His trade fusil is encased in an elkskin gun cover.

The warrior talking to the woods runner is typical of eastern woodland Indians. Fierce and proud, he made a sound friend and deadly enemy. He was often the blood brother or in-law of the coureur des bois. His clothes were influenced by his forest life style, and also show much influence of European traders. The shaved head and roached hair was common throughout the east. The trade shirt and trade wool clout were paid for with beaver and other skins. His hide leggings, held by bearskin garters, show tribal differences from those worn by the coureur des bois. His pipe bag of elkskin holds kinnikinnick tobacco about to be smoked in the French pipe tomahawk. The small buckskin shooting pouch is typical of Indian-made bags.

THE VOYAGEUR

Throughout the 18th and 19th centuries, much of the fur trade depended on river transport. Keel boats, North canoes or the massive 34-foot Montreal canoes — all were propelled by the hardy voyageur. These incredibly tough French boatmen could paddle all day, portage loads of over 100 pounds each, cordel up river and still find the energy to sing and dance around the campfire. The Yellowstone, the Missouri, the rivers of Canada, the Great Lakes; all the waters heard the happy French songs from voyageurs such as this. His knit wool toque is more than a hat; its color identifies his home province. He wears a colorful trade shirt tucked into a woolen knee breeches. His wool socks are held up by woven garters which match his waist sash. This woven sash was a trademark of the voyageur and he would have felt naked without one. He wears woodlands moccasins, the standard footwear of the forest. A pipe was as vital to the voyageur as a song: this boatman wears his in a gage d'amour around his neck.

The young woman being offered the Canadian style capote in trade is typical of eastern Indian women. Braided hair was almost universal among Indian women, who held a strange position within their own society. They were considered unequal to men, and yet most inheritance and lineage was through the mother's family. This woman is wearing a caped two-piece dress, although dress was often much less modest. The linen chemise beneath the dress is a trade item, perhaps earned on the same terms offered by the voyageur. Women's leggings, much different than a man's, almost cover her moccasins. The woman's bag holds fire tools, sewing gear and a whetstone. The beads on her clothes and at her neck indicate close contact with European traders.

THE MOUNTAIN MAN

"Waugh — I'm the meanest child in the mountains. I can ride a thunderstorm, outshoot and outfight any man alive. I am some." There was much truth in the mountain man's boast. The free trapper typifies the spirit of independence. Tough, crafty and fearless, he gave ground to only one living creature — the great grizzly. The mountain man quickly adapted to his surroundings, becoming more Indian than the Indians. The "older" man is wearing a Plains Cree hunting coat

over a cotton trapper's shirt. His fringed leather trousers nearly cover his hard sole moccasins. He wears a wide leather belt and Green River knife sheath, both heavily decorated with tacks. A voyageur style bag contains "fixin's" for his heavy plains rifle. In these fancy clothes a mountain man would have "shone" at rendezvous. His companion has been in the mountains for some time, and is dressed in Indian fashion. His war shirt of decorated elkhide may have been made by his squaw, as would his north plains leggings. This hivernant is wearing the soft sole style of moccasins. At his belt hangs a pipe bag with beaded decoration. His rifle is in a leather gun cover, while ammunition is carried in a fringed bag. Both men are wearing low crown felt hats. Aside from the color of his skin and the felt hat, the hivernant looks exactly like a Plains Indian.

Although the era of the mountain man was short, they left their moccasin prints across the history of the West.

THE WESTERN
INDIAN WOMAN

The western Indian was a skillful hunter and a deadly warrior. Often called "horseback Indians" because of their dependence on horses, the red men of the plains and mountains are a basic part of our history. The important role of the Indian woman, however, is often overlooked. Beyond the menial chores of cooking and camp life, western Indian women were skilled at many crafts. They excelled at bead and quill work and in fine tanning. In most tribes, the lodge and its furnishings were theirs. Many tribes had women's societies. These women show the wide tribal differences seen on western Indians. On the left is a typical Cheyenne dress of deerskin, Cheyenne leggings of buckskin, and hard sole moccasins. On her concho decorated belt, she wears a knife in a painted rawhide sheath and a whetstone case. In the center is a young Crow girl, wearing a Crow style dress made of calico. She wears wool leggings in a Crow pattern and soft sole moccasins. On her panel belt is an awl case and a fire tool pouch. On the right is a Blackfoot girl, wearing a classic buckskin plains dress. Her high topped moccasins, with soft soles act as both leggings and footwear. On her tack decorated belt is a plain knife sheath and a quilled bag. In her hand is a eagle wing fan.

Dressed in such finery, any of these young women would have been worth many horses from a man's herd, or the best of a mountain man's trade goods.

A FEW TIPS ON
18TH CENTURY TAILORING

Materials most commonly used were wool, linen, fustian (a cotton-linen blend), and; to a much lesser degree, cotton. Calcutta cloth (i.e. calico, a printed cotton material) was used by those who could afford it. Beware though! Today's calico is a great deal different from that of 18th century. The patterns then were spaced much farther apart and were usually one color on a contrasting background. Stripes are also "Calcutta" cloth.

Techniques differed "back then". Wool was always sewn on the raw edge. Cotton and linen, since they ravel easily, were sewn as we sew today, or, flat-felled. Sewing was all by hand since the sewing machine was not developed until after 1840. Sixteen stitches to the inch was considered fair, but a fine straight seam of 22-24 stitches per inch was expected of a good tailor or seamstress.

Coats, vests, bodices and breeches all fit very snug with the exception of the full seat in the breeches, which allows you to move. One reason buckskin was popular was that it gave as you moved. Tradesmen liked buckskin for its "stretch" qualities as well as for long wear. A leather breeches maker was a specialist. Not every tailor made clothing from leather.

As in all eras and places, the wealthy people set the patterns of fashion. The merchant class and tradesmen aped their styles and the poor folk took what they could get.

The old time tailor's techniques and customs remained pretty much in use until after the advent of the first commercial sewing machines in the late 1840's. Mass produced items then began to gain the ascendancy and only a very few of the old techniques persisted except in the skills of a few traditional tailors.

MAKING FRONTIER STYLE
FRENCH FLY TROUSERS

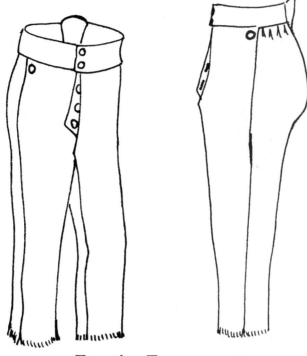

Frontier Trousers

*1750's style with
a French Fly.*

This is a correct style of trouser
for the period 1730-1760 (c) on the
Eastern Frontier. These may be made of
Fustian, Linen, or Buckskin.

There have been many articles on how to make this and that in the way of buckskinner clothing. One thing I don't remember is anyone saying how to turn a modern pattern into an old time pattern. I thought I just might make the attempt for you.

The first thing is to decide what you want to make. The next is to select the right pattern. I'll tell you how to make a pair of frontier style trousers of the Revolutionary War era. To keep them simple, I'll use the French influence and make them follow an early (1730-1750) French pattern with a button fly. The drawings will show what the pants will look like.

Making a Pattern

For a pattern take any men's dress pants pattern. Cut out the fronts and backs. Glue these to a large piece of brown wrapping paper. Then measure yourself and transfer these measurements, using a felt pen, to the pattern at the appropriate places. See Fig. 2.

Once the basic layout has been marked for size, draw the proper pattern outline. This should be your seam line. Now mark your cutting line outside the seam line. Allow ⅜ inch seams on leather if machine sewn — ⅛ inch seams if hand sewn. For cloth trousers allow ⅝ inch seams.

After the body pattern of the trousers is done, make patterns for the waist band, gusset and fly. The waist band should be as in Fig. 2A. Make an inner band also so that it is reinforced and, if leather, will not stretch. The band is your waist size plus about 1 inch overlap in front for the buttons and minus 1 inch per side in the back so the gusset can be drawn in. The gusset should be a round-top triangle about 5 inches tall and 4 inches across at the top. It is sewn in flat at the back as shown in Fig. 3. The fly is cut as in Fig. 1. It is approximately 2½ inches at its widest point, 1½ inches wide at the top and 9 inches long when folded lengthwise. If you wish pockets, their pattern should be made now.

Double check your pattern for style and fit. If all is ready, cut it out then lay out the pattern on your hides or cloth and cut out the parts. You are ready to begin assembly.

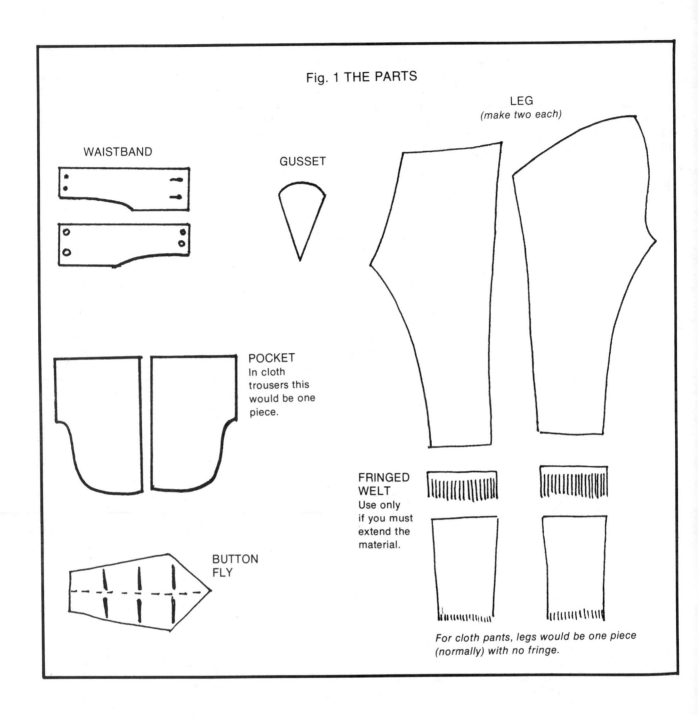

Fig. 1 THE PARTS

WAISTBAND

GUSSET

LEG
(make two each)

POCKET
In cloth
trousers this
would be one
piece.

FRINGED
WELT
Use only
if you must
extend the
material.

BUTTON
FLY

For cloth pants, legs would be one piece (normally) with no fringe.

Assembling the French Fly Trousers

1. If necessary, in order to make the pants long enough, sew on the leg extensions. Use a plain trimmed or a fringed welt.
2. Sew the crotch seams on the fronts and on the backs.
3. Sew the inner pocket pieces together (if necessary). Then sew them to the trouser backs. See Fig. 3.
4. Gather the rear panels to fit the waistband. Then sew the waistband on as in Fig. 4.
5. Sew the outer pocket to the trouser front. See Fig. 5.
6. Sew the backs to the fronts around the inseam.
7. Pin or staple the side seams and try the trousers on. Adjust to fit. *Leave the seat alone!* It's supposed to be huge.
8. Sew the side seams.
9. Sew the pockets.
10. Try the pants on. Mark the waistband for buttons (2) and button holes. Fit the fronts. Trim if necessary.
11. Sew the waistband to the pants fronts from the pockets forward.
12. Fold the button fly and sew both ends. Put in three button holes. Fig. 6.

13. Sew the button fly to the left side of the trousers (Fig. 7 & 8) so you can open and close it easily.
14. Lay the pants flat and mark for the buttons on the underside of the fly. Sew on the buttons.
15. Mark and cut the pocket button holes. Bind them with a button hole stitch.
16. Mark and sew on the pocket buttons.
17. Sew the gusset in place. Fig. 9. Mark for the thong

holes (3 to a side). Punch and button hole stitch them.
18. Measure the inseam. Trim and turn up and sew (cloth only). Leather may be fringed with a ½ inch fringe if you wish.
19. Cut a long thong and lace up the back.
20. Your pants are ready to wear.

Fig. 2 THE LAYOUT

Measurement A plus B should equal your hip size plus about two inches.

Then add the extra fullness in the seat.

Measurements C and D should add up to about your thigh size plus 1½"

E plus F should be your calf size plus two inches.

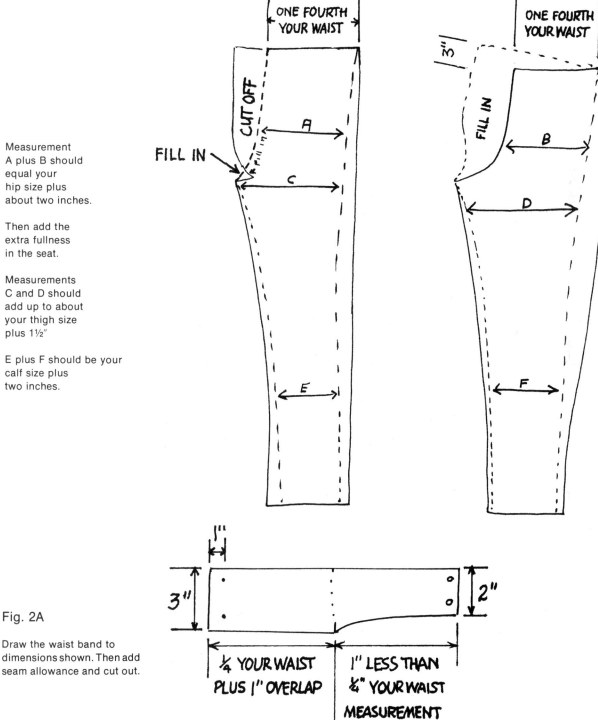

Fig. 2A

Draw the waist band to dimensions shown. Then add seam allowance and cut out.

108

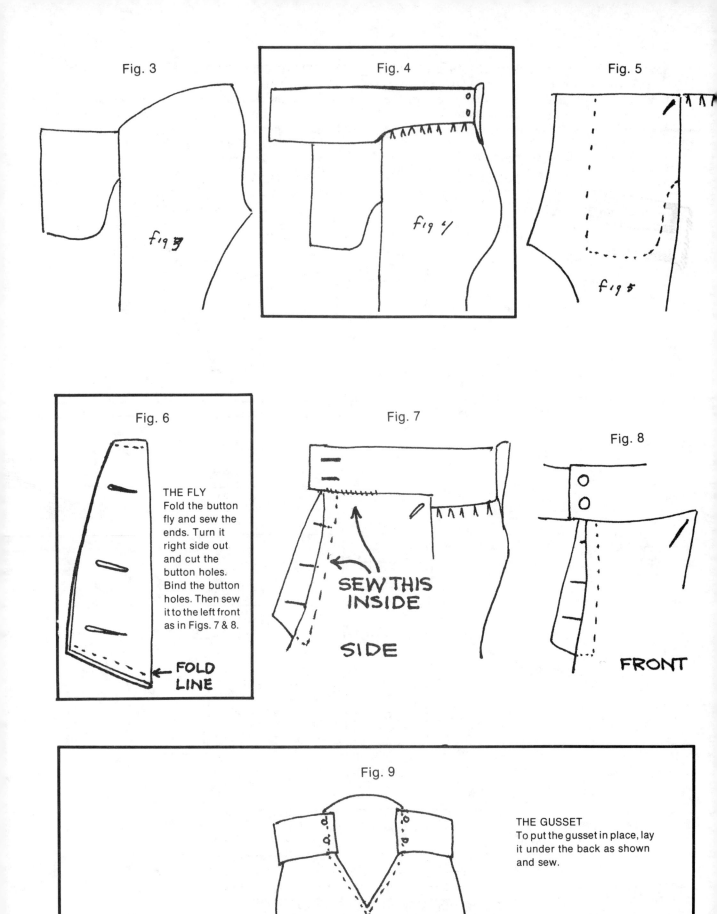

Fig. 3

fig 3

Fig. 4

fig 4

Fig. 5

fig 5

Fig. 6

THE FLY
Fold the button fly and sew the ends. Turn it right side out and cut the button holes. Bind the button holes. Then sew it to the left front as in Figs. 7 & 8.

FOLD
LINE

Fig. 7

SEW THIS
INSIDE

SIDE

Fig. 8

FRONT

Fig. 9

THE GUSSET
To put the gusset in place, lay it under the back as shown and sew.

MAKING THE PLAINS
INDIAN WAR SHIRT

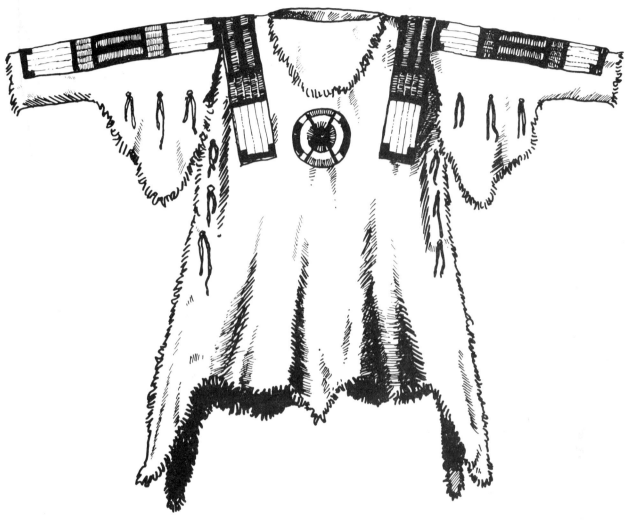

No matter what you call it, "the scalp shirt", "that ermine shirt" or "the war shirt", it brings forth a vivid picture of a magnificent garment. The war shirt of the plains and mountain Indians was and is one of the most impressive items of apparel ever designed and worn by any people. It was a symbol of rank and achievement. Not just anyone could own, much less wear, such a shirt in the olden times. The man who owned one was a man of distinction, no matter what his tribe.

The instructions provided will make a basic "north plains style" war shirt suitable for use with a costume of the 19th century. A particular tribe or a definite time period would be indicated by the trim and decorations.

If you cannot get to a museum to study originals, both the Museum of the American Indian in New York City and the Smithsonian Institution in Washington, D.C. have photos available of some of their collection.

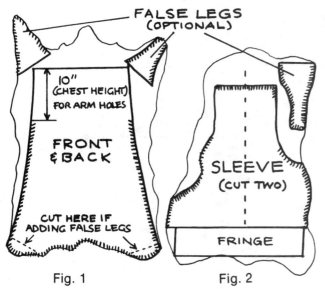

Fig. 1

Fig. 2

FALSE LEGS (OPTIONAL)

10" (CHEST HEIGHT) FOR ARM HOLES

FRONT & BACK

CUT HERE IF ADDING FALSE LEGS

SLEEVE (CUT TWO)

FRINGE

Materials Needed to Make the Shirt

Two large hides for the body of the shirt. These must be large enough to cut out a front and a back that are together at least 4 inches larger than your chest measurement. The shirt should be at least crotch length if possible (although many early ones were shorter). Most old shirts had the legs dangling down at the sides. If necessary, false legs were often added. See Fig. 1.

Two small (7-8 ft.) hides or one large one for the sleeves. If the hides are not wide enough for you to put "legs" on the sleeves, false legs may be cut and sewn on them as you do for the bottom of the shirt. The armhole fringe, if desired, should be cut from these hides also. Most old shirts did not have this. See Fig. 2.

Stretching the Hides

Now that you have selected the hides for your shirt, wet them thoroughly, wring them out and stretch them. See Fig. 3.

Laying-Out the Shirt

Either use chalk and work right on the material or make a pattern first. Be sure your measurements are right.

Cut Out the Shirt

Cut All of Your Fringing

Very short, fine (1/2" long × 1/16" wide) fringe is put down both sides of the shirt, across the bottom, around the legs and on the cuffs of the sleeves. The shoulder fringe is long (6"-10") and about 1/8" wide.

Assembling the Shirt

1. Sew the shoulder seams using a whip stitch. Leave a 12" wide neck opening for your head.
2. Sew the sleeves and arm hole fringe onto the body of the shirt. See Fig. 4.
3. Turn the sleeves inside out and sew the straight part closed with a whip stitch. See Fig. 5.
4. Cut 16 thongs (about 1/8" × 12") for both sides of the body.
5. Punch 5 sets of holes on each side of the body (using an awl, not a punch). Run a thong through each set and tie to hold the body closed. See Fig. 6.
6. Punch 3 sets of holes in each sleeve, lace and tie. See Fig. 7.
7. Sew the neck flaps in place. See Fig. 8.
8. Your war shirt is now ready to wear.

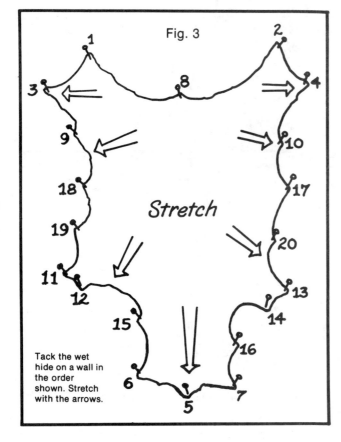

Fig. 3

Stretch

Tack the wet hide on a wall in the order shown. Stretch with the arrows.

Alternate styles of neck flaps are shown below.

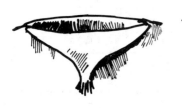

A very old style.

The triangle was typical of the middle plains tribes.

Blackfeet and Crow preferred the rectangle style.

Red and blue trade cloth sewn down with beads.

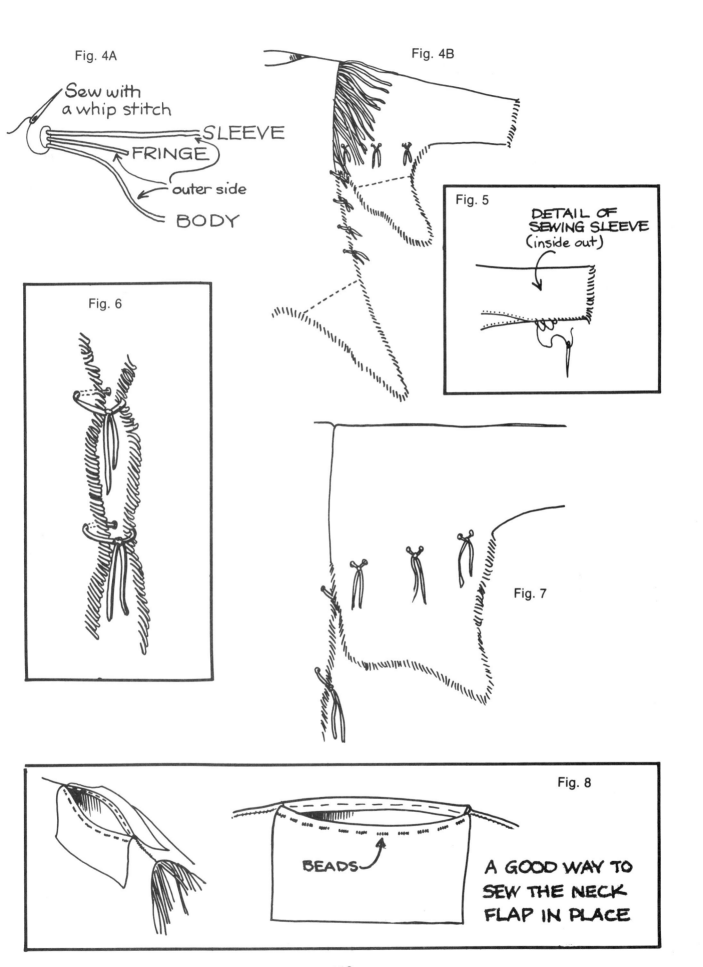

Fig. 4A

Sew with a whip stitch

SLEEVE

FRINGE

outer side

BODY

Fig. 4B

Fig. 5

DETAIL OF SEWING SLEEVE (inside out)

Fig. 6

Fig. 7

Fig. 8

BEADS

A GOOD WAY TO SEW THE NECK FLAP IN PLACE

MAKING THE PLAINS STYLE
HARD SOLED MOCCASIN

To make this western style moccasin you will need 2 pieces of leather for the uppers, 2 pieces of heavy leather for the soles, thread, needle, and instructions.

Making a Pattern
1. On a stiff piece of paper, draw around your stocking foot. Mark your instep and measure it. Write it down on the pattern. See Fig. 1. If your feet are different, then draw both.
2. Draw sole pattern using the foot drawing for size. Be accurate. Push the big toe over just enough to tighten it up against second toe. Draw the line ⅛ inch above the tip of the big toe and around the other toes just enough to allow movement. See Fig. 2.
3. Draw a line down the center of the sole pattern. See Fig. 3.
4. Take another piece of heavy paper and fold it down the middle. Lay it flat. Lay the sole pattern on the paper so that the center line and the crease line up. Trace the sole pattern lightly on the paper.
5. Mark the instep. Draw a horizontal line across the fold at the instep approximately ¼ inch less on each side than the width of the sole print at that point. This horizontal line will be your instep opening where you sew the tongue. To be sure it is in the right place look at Figure 4. Distance A-E (toe to tongue) should be somewhat longer (½ to 1 inch depending on the size than distance A-D. The width of your foot at the instep is the width of B-C (pattern width). D-F and D-G are each ¾ inch longer than A-B and A-C respectively. Mark line A-D and draw your pattern. Double check it for accuracy and then cut it out. It should look like Fig. 4.

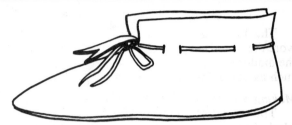

Cutting the Leather
1. Trace the sole pattern onto the sole leather. Be sure and get a right and a left. Cut out with a sharp knife.
2. Lay the upper pattern on the leather. Be sure the stretch is across the arch. Cut one right and one left.
3. Cut 4 strips ½ inch wide or so by the length of the moccasins for welting.
4. Cut out 2 tongues. See Fig. 6. Tongues a or b are best for the old style.

Sewing the Moccasin
The best stitch to use all the way through is the overcast or whip stitch. *Sew Tight.*
1. First lay the pieces of the moccasin as shown in Fig. 5. The moccasin is sewn inside out. The upper is laid on the edge the same way. The sole is laid with the inner (rough) side up. Start sewing at the toe; first one side and then the other, to the center of the heel. Be sure you are sewing this straight and even.
2. Now trim the heel so that the two sides just meet. Sew up the back. Use a welt here, too, if you wish.
3. To finish the moccasin, sew in the tongue. Repeat for the second moccasin.

Before beading, consider the tribe and time period you wish to represent by studying originals or pictures.

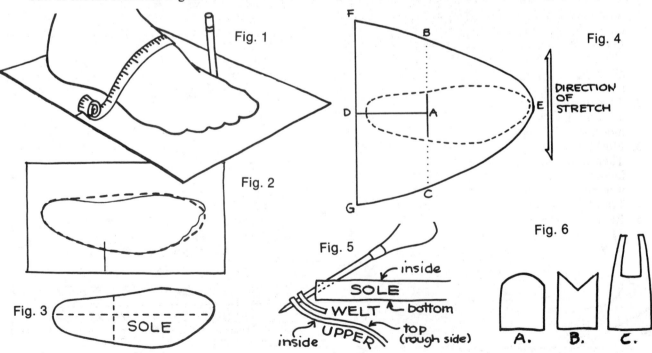

MAKING THE
WOODLAND MOCCASIN

The longhunter of the eastern frontier generally wore the woodland moccasin made of buckskin. But for the modern longhunter with tender feet, a thicker hide such as cowhide might be a better choice.

Making a Pattern

Trace your stocking foot on a piece of heavy paper. Mark the instep with a line. Measure at this point over the arch and mark the measurement on the paper. "C" is your arch line. Distance C-C should be the distance over your arch plus the width of your foot at that point. Distance A-B is about one inch. D-D is the same as C-C. E-E is the distance around the ball of the foot. When you have these points marked, sketch in the outline of the moccasin and cut out your pattern. The flaps will usually have to be cut separately from the bottom of the moccasin. See Fig. 2 and Fig. 3.

Make a Prototype

Before cutting your leather we suggest you make a cloth moccasin and try it on. This way you can check the fit and correct the pattern before cutting up the hide. Remember though, cloth won't stretch like the leather so it won't fit as well.

Cutting the Leather

When you are sure your pattern is correct, you can cut out your leather, but follow these instructions and do the cloth moccasin first. Cut out a right and left moccasin. Be sure the stretch is *across* the arch. Now cut out the flaps unless you were able to cut the moccasin in one piece.

Sewing the Moccasin

1. Sew the moccasin inside out. Start at the V of the notch (A) and sew the moccasin using a whip stitch. Gather the seam around the curve of the toe (Fig. 4). Then sew the balance evenly without pucker. Sew all the way up the vamp (toe area) to C-C. Pull the stitches *tight*.
2. Turn the moccasin right-side out. Work the toe over a broom handle and then work your foot into the moccasin. Pull and stretch it until it fits.
3. Mark, then trim the heel to fit and sew up the back. Then trim the heel tab so you have only about 1½ inches at the center. Fold it up over the back and sew it in place all around the edge. See Fig. 5.
4. Trim the flaps to fit and sew in place. See Fig. 6.
5. Repeat for the second moccasin.

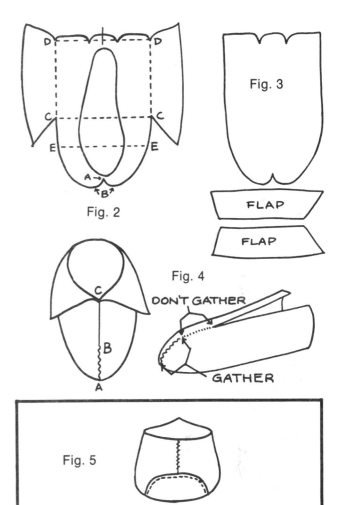

Fig. 2

Fig. 3

FLAP

FLAP

Fig. 4

DON'T GATHER

GATHER

Fig. 5

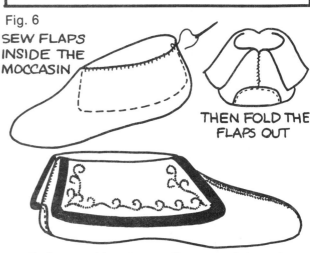

Fig. 6

SEW FLAPS
INSIDE THE
MOCCASIN

THEN FOLD THE
FLAPS OUT

DECORATE MOCCASIN IF YOU WISH BY BINDING THE FLAPS WITH RIBBON AND BY BEADING THE TOE AND/OR FLAP. (See "Ojibwa Crafts" or "Iroquois Crafts" by the U.S. Government Printing Office)

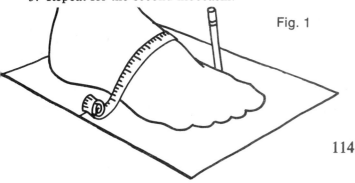

Fig. 1

114

MAKING THE
PIPE BAG

The pipe bag is simple. It is basically a fringed tube made to carry a pipe and the "fixin's". To make your pipe bag, just follow these simple steps.

1. Cut the pieces out of the leather. You should have 2 pieces approximately 16 inches long by 6½ inches wide for the body of the bag and one piece about 6¼ inches wide by 6-8 inches long for the fringe.

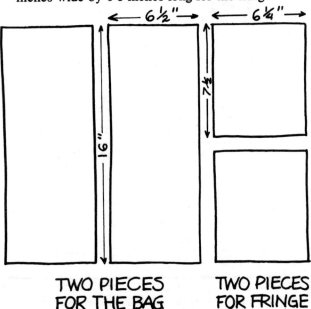

TWO PIECES FOR THE BAG **TWO PIECES FOR FRINGE**

2. Sew up both sides of the bag to form a long tube. Be sure to sew it inside out. Use a whip stitch about 16-20 stitches to the inch.

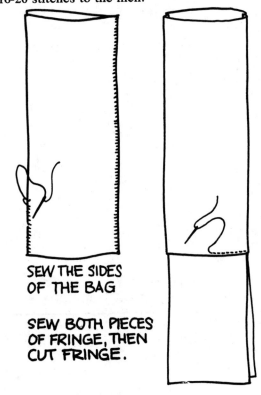

SEW THE SIDES OF THE BAG

SEW BOTH PIECES OF FRINGE, THEN CUT FRINGE.

3. Turn the bag right side out. Insert the fringe piece about ⅜" into the bottom of the bag. A small amount of glue would help to hold it in place. Using a fine running stitch, sew the fringe to the bag.

4. Cut the fringe about ¼ inch in width.

The basic bag is now finished. If you wish, you may bead a design such as that shown in the drawing on the front of the bag.

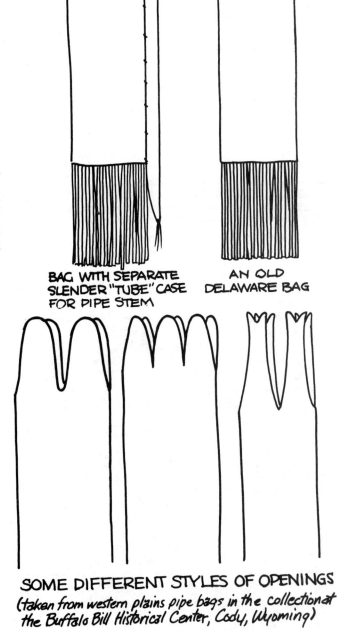

BAG WITH SEPARATE SLENDER "TUBE" CASE FOR PIPE STEM   **AN OLD DELAWARE BAG**

SOME DIFFERENT STYLES OF OPENINGS
(taken from western plains pipe bags in the collection at the Buffalo Bill Historical Center, Cody, Wyoming)

CONCLUSION

Whatever you choose to do, I hope you will choose to do it well. Anyone can say, "If they'd a had it, they'd a used it." However, it does add a lot to an adult activity to have things done as well as possible. A strip of cotton cloth and a pair of "lace 'em up" moccasins may be OK for a small child. Are they good enough for you?

Accoutrements & Equipment

by Tony Hunter

TONY HUNTER'S INTEREST IN muzzleloading began at an early age. When he was about nine years old, living in a suburb in northern Ohio, he became entranced by the Walt Disney T.V. series about Davey Crockett. Using a broom stick for a rifle barrel and a board from a box sawed into a stock, he made himself a long gun.

After graduating from St. Joseph High School in Cleveland Tony went into the monastery which proved to be a great mistake for him. After five unhappy years behind the walls which blocked out the real world, Tony left. He completed his education at the University of Dayton and Western Reserve University and majored in American History. After his graduation Tony embarked on a series of pack-on-the-back wanderings which took him to South America, the British Isles and a couple of trips through Europe.

For the next 11 years Tony worked as a teacher for the Cleveland Public Schools. During his first year of teaching he happened to see a fellow at a flea market who had a flintlock rifle for sale. This immediately awakened his long gun interest from his youth. The fellow explained that he built the rifle himself, that it actually shot and that there were muzzleloading clubs where fellows came together for this purpose. Tony was absolutely amazed! Why had he not heard of this before? The flinter was bought from the fellow and Tony joined the National Muzzle Loading Rifle Association and sought out the most primitive muzzle-loading club he could find in his area.

Later, Tony tried putting some of his muzzleloading experiences into words and photos and wrote several dozen articles for *Muzzleloader* and *Muzzle Blasts* and a couple of years ago was invited to become the Historical Editor of *Muzzleloader*. His column appears in every issue and is called *Cache Of The Hollow Tree*. Tony is also interested in the water and has written articles for yachting magazines and is involved in marine photography.

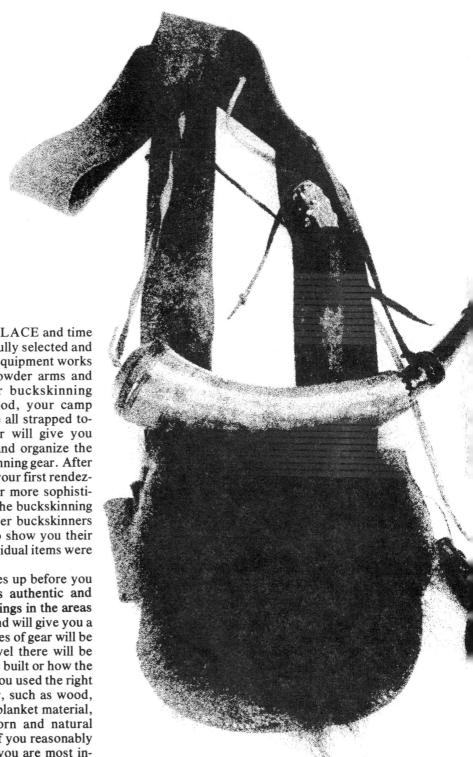

THE RENDEZVOUS IS THE PLACE and time when you bring together all your carefully selected and built buckskinning gear to see if your equipment works as a harmonious unit. Your black powder arms and accouterments team up with your buckskinning clothes, with your shelter, your food, your camp equipment and blankets and these are all strapped together into your pack. This chapter will give you suggestions on how to build, select and organize the most important pieces of your buckskinning gear. After you have put together the basic items your first rendezvous will give you a flood of ideas for more sophisticated and involved gear. It is part of the buckskinning tradition to "borrow" ideas from other buckskinners and they will be happy (with pride) to show you their gear and explain how some of the individual items were made.

One of the big questions that comes up before you get started is how to know what is authentic and what is not. Well, your historical readings in the areas that most interest you is a good start and will give you a general feel, but although specific pieces of gear will be mentioned in the history book or novel there will be little explanation on how that item was built or how the fellow came by it. I would say that if you used the right authentic materials to build your gear, such as wood, leather, raw hide, homespun wool or blanket material, copper, brass, iron, steel, bone, horn and natural thread, that you cannot go far wrong if you reasonably understand the historical period that you are most interested in.

Almost anything that you can think of that can be built with these materials was built with these materials to the limit of the technology of that historical period. This seems to be a broad statement, but the following dezvous took on a military meaning and later the word took on a western connotation in reference to the great Rocky Mountain rendezvous. But whether east or west or what period of history the word is used in, the rendezvous stands for a gathering of men in the bond of fellowship and common interest.

More than anything else the rendezvous is an art form. It is the reliving of one of the richest and most unique pioneer traditions of any country in the entire world. The buckskin rendezvous can give us a better understanding of the independence, skill and craftsmanship of those who brought this country into being and who gave us its spirit.

There are a thousand different ways to build and organize your rendezvous gear. The selection of the articles you think you need is a highly personal choice. No two buckskinners have exactly the same gear or would want to. What works for one fellow may be a curse for another fellow. The buckskinner shows his individuality, his taste and his craftsmanship in the items he selects to build. Also, his common sense is reflected in his equipment.

There is only one good way to build your rendezvous equipment and that is very slowly. If you take one item at a time, think it out carefully, borrow ideas from other buckskinners, choose good natural materials and build with care, you will have a piece of gear that you can be proud of and which will last you a long time. John Swett of Ohio is a good example of a buckskinner who builds his gear with great care. At one rendezvous the wigwam was dark and John figured some light was needed. He went into his pack and pulled out a muslin bag. Opening it he pulled out several layers of tin all folded neatly one on top of another. When he opened them up, the tin layers, all hinged together, formed a candle lantern complete with mica window. John had spent many hours figuring out on paper how a candle lantern could be made to fold up into one flat piece and after several false starts he finally perfected the device. This example shows what great pains some buckskinners take in the building of their gear. Every time John pulls out that candle lantern it never fails that the lantern comes under close scrutiny by those buckskinners present who have not seen it before. This lantern was well worth the time and effort it took to build it and is a first class piece of rendezvous gear.

Some pieces of gear you can't make or don't have to make. Some buckskinners specialize in making one fine item of great quality. It would be worth your while to see if these fellows would be willing to trade one of their items to you if you think that item would be an asset to your gear. Also, keep your eyes open at flea markets and junk shops for the items you need. Old fur caps and coats have a habit of turning up at garage sales. I remember seeing one buckskinner turn up at a rendezvous with a full length raccoon coat that was left over from the 1940's. Many times you will come across a one-of-a-kind item that fits in with your gear perfectly whether it be an old iron belt buckle or a strange looking tin pot. Also the trade blanket is a good place to get items you need. What doesn't fit in another buckskinner's gear may fit perfectly into your own. You may want to consider purchasing inexpensive buckskinning

little story will give you an idea of what I mean.

An experienced buckskinner of many seasons turned up at a winter rendezvous about 10 years ago in Ohio. The snow was half a foot deep and only five fellows turned up (sometimes these small rendezvous can be the best of all) because of the cold weather. The buckskinner's name was Pete Peterson of Michigan. Since this was my first rendezvous I marveled at his fine gear right down to the hand stitched quilt neatly folded on top of his pack basket. His "Long Tom" rifle barrel (exceptionally long) was bought as a smoothbore and he built his own rifling machine and rifled the barrel himself. Pete had a small knife hung around his neck on a leather thong. The arrangement was sort of a necklace with the leather sheath acting as the center piece and with beads strung on the thong on either side. It was a great idea to have a small camp knife with you at all times for cooking and cutting and a handy way to carry it. This neck knife fit all the criteria. It seemed a perfect piece of gear, an item that was functional, well made and decorative. After the rendezvous I made a neck knife and it soon caught on to the rest of the club until a neck knife was almost a standard piece of equipment for our local stamping grounds.

Was this item authentic or not? Even though these knives were made up with authentic materials, was the knife itself authentic? About a year later I saw an art show at the Cleveland Museum called *The European View of America*. One grand original oil painting (three hundred years old) showed a British Indian agent decked out with red military coat, moccasins, buckskin leggings and trade musket. And guess what hung around his neck? Sure enough, it was a neck knife almost a carbon copy of the one Pete had made up, yet Pete never saw this painting. The two ideas were arrived at independently several hundred years apart.

The human mind is sometimes more creative than we generally believe. What ideas you come up with while building your gear, you can be pretty sure dozens of original buckskinners built their items in nearly the same way. If the item is built well, does its job, is reasonably correct to the period of history that you are most interested in and uses natural materials in its construction, then that item is authentic.

The rendezvous, where your gear will be tested and put to its maximum use, is an ancient American tradition. The word "rendezvous" comes from the French, meaning to betake yourself. The French trappers as early as the 1600's used the word to mean a place for a meeting, to link up with other trappers, Indians or traders. During the French and Indian Wars the word ren-

This painting shows some of the equipment that the western mountain men carried including beaded rifle case, beaver trap and Santa Fe saddle.

PAINTING BY DAVID WRIGHT

items that you come across that you cannot use at the moment, but are sure that other buckskinners would be interested in. These are good items to put on the trade blanket and through these items you may be able to pick up the items you need.

When you are selecting and building your gear keep in mind the weight of the objects. The weight is less important if you intend to come into camp leading a fully packed mule, but for many rendezvous you will have to carry everything in on your back over hill, creek and dale. Every ounce in your pack will feel pounds heavier by the time you trudge into camp and cast your load to the ground. So, the number of items you select and their weight should be carefully considered. I recall one buckskinner who insisted on cooking in a cast iron frying pan for he claimed that his victuals tasted better in iron, but he had to pay the price in carrying that pan which weighs 5 times that of a sheet metal pan. You will find yourself going through your gear periodically to eliminate unnecessary and heavy items, especially after a long rendezvous walk in which both ways seem to be uphill.

Before we go into the actual building and selecting of the key items you will need, let us consider the organization of all your items. After you have completed your gear, if you lay it out you will note that it is easily divided into three different sizes. There are the large things like the blankets and lean-to cloth; there are the middle size items like your frying pan and water cask, and there are a host of small items from fork and spoon to small muslin bags. These small items are the hardest to organize and if they are left loose in your pack they will be difficult to find when you need them. Dick Nezat organizes this small gear in a parfleche box, while Bill Wunderle divides this gear into several larger bags. Pete Peterson puts all this small gear in his stew pot and John Swett uses a tin box something like a large tea tin. I use a wooden, dove-tailed box which can be bought at most craft shops. After adding brass hinges and hasp the inside lid can be fitted to hold an antique fork and spoon. I tried to make this box resemble the mess kit that George Washington used in the field during the Revolutionary War.

The back pack is the final organizer. One old buck-

120

skinner once said that a good pack is nothing more than a large bag stuffed with a lot of little bags. If you like basket packs you can store-buy these. L. L. Bean is one place to obtain a quality basket pack. Since they are ridged on the sides it is easy to get into them to get your gear out. If it rains you can simply throw a hide or piece of canvas over it for protection. Some buckskinners simply use a large split cow hide bag with straps sewn on it. This works very well and all gear can be stored inside without having to tie items to the outside of the pack. The sides can be rolled down when filling the bag to get at the bottom. A drawstring at the top pulls the whole pack tight.

Others have made parfleche boxes with straps on them. These are heavy but will last a hundred years. Jack Perry of Michigan hiked into the Saltillo Rendezvous a few years back with a pack box made out of birch bark which was a very unique piece of gear. The materials you can use for your back pack are wide and you have a large choice.

A buckskinner relaxes in camp amid guns and equipment. A basket pack as mentioned in the text can be seen in the background.

THE RIFLE COVER

This chapter will presume that you have your buckskin costume and shooting gear in order and that it is arranged so you can shoot in the field out of your pouch with powder horns, measure, bullet starter, patch knife etc. To complete your shooting gear one of the first pieces of rendezvous gear you will want to consider is the making of a rifle cover to protect that valued possession.

The rifle cover will protect your rifle from bangs and bruises during a day of shooting. When camped out at night it will keep much of the wet off your rifle which produces that damaging rust that you find on the barrel and lock in the morning which is quite time consuming to clean off. The main problem with making a good, well-fitting rifle cover is the shape of the lock on any muzzle loader. Some of the lock parts stick up and the rifle cover is difficult to fit over this area. Also it is difficult to find a practical and primitive way of tying the cover around the stock to give a tight fit to keep out moisture. The slip-on cover only does part of the job.

One method of overcoming these difficulties and still have a primitive cover is to make a fold-over rifle cover. When laid out the top edge of this cover is straight. The bottom edge follows the lines of the bottom edge of your rifle. This edge can be stitched on the outside of some thin hide or the hide can be turned inside out to produce an inside stitch. A liner of water proof canvas would insure that the moisture stays off the rifle. Also, instead of hide or canvas a wool blanket part would make a good cover, for it will repel moisture. The stitching should be tight with all these materials and it would be a good idea to use waxed thread.

After inserting your rifle in the finished cover the top edge over the stock area is pulled tight and folded over the side of the stock to form a tight fit. A thong is then tied around the cover at the wide part of the stock to hold the cover in place. The leather thong should be stitched to the cover for convenience. Decorative elements are easily added to this type of cover. The fold-over rifle cover will be one of your most practical pieces of rendezvous gear.

THE TOMAHAWK

Besides backing off 7 paces and throwing at the hawk target the tomahawk has many camp uses. Most of the time the hawk finds a home sunk in a log next to the cook fire where it is handy for breaking up fire wood. At other times it is carried by the buckskinner thrust through his belt in the middle of his back. A brass ring or leather holder is sometimes used for carrying the hawk and a leather blade cover can be tied on the hawk head to keep the blade from cutting the wrong hide.

The tomahawk goes way back in history to the medieval battle axe and even before that it was a favorite weapon of the ancient Roman warriors. Also the famous boarding axe of the British Navy is identical to the standard tomahawk that most buckskinners use. Well made items and good ideas have a way of lasting through the centuries.

The buckskinner is mainly concerned with that type of steel, iron and brass tomahawk used on the American frontier. There is a steel tomahawk that you see at every

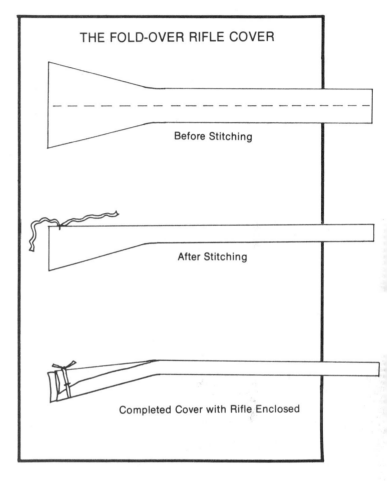

THE FOLD-OVER RIFLE COVER

Before Stitching

After Stitching

Completed Cover with Rifle Enclosed

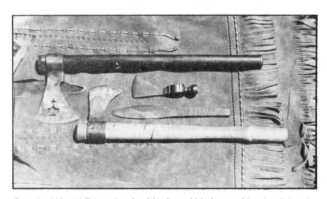

Standard H and B tomahawk with pierced blade, smoking hawk head, throwing knife and hand forged hawk with hammer handle.

Besides being a useful tool, tomahawks are a lot of fun to throw. Each 'skinner has his own style as shown by Russ Sidebottom.

rendezvous and this type of hawk is used by more buckskinners than any other type. This standard hawk is a direct copy of ones carried during the American Revolution. In fact if you see an original hawk of this type in a museum it would be hard to tell the difference between it and a modern-made standard hawk. These standard hawks are commonly called H and B after the company that makes them, but there are several companies that make similar hawks of the same style. The head is made of mild steel with a dark finish with natural heat scale and hammer marks that gives a very original appearance.

The hickory wood handle is tapered and is inserted from the top of the hawk head. The more force that is applied to the blade the tighter the handle locks on to the head. If you do a lot of hawk throwing it would be a good idea to have at least one spare handle handy. The handle will get nicked up a bit and it will eventually break with throwing use. If you need a hawk handle and cannot get to the muzzleloading shop, you can take your hawk head to a local hardware store and look for a large hammer handle. The right hammer handle turned upside down will fit your head in a pinch. It will look a little strange, but this handle will do the job.

You can alter your standard hawk for the better by welding a piece of flat steel to the back of the hawk head to make a sort of hammer. This flat can then be used to pound in shelter stakes, pound your bent throwing knife flat again and anything else you would generally use a hammer for. It makes a good tool even better. If there is no way you can weld the flat on, a blacksmith can heat weld a flat for you in a few minutes and he will have the metal stock to do it.

Also, it is possible to alter your standard hawk in a decorative way by piercing the blade with a design. Few tools are needed to do the job and it can be done in one evening. You may already have the necessary tools on your bench to complete the job. First you need a masonry drill bit about 3⁄8 inch in diameter. Mount your hawk head in your vise and drill through the blade with the masonry drill and your power drill. It may be tough going depending on the hardness of the steel, but the masonry drill will cut it. Use some oil on the bit. Drill the hole in the center of the area that you want the design to be in. Now, using the hole as the center of your design make a simple line drawing with a pencil right on the blade.

After the drawing on the blade is complete take a

tungsten carbide hacksaw, which you can find at your local hardware or discount store for about $2.50, and place the rod through the drill hole. Then hook up the rod to your standard hacksaw frame and begin cutting out your design. Note that as you cut you are actually making two edges because of the thickness of the rod hacksaw blade. When the design is completely cut out just remove the rod and file and sand down the rough spots. A rat tail file helps in cleaning up the drilled hole.

Besides the standard camp hawk there are dozens of other types in steel, iron and brass. Some are smoking hawks with a tobacco bowl opposite the blade. These can be highly decorated and down right beautiful to behold. Many are of excellent craftsmanship. To own a fine brass smoking hawk is a real pleasure and some buckskinners collect them, but these are certainly not for throwing or general camp use. You cannot beat the standard camp axe for your first hawk. If you select it carefully it will serve you well and will be impossible to wear out. You will find them in any muzzleloading shop along with plenty of hickory handles.

THE POSSIBLES POUCH

Traditionally buckskins do not have pockets, so the possibles pouch is used to hold those items that usually would be held in the pockets of your pants. For modern buckskinners that includes items like keys, cash and wallet. You meet a lot of new people at rendezvous and it would be a good idea to also carry pen and paper in your pouch for the exchange of addresses and the writing of short notes on new ideas you encounter. A pen or pencil is also handy for keeping score or marking your targets. In short the possibles pouch is for any small items you think you will need that will be immediately at hand.

Possibles pouches come in any size and shape the owner decides is proper for himself. Some are square while others are long and rectangular. Some hang from a strap over the shoulder and across the body on the opposite side of the shooting pouch, while others are attached at the waist to the buckskinner's belt. Some are highly decorative with long fringe hanging off the bottom, bands of intricate bead work or even porcupine quills. Other possibles pouches are small in size and quite plain with a simple fold-over flap.

The materials to choose from to build your possibles pouch are vast and range from split cow hide to a rich fox fur. Your personal needs will help you decide the size, shape and materials you will use in the making of your possibles pouch. It should be stitched extra strong for it will receive a lot of wear in the wilderness. Small stitches with waxed thread will do it up just fine.

THE PIPE AND PIPE CASE

Since cigarettes are not acceptable at rendezvous, many buckskinners burn their tobacco in pipes. Outside of the tomahawk smoking pipe and large peace pipes there are the smaller individual pipes that a buckskinner might carry stuck in his cap. Of these small pipes the white clay pipe and the red catlinite (soft red stone) pipe are among the most popular. Since these pipes are somewhat fragile some buckskinners use pipe cases made of wood for protection. They are simply

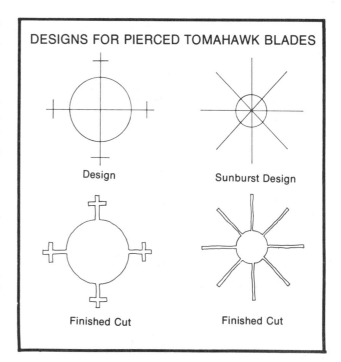

DESIGNS FOR PIERCED TOMAHAWK BLADES

Design

Sunburst Design

Finished Cut

Finished Cut

Buckskinner's wide belt and iron buckle, square possibles pouch and *japaned* tin containers.

two pieces of wood cut to the general outline of the pipe and hollowed out to fit the pipe. Two small leather hinges tacked into the wood allow it to be opened and a leather thong about the middle holds the case closed. A loop of scrap leather holds the case to the belt. I imagine a simple slip-on pipe case could also be made out of any stiff hide.

THE BUCKSKINNER'S KNIFE

To complete the gear that is generally carried on your person and before we turn to the gear in your pack we must bring up the subject of the buckskinner's knife, or more properly his knives. This is a vast topic and you should do some research to find out what style knives fit your period of historical interest and your needs.

I believe the buckskinner's knives can be broken down into four rough groups, the patch knife, the general utility knife, the throwing knife and the decorative fighting knife. The only requirements for the patch knife are that it be razor sharp, used only as a patch knife and it should be generally of small size for easier handling. As far as what it should look like — the sky is the limit. You will see dozens of different types with dozens of different materials used in making the handles.

The general utility knife is the real work horse. It is usually worn on your belt in a full length sheath that covers all but the butt end of the handle. It has a blade of medium thickness that is between 4 and 8 inches in length and has a comfortable handle. This knife is one of the buckskinner's most important and most often-used tools. It can be used for cutting wood, rope, hide, canvas and in the old days was used for cutting hair also. It can be used for notching, hacking, stripping bark off of branches and for the repairing of other gear. Also, this knife can double as a tool for cooking as well as for cutting your meat. The blade is relatively short so it can be controlled and good leverage can be used for cutting. A large knife would be awkward to use in this type of work and could not perform the functions of a good utility knife.

As far as style goes, check the knife books at your local library for there are hundreds of different types. The Green River knife is a good example of a fine utility knife for its particular historical period. If a buckskinner only had one knife, I'm sure he would choose a general utility knife for it can do anything he might desire from its use.

The throwing knife is the crudest knife of them all. It takes a great beating, bouncing off targets, rocks and other knives and hawks. Some types with soft steel blades will have to be straightened out periodically with a good pounding from a tomahawk. In its simplest form a throwing knife is just a piece of steel with a point at one end and some leather and thong tied on for a handle at the other end. The knife should be of medium to heavy weight for a light blade is impossible to throw. A piece of mild steel stock 1½ to 1¾ inches wide and 12 to 14 inches long and ¼ inch thick will make an excellent throwing knife and will practically be indestructible. No pounding necessary on this baby to straighten it out. A simple handle of wood, bone or leather and a point on the steel tip and you are in business. You can refine it as much as desired or leave it mean and crude. This type of

125

throwing knife will meet N.M.L.R.A. rules and be accepted at almost all local events.

After the first throws at about 5 paces your throwing knife will start to pick up some "character" — nicks, scrapes and bangs. If you would rather not make your throwing knife you will find an assortment of throwing knives at your local muzzleloading shop. Get the toughest one you can find.

The last of the buckskinning knives is the decorative fighting knife. They are usually large knives and in the days of old were actually used in battle, but now grace the buckskinner's belt as more of a part of his costume then a piece of practical gear.

In the west, large Bowie knives that found their way into the Rocky Mountains and the long knives of George Rogers Clark and his men fit this type of knife. In the east, the long rifle knives used by riflemen during the American Revolution fall into this category. Since these knives are mainly for show many of them are beautifully crafted with the finest antler and bone handles and blades that shine like the sun. You will have to decide for yourself whether your costume will lend itself to this type of decorative fighting knife.

While speaking of knives we must not forget the whet stone which should be carried in your pack or possibles pouch. A little spit and a few strokes and that blade will win back a fine edge.

THE WOOL BLANKETS

Now we can go on to the items you will need for your pack. We might as well start with the largest and work down. By far the largest items in your pack are your wool blankets. They are the buckskinner's friend. Nothing is more friendly than a warm woolen blanket wrapped around you while tending the fire at a winter rendezvous on a cold clear night. Wool has very special properties that make it an ideal material for use in the woods. Wool is a natural fiber with a long historical tradition of friendship with frontier people. It has great strength and wears long and hard. Wool is resilient which enables it to snap back to its original shape after it has been crushed. Wool reflects warmth and feels warm to the touch. Its dense fibers trap air which in turn insulates. After a driving rain you can take a wet woolen blanket and wring it out and it will still give warmth. Cotton on the other hand does just the opposite. Wet cotton takes warmth away from the body.

Wool tends to repel moisture. The frizz on each fiber is so dense that water has a hard time penetrating. Dirt also has a hard time getting a grip on the wool fibers so most dirt can simply be brushed off.

The basic item most of your wool gear will come from is the wool blanket. When buying a good wool blanket make sure it is of virgin wool (new wool) and note the weight of the blanket, size and thickness. Virgin wool blankets are expensive, but you can cut down on the cost of a good blanket by buying one made of reprocessed wool. These are warm and long wearing and usually are 85% wool, but they do not have quite as much warmth as the virgin wool blankets. The low cost of the reprocessed wool blankets compared to the virgin wool makes them a wise buy. You can get four or more reprocessed wool blankets for the price of one virgin

wool blanket. These reprocessed wool blankets are usually dark in color and are solid with no stripes.

When buying a wool blanket do not be overly impressed with the brand-name blanket. Many times when you buy an expensive brand-name blanket you are putting your dollars into the name and not into the wool where it really counts.

After you have selected your sleeping blankets (a good size is somewhere around 60″ × 80″) select a blanket for your capote. The capote takes a tremendous amount of hard wear in the woods, so a reprocessed wool blanket is probably your best bet. You will have blanket parts left over from making your capote and you can use these for making a capote sash, mittens, moccasin liners, rifle cover or a blanket vest to wear over your muslin shirt in the winter. I have seen buckskinners hike into a rendezvous wearing blanket material leggings, using pieces of wool blanketing to throw on the ground to sit on in front of the fire or to wrap around your feet at night. When your water cask begins to freeze up on a winter rendezvous, wool certainly becomes one of your best friends.

One problem with your wool blankets is that they will tend to creep off of you while you sleep no matter how carefully you wrap yourself up. Some buckskinners solve this problem by folding their blankets in half the long way and stitching across the bottom and about half way up the side. Then you have a warm envelope of blanket to sleep in. You can do this with several blankets and then have the option of sleeping under one layer, or two or more layers. Sometimes you will want to have more layers under you and sometimes more on top. This is a practical arrangement that will give you warm comfortable nights.

THE GROUND CLOTH

While we are discussing sleeping gear we must say a few words about a functional ground cloth. Most buckskinners simply use a piece of canvas that is about 2 feet longer and wider than their blankets that are folded the long way. The canvas can have frayed edges all the way around or it can have a sewn finished edge. It would be best if this canvas was waterproofed to keep the dampness of the night from you and your blankets.

The most authentic ground cloth I have seen was a piece of pillow ticking that was tacked to the barn wall and painted again and again with linseed oil. Each coat was allowed to dry for several days. This makes a very fine waterproofed ground cloth which is light in weight.

When making your ground cloth you might want to construct it wider than usual so that you can fold over a long pocket (stitch it up) on one edge so that you can slip your rifle in to give it added protection from the night dampness.

RENDEZVOUS SHELTERS

The tipi is probably the best tent ever designed by man for it has a fire and smoke system that allows you to cook and obtain warmth without getting smoked out of the tent. The best book on the subject is by Reginald and Gladys Laubin and anyone who is considering making a tipi should study their book carefully. You can find it in most public libraries.

But for the lone buckskinner the most common type of shelter is the lean-to and the lean-to cloth is probably the next largest item in your pack after your blankets. There are many ways to use this cloth. If a rendezvous in the fall or winter is a few hours drive from your home, by the time you leave work on a Friday afternoon, get your gear from home and drive to the rendezvous site, it will probably be dark and late. After working all day and hiking in with the full basket pack and candle lantern, you will probably be one tired buckskinner. One of the last things on earth you will feel like doing is searching around in the woods with your candle lantern trying to find and cut lean-to poles and then put up the lean-to. Also you will not be able to see the lay of the land very well and probably will not select a very good camp site.

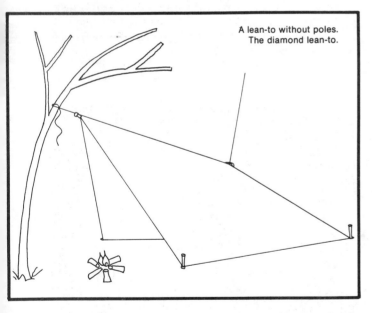

A lean-to without poles.
The diamond lean-to.

In this situation some veteran buckskinners simply use the envelope shelter for the first night. Find a flat and slightly high spot of ground, spread your lean-to cloth and lay out your ground cloth and blankets on one half of the lean-to cloth. Then climb into your blankets and pull the other half of the lean-to over you like a large envelope.

This shelter will protect you in most any weather and if it rains or snows you can keep dry by folding under the open edges of the envelope so that water will not trickle in. In the morning you will be able to find a better spot to set up your regular camp.

There is a great range in types of cloth that buckskinners use in making their lean-tos. It is generally accepted that tarp type canvas is too heavy for lean-to use. A light canvas duck will work fine. For an even lighter lean-to, Indian head cotton works well and I have seen a group of veteran buckskinners from Michigan use a heavy grade of unbleached muslin for their carefully designed lean-tos. All of these should be water proofed with a compound you can get at the local hardware store. Also if the color of the cloth is light you will have more light in your lean-to during the day. This light color will not hurt the shading effectiveness in sunny weather.

There are hundreds of different types of lean-tos in many different sizes from the large family size down to the lone trapper size. Some require many poles and some require very few. While at a rendezvous you will have to look around and see if you can find a lean-to that will fit your needs and a style you like and would enjoy making.

One of the simplest and best all-around shelters known to buckskinners is the diamond shelter. It requires only one sapling or one pole to string from and can be set up in five minutes. The diamond shelter is a piece of cloth about eight to ten feet square. One corner is staked to the ground. The opposite corner, diagonally across the cloth, is tied with a line which is run and tied to a sapling about six feet from the ground. This sapling is bent slightly to act as a spring to keep the lean-to tight. The other two corners are then stretched out tight and staked to the ground. A line can be run from a tie in the middle of the cloth and tied to a nearby limb. This line will lift the center of the shelter and prevent it from sagging.

Your bedroll can be laid across the mouth of the shelter and your gear can be stored behind this. Your cook fire can be built under the point where the corner is tied to the line. It is possible with such an arrangement to cook your breakfast without leaving your blankets. In cold weather the fire can be moved closer into the shelter.

This diamond shelter is very easy to construct. It is simply a square piece of cloth with leather ties stitched to each corner and one in the center. Also, if the need arises this cloth can be fashioned into many other types of shelters. All of these shelters should generally be put up with the back of the shelter facing the west. This is the direction that most weather will come from.

If you find yourself in an area where there are no saplings to tie from you can cut a single pole, stick it as deep as you can in the ground and run a short line from the middle of the pole and stake the line to the ground about six feet from the pole. You can then run your regular diamond shelter line from the top of the pole in the opposite direction from the short line. If there are no limbs around to tie the center line of the shelter to, you can cut a three foot prop, place a piece of leather over the top and stick it in the center of the shelter. The leather piece will prevent the prop from poking through the cloth.

Several diamond shelters can be strung from a single

pole and it is possible to enclose an area completely with four diamond shelters of about the same size and all strung from a central point. A common fire can be built and the smoke will escape through the upper openings. For several buckskinners who each have a diamond shelter this type of common shelter works very well for a deep winter rendezvous.

The wigwam shelter is another type of common shelter that could be used to house a group of buckskinners. The wigwam was developed and used by several Indian tribes of the Great Lakes area. It was a hemispherical dwelling with a basic structure of bent sapling poles covered with sheets of elm or birch bark. The buckskinner can use some of the basic features of the wigwam shelter to make an excellent summer or winter shelter which can sleep from two to fifteen fellows depending how large you make it.

To put the dwelling up, fresh poles are cut and three foot long stakes are driven half way into the ground in two parallel lines. Then the poles are lashed to the stakes at their top and bottom. The poles are then bent toward the center line of the dwelling and lashed to the opposite pole to form a large wicket. After you have erected a series of wickets you can tie longitudinal poles on either side to stiffen the wickets up. Then the fellows can use their lean-to cloths to cover the dwelling leaving a smoke hole of about two feet square in the center of the roof.

Some individualistic buckskinners don't hold with the conventional lean-to and have experimented with other dwellings. Marvin Sowers showed up at a rendezvous two days early and built himself a bark hut. It had taken him several weeks to collect enough bark from large dead trees in the area. He also built himself a bed made of logs with a woven rope mattress.

Not to be outdone, Lester Dumm, a friend of Marvin's, built a permanent small log cabin at a regular rendezvous site on his land. The logs were mud chinked, the roof was laid with sod and the cabin had a stone fireplace. So you can see that the stars are the limit as far as rendezvous shelters go and some fellows prefer just the stars.

WATER CONTAINERS

The next largest item you will find in your pack is a primitive container that will hold a most important supply — your water. Before embarking on a rendezvous it is a good idea to find out if drinking water is available at the site. Many times this information will be mentioned on your rendezvous invitation. If water is available then you can hike in dry which will save a lot of weight in your pack. If water is not available you will have to pack it in. Sometimes water can be used for drinking from small streams called run-offs. It is best not to drink from larger streams (over two feet wide) for they travel a long way through many woods and farms and under many cows, sheep, horses and goats.

You will have your choice of several types of water containers and some can be hand made. Round wooden canteens were popular in the military from the Revolution to the Civil War. These can be made from scratch or from kits and they come in several sizes. You will find a tin canteen at your local muzzleloading shop of the type used by the British during the American Revolution. A nicely shaped earthenware jug is another possibility, but they are on the heavy side. Also, I know of at least one buckskinner who planted gourd seeds in his garden, grew a large gourd and made a fine light

Tin, glass and wooden water containers.

128

canteen out of it that held almost a gallon of water. So, there are many possibilities for carrying your water supply and you may be able to come up with some new ideas for a primitive canteen. Also a large modern water container in your car would be a good idea for refills.

CUPS AND TIN WARE

You will find that a small tin drinking cup will be one of your most used pieces of gear. You can make coffee or tea in it and push it right into the coals of your cook fire. Also, in a pinch you can actually make a small stew in this miniature pot.

Copper cups are fine for cold drinks, but they can be unhealthy to drink hot liquids from unless they are tinned inside. You can do this yourself by scrubbing the inside of the cup thoroughly and heating a small cube of pure tin and spreading the liquid tin around the inside with a stick. If you use a copper cup it would be a good idea to wrap the handle in leather for copper cups can be hot to hold.

There is a military size (large) tin cup that is the big brother to the regular tin cup. This large cup can be used for drinking and cooking and can be a good substitute for your stew pot. You can find them at your local muzzleloading shop next to the regular tin cups. Some fellows have made lids for these large cups out of wood or sheet metal which makes them a perfect miniature pot.

Some buckskinners have made drinking cups that can be carried on their belts. A round growth on the trunks of some large trees can be cut off and hollowed out to form a wooden cup which is suitable for carrying on the belt. Also a neat belt cup can be made from the shell of a small turtle.

At some old-fashioned hardware stores you can find a variety of tin pots. They are really made from sheet steel, but are light in weight and do a good job of cooking up your favorite stew. These pots are about 8 to 10 inches in diameter, are about 6 inches deep and have a flat bottom and tin lid with a wire handle. This type of pot is also great for protecting breakable food, like eggs, while carrying your pack or you can freeze your red meat solid and place it in the pot for transport into the rendezvous site. The pot can be your water carrier, hot water maker, all around cooking pot and the lid can be used for a plate in a pinch. The tin pot is one of your most practical all around items.

Also, at some hardware stores, you will find sheet

Plain copper cup, copper cup with wrapped handle and tin insides, large military tin cup, regular size tin cup and utility knife in sheath.

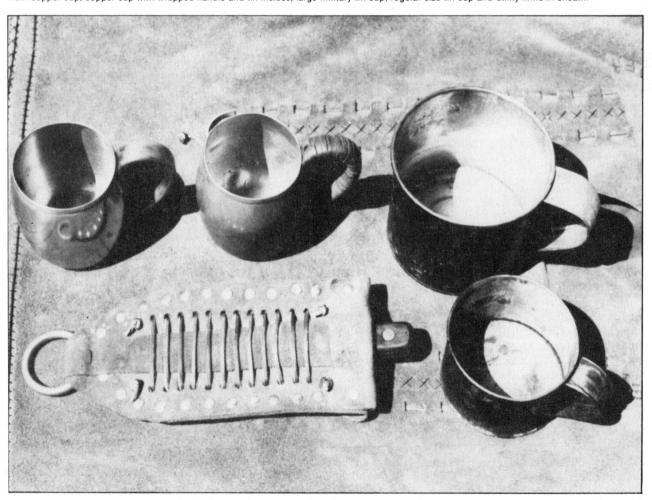

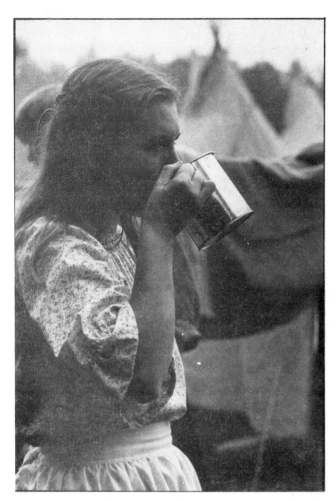

This pretty young lass takes a drink from the large (military size) tin cup.

This drinking cup that hangs from the belt is made from the petrified shell of a small turtle.

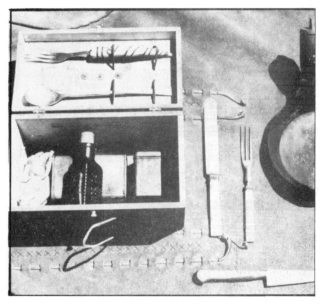

Wooden cooking box with spoon and fork secured in lid, original Green River Forge knife and fork, sheet-metal frying pan with wooden handle and cooking knife.

metal frying pans. They have a modern metal handle, but you can cut this handle off and add a short wooden one made from a broken hawk handle or any hard wood. A frying pan about 8 inches in diameter will hold a couple of eggs and some sausage for your breakfast or a slice of red meat for supper.

Your tinware can easily be cleaned in the creek with a bit of soap and sand. It is a good idea to carry in your pack a scrap piece of cloth to use as a cleaning rag for your cooking items. Just tear a section off and when it gets greasy discard it into the cook fire.

While shopping in the supermarket be on the look-out for products that are packaged in tin containers. Some imported teas are so packaged and items like dry mustard from England come in tins that you can use for storing your sugar, salt, tea, coffee and dried beans etc. You can *japan* these tins by placing them on the fire or stove and burn the surfaces inside and out. A piece of steel wool will remove any remaining ash and to protect the tin from rust you can give it a few coats of liquid floor wax. A coat or two every month after that will keep the rust away permanently. Some buckskinners prefer to use horns for their sugar and salt. Sometimes a discarded or unfinished powder horn makes a good sugar or salt horn.

THE FORK AND SPOON

These eating items can easily be found at flea markets or junk shops at little expense. Some have bone handles and some are of wood. A three tine fork will service you better than two tines and a medium size spoon is better than one that is too large or too small. Some blacksmiths can pound you out a fork and spoon from steel, but you may find these more difficult to actually eat with. Some fine hand cast pewter spoons have turned up at rendezvous which would be a neat item to trade from off the blanket.

COOKING OIL AND RIFLE OIL CONTAINERS

Also at flea markets look around for old bottles. A small antique glass bottle with a cork stopper is good for your cooking oil and you can stitch a leather cover over it if desired. A smaller bottle would be right for carrying your rifle oil which could be kept in your shooting or possibles pouch.

Hand-forged iron dinner ware can be found on trade blankets at most rendezvous.

CLOTH BAGS

To round out your cooking items you can stitch together some small muslin or leather bags with draw string closures. These are good for holding small items such as your in-the-woods repair kit which would contain needle, thread, small scissors, scraps of cloth and leather. Some fellows prefer a small leather salt bag to the tin or horn.

Larger muslin or leather bags can be stitched up for a food bag and a cold weather bag that would be carried in winter with wool mittens, extra pair of long underwear, extra wool socks and wool cap.

THE BUCKSKINNER'S FOOD

There are some buckskinners that do an exceptional job of cooking in the woods. I have seen fellows make biscuits from scratch, cook pancakes for breakfast and cook elaborate meals for supper on an open fire. At one rendezvous a three foot deep pit was dug and coals were set into the bottom and a thirty pound turkey was coated with creek mud and laid on the coals. More coals were added around the bird and on top. Then the bird was covered over with earth and left to cook for twelve hours. When the turkey was dug up the whole camp feasted on this unusual treat. The creek mud simply hardened and was broken off the turkey. If you like to cook, your best bet is to seek out these fellows who excel on the open fire and learn some of their secrets. They will be glad to help you out.

On the opposite end of the lean-to pole there are fellows who don't cook at all. Some jerky (dried beef cut into thin slices) from a cloth bag or a few bits of pemican and some coffee or tea and an apple or pear will do them just fine. Most of the fellows are in the middle and do some simple cooking. Then there are the "gatherers" who do not bring their food but roam the woods looking for their meals such as may apples, wild onions, mushrooms and sassafras tea. So, there are plenty of cooking styles to accommodate a great variety of buckskinner stomachs.

The easiest way to "gather" your rendezvous food

is at the supermarket. Just roam up and down the isles and try to find those foods that were around in the 18th century and that appeal to your taste. Apples are always good. Eggs and sausage or bacon are great for breakfast. You can find loaves of unsliced bread that look like Martha Washington baked them. Goose liver, all types of red meat, pears, peaches, dried beans, carrots and a hundred other items are all good possibilities.

Some buckskinners cook their red meat without a pan. They let the cook fire burn down to coals and then lay the meat right on the coals. When cooked to suit they dust the ash off the meat and cut it up for eating. Buckskinners from Michigan delight in bringing hams into camp which they slip a small piece of wire into at their tops. They hook the wire loop onto their tripod chains and cook the ham very slowly over a low fire. When the ham is done and you need a meal you simply take out your utility knife and cut off a slice.

You may want to start off your rendezvous cooking simply and after gathering ideas from other fellows you should be able to develop a cooking style of your own which will fit your tastes. Remember that the more cooking items you carry in, the more items you will have to clean up and the more you will have to haul out.

THE CANDLE LANTERN

The main job your candle lantern performs is to give you light while you are hiking into the rendezvous site at night. If you do not intend to arrive at the site after dark you may not need a lantern. The lantern also provides light around your camp area in the evening beyond the light from your camp fire, but this is not completely necessary and many fellows don't even carry a candle lantern in their packs.

If you believe a candle lantern belongs in your pack, check out two main types. The window lantern has a mica (natural mineral) or glass pane that lets the light from the candle shine clearly through. The pierced candle lantern has no window, but the light shines through numerous piercings in the sheet metal sides. Many times these piercings have a fine design quality. This lantern gives less light and is simpler in construction than the window lantern, but it provides enough light to let you find your way down a dark trail.

Both of these lanterns can be made or you can find them on the trade blanket and in the muzzleloading shops. Books at your local library on lighting fixtures will clearly show these types of candle lanterns. If you build your own, make sure to construct the body of the lantern large enough so that the heat from the candle does not build up inside. If it does the candle will melt quickly within a few minutes. Also put a lot of air vents at the bottom and top of the lantern so that cold air can enter at the bottom and hot air can escape quickly from the top. Even though a candle lantern is not a completely necessary part of your gear it sure does make a fine decorative item hanging outside your lean-to on a starry night.

FLINT AND STEEL

Three shadowy figures moved through the wood stamping half a foot of snow under their moccasins.

They were hunched over, leaning hard into the straps of their heavy packs with long guns cradled in their arms. A tin cup rattled against a powder horn and snorting faces could be heard across the wood.

They stopped up short, looked around to survey the lay of the land and felt the earth beneath the snow with their feet. They decided and flung their burdens down. One figure took a leather bag from atop his basket pack, put it in his teeth and knelt religiously in the snow. With mittened hands he brushed the snow away to bare ground. Then he opened the leather bag and took from it a steel object, a stone, some bits of cloth and a bundle of rope. He struck the stone against steel with a single metallic click and sparks jumped against a small black piece of cloth set in a maze of frayed rope. The black cloth began to glow with a small orange spot and the figure grasped the bundle and raised it ceremoniously over his head and blew hard into the bundle. White smoke poured forth and finally red flame sprang to life and he cast the bundle down onto the frozen earth.

Concealed in his left hand were dry twigs and he now threw them onto the flame. And the flame caught and grew. The two other figures now appeared with dry wood they had collected, set their wood upon the flame and the flame grew larger still. The ends of some fallen limbs were laid into the fire and the warmth of the blaze was reflected in the faces of the three figures now huddled close around the fire. Meat and pipes were fetched out and they were satisfied.

Flint and steel fire building works on the principle that a sharp piece of flint can be struck against a piece of hardened steel and this action cuts off minute bits of steel which instantly turn molten because of the intense friction that is generated. Charcloth is used to capture these molten bits of steel (sparks) and the cloth will begin to burn with an orange spot. The charcloth on the tinder is then blown into a flame.

You can find flint on the ground in several states, especially Texas and Ohio. It also can be traded off the blanket or bought from your muzzleloading shop. Any piece of hardened steel can be used as a striker. Old files that have the rough surface smoothed down are good. Some strikers are constructed in a horse shoe loop so that you can hang on to them better when striking. Some are simply straight pieces of steel while others are exact copies of historical strikers found in museums.

The carbon in the steel makes it hard and steel can be hardened by heating it red hot and quenching it in oil or water depending on the type of steel it is. Also you can harden steel by adding carbon. The purest form of carbon in nature is burnt sugar. You can place sugar on steel and heat it to increase its carbon content and then quench it in the proper substance of oil or water.

You can make charcloth yourself in the field or at home. Pure cotton cloth works well. Just cut up an old cotton garment (T-shirts are good) into 3 inch squares and put them in a tin can with some type of lid on it. A stone or piece of wood or tin cover will work fine. Leave a small gap open so that the smoke can escape from the can. Place the tin on a fire or stove for about half an hour. Smoke will pour forth from the gap and when the smoke begins to stop remove the tin and let it cool for about 10 minutes. If you open the tin too quickly air will rush in and ignite the charcloth. Check the charcloth to make sure all of it is charred black. If the cloth still has natural color spots in the middle of each piece then it was not heated long enough. If the cloth has turned into a bunch of ash then it was heated too long.

The best all around natural charcloth yet discovered is cut from cotton bath towels. The spark will burn hot and long which is a great help when trying to make a fire in the wet. For tinder you can collect different pices of natural rope or binder twine and test them on how well they burn after they have been frayed into a bird's nest shape. Frayed grape vine also is good tinder and you can find it in the woods.

To make your flint and steel fire, strike the flint (sharp edge) against the steel as if you were using the flint as a knife to hack off a bit of the steel. Arrange the charcloth in the center of your tinder (bird's nest) and when the spark is caught on the charcloth pick the bird's

Flint and steel container, rope tinder, charcloth, steel striker, flints, steel pot for melting lead, rifle lead carried on a thong and copper ladle for pouring balls.

133

nest up and hold it over your head to keep the smoke from choking you and blow into the bundle until it flames. Then cast it down on the ground where you want your fire to be placed and add small dry twigs immediately. With larger dry wood you can quickly build the blaze into a cook fire.

Most fellows start out using a *japaned* lozenge tin to hold their flint and steel kit, but they soon find it is only large enough to make a few fires and the tin is not water proof. A better arrangement is to use a tin that has a semi-screw top lid and that is about 4½ inches in diameter and about 3 inches deep. This type of tin is what a brand of shop hand cleaner comes in and it will seal air tight to keep your makings dry after it is *japaned* and coated with floor wax.

Besides your several pieces of flint, your steel, tinder and charcloth you should also carry in that tin some dry twigs for those times when dry wood is hard to come by, a candle stub and a special fire bundle. This bundle would include twigs, wax, tinder, birch bark or any other item that will burn well. The fire bundle is for those rainy or snowy days when it is almost impossible to get a fire going by ordinary means.

As you can see from the preceding pages the making and collecting of buckskinning gear is pretty near a limitless topic. But in the construction of your own gear there will be a definite limit to what you choose to carry on your back. You will find that your gear will continuously change for you will see and read about new ideas and you will add and trade off items.

One buckskinner worked hard to make and collect his gear and just as he thought he had everything organized just right a fellow laid a beautiful long gun in front of him and a trade was made after hours of talk. The buckskinner gained a fine rifle, but he sacrificed all his hand built gear and he had to start all over again. So, the perfect permanent set of items does not exist. You will find your gear is in a state of evolution and that evolution will be influenced by your ideas, what you see and what you read.

There are a few books that can help you with the construction of your gear. Most of these and many more can be found at your local muzzleloading shop. *Sketch Book 76* will give you details of a haversack, an 18th century folding knife, tomahawks, wooden canteens, tin military canteens and tin cups. This book has many drawings and was written by Robert L. Klinger. Also, it has details of moccasins, rifle shirts plus a lot of military gear.

The Mountain Man's Sketch Books Vol. I & II by James Austin Hanson have much information about clothing, weapons and tools of the fur trading era.

These sources will help you with your gear, but the best place to see the gear in use and to collect your own ideas for your gear is at a rendezvous. If you join a muzzleloading club that has a keen interest in this art form (some clubs do not, so choose carefully) the club will guide you into this buckskinning experience and you surely will not regret it.

The Skills

Warren "Hawk" Boughton

WARREN "HAWK" BOUGHTON IS well known in the primitive area of buckskinning. He personifies what it is really all about. He loves shooting, hunting, camping, backpacking and canoeing — all primitive style, of course! He has pursued these activities in the wilderness areas of California, Utah, Wyoming, Montana, South Dakota, Colorado, Missouri, Arkansas, Illinois, Kentucky and Tennessee.

His greatest interest lies with the history and life styles of the mountain men, longhunters and Indians, with emphasis on their hunting, warfare and survival methods. Wherever he has lived or traveled he has made a point of learning and practicing the primitive survival skills that apply to that particular area and the people who lived there.

Boughton is a life member of the National Rifle Association and the National Muzzle Loading Rifle Association. He is also a member of The American Mountain Men and now serves as their Eastern Territory Segundo for all states east of the Mississippi plus the states of Iowa, Missouri and Arkansas.

Hawk has won numerous primitive matches, but he has won the biggest of them all, the Mountain Man Aggregate of the NMLRA on three different occasions and placed second three other times. This match involves making a fire with flint and steel in the fastest time possible, three difficult rifle shots, three throws with the knife and three with the tomahawk. The winner is judged on his composite score in all the events.

Although he was christened Warren L. Boughton, Jr., his friends call him Hawk which he thinks is rather appropriate because "I have sharp eyes for shooting, I throw the "hawk" fairly well, and finally, in a political sense, I am more hawk than dove. I am for and with this country over all others, all the way, regardless of where it leads."

THE CITY DWELLER WHO DRIVES through a wilderness area views it as a hostile environment — a place of mystery and the abode of evil forces capable of dealing out death through hunger and thirst, by drowning, by exposure to the elements or to wild animals, or to the debilitating effects of being hopelessly lost. But to the man of the wilderness the fears of the city dweller are utter nonsense, not because he has conquered the wilderness but because he has learned to live with it. He is at home there. To those who prefer the far lonely places, whether in the mountains, the desert, or the forest, the wilderness is a source of shelter and clothing, food and drink, and even of entertainment.

But this high level of compatibility with the wilderness was not attained by white men in the earliest of Colonial times. Rather, it began with their first contacts with the Indians. It made great strides prior to the American Revolution, and reached its zenith with the frontiersmen of the east and mountain men of the far west.

By today's standards neither the frontiersmen nor the mountain men would be classified as skilled workers, yet their occupations required combinations of many skills. When the Indian fighting frontiersmen and borderers went west to the shining mountains they took with them the skills learned in the east. Over the next 50 years they acquired new ones in their dealings with the Indians of the prairies and mountains. Not all men knew all things but an old hand, a hiveranno, was an expert hunter and marksman; he could skin any animal, large or small, and if need be, tan its pelt for future use. He could track an animal or a hostile Redskin, and if the tables were turned, evade the Indian, circle back, ambush him and go on his way.

The hiveranno could find dry wood in the wettest weather and start a fire with flint and steel, or with his rifle. Far from his squaw's tepee or his party's camp he could make a warm dry shelter with a square of canvas or the stones and wood at hand. He could cook a meal in utensils made on the spot, or with none at all. He could catch a wild mustang, pack his mules, and ride a horse over the roughest terrain. He could build a dry underground cache, paddle a canoe, make his own clothing, and find his way without a compass. In an emergency the old hand could survive on edible plants and the game caught with snares, pitfalls and deadfalls. He could build a cabin, a dugout and a bull boat. If all these skills weren't enough to tax the abilities of any normal man the hiveranno had, at times, to be his own doctor, surgeon, and veterinarian!

There are very few men living today who practice all the skills of the old time mountain man, but there are many who practice most of them. Given the same conditions and circumstances today that prevailed on the frontier 150 years ago, I have no doubt that these men

would soon master those skills which they now lack.

In every war in which our country has been involved, some of these skills have proven invaluable to the fighting men. Likewise, the civilian populations of war-torn countries have sometimes been forced to rely on primitive skills in order to survive. Primitive techniques are sometimes life savers in times of peace. All too often we hear of the airplane forced down in a wilderness area; or the canoeist who capsizes and loses his equipment while many miles from the nearest help; or the ill-equipped camper who is snowbound by a sudden blizzard while far back in an isolated mountain area.

With this in mind we will attempt to set down on paper a few of the techniques that helped our forefathers survive on the frontier. By study and practice the reader will be enabled to master these techniques, then go on to learn many of the other skills, which are, for the most part, the almost exclusive province of today's mountain men.

AUTHENTICITY

No self-respecting modern day mountain man would want to be found dead in a camp with any of his clothing, equipment, food, or any other item that was not known on the frontier before the year 1840. Banned from all primitive camps are plastic wrap, aluminum foil, white paper wrapped cigarettes, lighters, modern tin cans, screw cap bottles, ice chests, wrist watches, flash lights, styrofoam, air mattresses, modern shoes, blue jeans, synthetic cloth, plastic buttons, most rubber products, and imported food, the most notable exceptions to this last item being tea and coffee.

It takes much thought, considerable research, and some doing in order to find authentic substitutes for the camp gear found in today's marketplace — but it can be done. Replace plastic wrap and aluminum foil with greased brown paper. Choose foods that were either available in the area where your gathering is held, or were supplied at the old time rendezvous. Transport and store food in boxes, cans, cloth bags, earthen jugs and crocks.

Most camps and rendezvous allow enameled cookware even though it did not become popular until after 1840. On the trail and in camps of short duration the veteran buckskinner gets by very well with no more than a sheath knife, a spoon made of wood or forged iron, a small pressed steel skillet, which also serves as a plate, a small pail, a tin cup or wooden noggin.

Gourds, although now much neglected, were once a valued source of camp and household utensils. Most useful for our purposes are the bottle, canteen, and dipper gourds. To make a good container for both wet and dry materials cut off the top of a dry bottle gourd, remove the seeds and filament from inside the gourd and install a stopper made of wood. Bottles such as these are handy in a semi-permanent camp for the transportation and storage of water, flour, beans, rice, etc. Smaller bottles make good containers for such things as powder, balls, shot, oil and salt. Bill Estes, a Kentucky mountain man, once received in trade for gunsmithing work, a bottle gourd containing black powder. A sheet of rolled-up newspaper which formed the stopper was dated in the 1880's. The powder was still useable.

Excellent dishes and bowls are easily made of bottle gourds by sawing them off one to three inches above their flat bottoms. Complete the dish or bowl by rounding off the sharp edges. This type vessel can also be used for brewing coffee, boiling water, and cooking vegetables, roots and herbs; more about that later.

It is easy to make a serviceable basket for carrying mushrooms, roots, herbs, nuts, fruit and berries. Saw a bottle gourd off four or five inches above its flat bottom; make the cut at, or near, its widest diameter. On each side of the gourd about one inch down from the upper edge, cut a ¼" × 1" slot. Weave a carrying handle of rawhide thongs or thin strips of the inner bark of hickory or basswood, which is another name for the linden tree; or use the outer bark of young willow. A handle can also be woven of fibers from pounded dead leaves of the yucca plant, or from stalks of the sunflower and the wild hemp plant. Complete the basket by rounding all sharp edges and tying the handle in the slots.

As its name implies, the dipper gourd is shaped like a dipper and is easily made into one merely by removing somewhat less than half of the upper part of the gourd body. Save the piece removed and later convert it into a large cooking spoon by reducing it to the desired size and adding a handle carved from a non-resinous, non-aromatic wood such as maple or basswood. Add an authentic touch to your handiwork by attaching the spoon bowl to the handle with two or three hand-carved wooden pins. Make the shanks of the pins ⅛" in diameter and the round heads slightly larger.

A light-weight convenient cup that is suitable for attaching to your belt can be made from a dipper. Using a completed dipper, shorten the handle to within one inch of the cup. Select a fork of a tree limb and saw it off as indicated in the drawing. Make sure that the part which is to be inserted into the handle hole is approximately ¼" larger in diameter than the inside diameter of the hole. (See diagram.)

HOW FORK OF TREE IS USED FOR CUP HANDLE

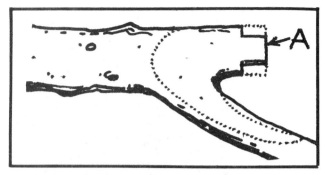

Remove the bark and carve the area indicated at "A" to fit hole in cup. Finish shaping and sanding the wood. Make three wooden pins of the type described for the spoon. Drill three equally spaced holes through the gourd shank and into the wood. Make the holes slightly smaller in diameter than the pins so the pins can be pressed in and be friction tight. Complete your cup by drilling a hole at the end of the handle in which to tie a leather thong.

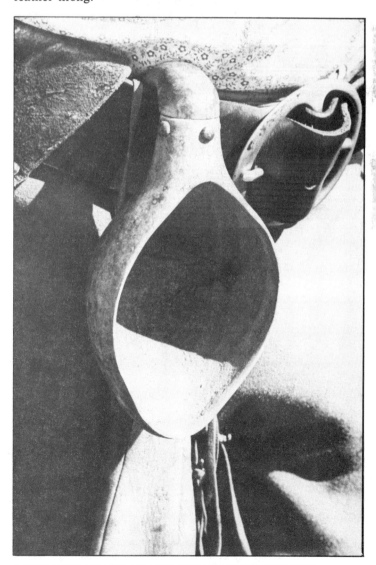

A gourd drinking cup with a tree limb handle fitted as described above.

138

The mountain man had to be alert when in hostile Indian territory and often had to use his skills to keep his hair.

Sir William Johnson was served his food in a sterling silver trencher. Middle class families ate from pewter trenchers, while their backwoods cousins used wooden trenchers or tin plates. Trenchers were too heavy and cumbersome to be carried by frontiersmen and beaver trappers so they ate directly from their skillets or from light-weight tin plates. You can easily make a wooden trencher by slabbing a piece of wood about one-inch thick and cutting or scraping a shallow depression in its top surface. It makes no difference whether your trencher is round, square, rectangular, or oval.

In timber country when you have no metal cooking pot, improvise one with a billet of wood and a tomahawk. Cut a section of wood 10 or more inches in diameter by 12 to 14 inches long. Flatten two opposite sides of the billet, then chop and remove enough wood from the upper surface of your soon-to-be pot to accommodate the food you wish to cook.

The inside surface of this vessel need not be smooth if it is for temporary use only. If it is to be used for several meals it must be smoothed to make cleaning easier. The smoothing operation can be done with a "crooked" knife, or, lacking this, by scraping the inside with sharp-edged chert or flint stone. Another, perhaps easier method, is to burn out the irregularities, then scrape away the charred surface in the manner used by southeastern Indians in making their dugout canoes called pirogues (pee-rows) by Louisiana Cajuns.

Harriette Simpson Arnow in her book, *Seedtime on the Cumberland*, recounts the story of a Tennessee borderer returning to his camp with a deer across the back of his pack horse. Stopping by the trail to cook a meal he dug a bowl-shaped depression in the earth, pressed the fresh deer hide into it, hair side down, and had a pot ready for mixing of bread dough or cooking of food.

Long before the Indians acquired metal utensils from the whites they learned to utilize the membranous sacs and bladders of the animals they killed for food and water storage and for cooking. Lewis and Clark, George F. Ruxton and others, documented their use as cooking utensils. The paunch of a buffalo, for example, could be turned inside out, washed, scraped and used as a container for water or for cooking of food. Although smaller in size, the bladder, the scrotum and the sac enclosing the buffalo's heart was also used. Even the lowly gut made a good waterproof utensil. It required a minimum of effort to rinse it out, tie one end, fill it with water and tie the other end to convert it into a useful item for camp or trail.

In northern climates where the paper birch (also called canoe birch) grows large, the Indians and some whites make many useful items of the bark: Canoes, pack baskets, berry baskets, sugar maple sap buckets, fish creels, pemmican storage boxes — and what is more pertinent to our present subject — dishes, bowls, and cooking pans.

Removal of the bark kills the tree. As a rule, when a canoe or several large items are to be made, the birch tree is cut down to make peeling of the bark easier. This practice, of course, cannot be followed now unless one owns the tree or has permission of the owner. It should be noted that the bark from beech, tulip poplar, basswood, and several other species, are also suitable for construction of utensils.

PATTERN FOR FOLDING BARK COOKING VESSEL

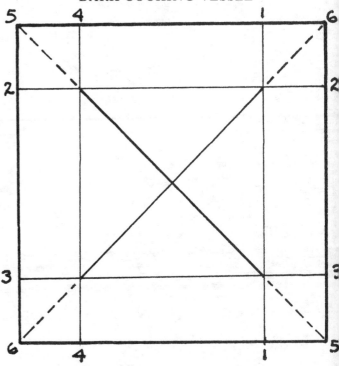

To get the hang of folding bark, cut a piece of heavy paper (a grocery bag is satisfactory) 15″ × 15″ square. On each of the four sides draw a line (See Numbers 1, 2, 3, and 4 in Figure 2). Make each of the lines three inches from, and parallel to, the edge of the paper. Draw diagonal lines 5 and 6. Fold and crease the paper along lines 1, 2, 3, 4, 5, and 6. Starting at the upper right-hand corner of the paper, raise it at points 1 and 2 while at the same time pressing in along dashed line 6 to form a folded pleat. Hold the pleat in place with a straight pin. Repeat this procedure at the remaining three corners. You now have a mock-up of a pan that measures 9″ × 9″ square and has 3″ sides. A bark pan is made the same way except instead of drawing pencil guide lines on the bark you must deeply score it with a sharp-pointed stick or thorn, being careful not to cut all the way through. It is not necessary to score the *diagonal* lines all the way across; just at each of the 3″ corners is sufficient. To hold the corners of your bark vessel in place punch small holes near the upper edge of the bark and secure the corners by lacing them with green root or pin them down with thorns.

This fanciful old engraving shows the buffalo which was one of the primary food sources of the mountain man.

compressed, this blanket should be about one-inch thick. Cut a three-inch thick slab of meat, wrap it in damp leaves and place it in the hole. Cover this with another blanket of damp leaves and grass to a depth of two-inches. Rake the pile of hot coals and ashes back into the hole and cover these with a five-inch layer of earth.

It will be two and one-half to three hours before the meat is done. Until then you may want to build another fire in the remaining four or five inches of the hole and cook a meal; or, you can go hunting for more meat; or you might want to shoot at a mark, trade, or just plain palaver with your friends. Being able to cook without having to be continually puttering around the fire is one of the good features of this kind of cooking. Another is, you seldom burn the food you are cooking. Still another good point is that you can cook other things in the same hole while the meat is cooking — fish, vegetables and eggs — for example.

In all honesty, however, there are at least two negative features. One, you can't tell when the meat is done unless you uncover it and look. (If the meat isn't done to your taste, replace it, cover it again, and build a fire above it and let it cook a while longer.) Two, you are bound to get some dirt and/or ashes on the meat when you uncover it, but this is easily removed by scraping it off with a knife, or by removing and discarding a thin slice of the meat.

You can cook eggs in the shell by placing them in the ashes near the edge of the cook fire and turning them occasionally. A novel way to cook an egg is to make a small hole in each end of the egg and pass a small clean stick through it from one end to the other. Don't let the egg get too hot too soon or it will either explode or its contents will be slowly forced out of the holes and into the fire.

There are two ways of boiling food in gourds or in thin-walled bark utensils: One, heat clean stones red hot and drop them into the vessel. This is an efficient method of cooking because all of the heat of the stone is absorbed by the liquid. Two, place the pan directly on the hot coals. Cover the embers around the bottom edge of the pan with dead ashes so the fire cannot blaze up. The sides of the vessel will not ignite so long as flames do not rise above the water level. The bottom will not ignite because the temperature there can increase only slightly above boiling temperature. All heat above that temperature is absorbed by the liquid in the pot.

Incidentally, something our ancestors knew but is now all but forgotten is that wood ashes are a direct substitute for baking soda. For example, if your recipe calls for one teaspoonful of baking soda but you have none, use one teaspoonful of white wood ashes. Any kind of white wood ashes will do but the best are those from hardwood trees such as dogwood, pecan, hickory, maple, beech, and ash.

Another little known fact that you may find useful when you are far from civilization is that snow can be substituted for eggs when eggs are listed in a recipe. Eggs are needed in some mixes because of their ability to trap air in thousands of tiny bubbles when mixed or beaten. Fluffy, unpacked snow seems to do the same thing, that is, it retains its shape long enough to trap air in the dough or batter, thus increasing its volume. Substitute two tablespoons of snow for each egg called for in the recipe.

Cleaning Up

Cleaning up after cooking and eating can be quite a chore, especially if you would rather be doing something else, — and who wouldn't? But it is not such a bad job when you know a few tricks. To clean a greasy tin plate: Pull up a clump of grass, roots, dirt, and all. Scrub the plate with the roots and dirt and finish by wiping it with the grass. Rinse it off with water if you have plenty.

Never scrub a well-seasoned skillet with any kind of abrasive. If you do, the skillet will have to go through another breaking-in period during which foods tend to stick to the bottom. To clean a dirty skillet, just wipe it out with leaves or grass. If it won't come clean by this method, fill the skillet with water up past the cooked-on food line. Mix the water with wood ashes until it is about the consistency of mush. Place the skillet over the fire and bring the mixture to a rolling boil. Ashes combined with water make a weak lye solution which, aided by the heat, will cut through the most stubborn grease and cooked-on food. To complete this cleaning job, pour out the water and ashes, wipe the skillet out with grass or leaves, and rinse it with water.

FIRE MAKING WITH
FLINT AND STEEL

Film directors apparently believe that fire making with flint and steel is an art that died out in the 20th century. If not, then why, when the script calls for a pioneer type to start a fire, the camera invariably pictures a man building a pyramid of sticks and leaves, then it shifts momentarily to another subject and when it returns to the fire maker we see that the fire is already blazing merrily away? It wouldn't require more than about five minutes time to show how the man actually makes his fire with flint and steel.

The reason he is not shown making the fire is surely not because it would require too much time. In timed contests I have seen fires started in six seconds, and occasionally in as little as five seconds. This is elapsed time that began with the first strike of steel against flint and ends when the contestant blows the charred cloth and tinder into a flame.

In the writing of Rudolph Freiderich Kurz we have indisputable proof that a fire steel was one of the mountain man's most valued possessions. Kurz was a Swiss artist who went to the American west to paint Indians, a subject which, at the time, had captured the imagination of the civilized world. To support himself while painting, he worked as a clerk at various fur trade posts. During the winter of 1852, he was employed as a clerk by the Booshway at Fort Union in what is now the state of Montana. On January 20, 1852, Kurz made the following entry in his journal: "Smith wants my fire steel for his benefit early in the morning: he is going on a hunt. Throughout the entire fort not a fire steel, a uten-

sil of such importance . . . in so extended an enterprise as this fur-trading business. Hunters find their flint and steel indispensable; matches are too easily affected by dampness to be practical and, furthermore, we have no supply in stock. So Smith is at a loss unless he can get mine. . . . I made him a present of my flint and steel. In doing this I was perfectly aware of the fact that in this place a man never knows where he will sleep the next night or whether he may not be sent unexpectedly into the open where a fire steel is just as necessary as knife and gun."

Our primitive fire making equipment consists of four necessary items; five, if we count the box, bag, or leather folder in which to carry them. The fire kit should contain flint, a striker (fire steel), charred cloth, and tinder. Because your life may sometime depend upon your ability to make a fire, you should not be satisfied with anything but the best components in your fire kit. The flint you use should throw hot, yellow (not orange) sparks that snap and pop two or three feet through the air before they are extinguished. I prefer the black English flint that Dixie Gun Works imports from southern England. It comes in one- to two-pound nodules and is covered with a thick white layer of chalk just as it is taken from the ancient flint mines. The light-colored French flint is also good, although I have never used it for striking a fire. In this country, there are several good sources of flint, some of the best being from the quarries at Flint Ridge, Ohio, where it was discovered by the Indians.

The stone carried in most fire kits is not flint at all, but a variety of quartz called chert. Chert is found in this country from border-to-border and from coast-to-coast. If ever you stand in need of a flint for your rifle or a good fire striking rock, you won't have to look far to find plenty of chert that will serve your purpose very well.

Good fire steel in all the traditional patterns are available from most muzzle loading supply houses. There are many blacksmiths around the country who specialize in making muzzleloader supplies. They will make, to your specifications, such items as fire steels, tomahawks, and knives. But perhaps you would rather make your own fire steel. This isn't difficult provided you have the time and a few common tools. Lacking a forge for bending and shaping the steel, you will have to rely on a blow torch, a bench grinder, and mill files. The steel used must, of course, be a high carbon type. A satisfactory steel that is available to most everyone is found in an ordinary file. An old file will do as well for this purpose as a new one, the only requirement being it should be at least 1″ wide and 3/16″ thick.

A traditional style striker shaped like a flat-backed letter "C" can be made at home as follows: Using a hammer and cold chisel, cut the file straight down the middle. While the steel is still in a "soft" state, grind and file it to the desired width and shape it. Then bend the ends so your steel is shaped like the letter "C". Reheat the steel to a cherry red color and quench it in water. The entire piece is now hard, so much so that if you should drop it on a hard surface it would break. To temper the steel, polish one side with abrasive cloth. We want the ends to be unbreakable and "soft" as compared to the striking surface, which must be left hard. So apply heat to each end of the striker and watch the change of colors as the steel is tempered. As each end turns blue and colors start to flow into the polished center portion of the striker, quickly quench it in cold water. This halts the tempering process at that particular temperature. The hard center portion of the steel will now throw a shower of hot sparks, yet rough usage will not cause the narrow diameter ends to break. Your fire steel is complete.

By far, the most critical item in the fire kit is the spark catcher which, in most cases, is charred cloth. It must be nearly perfect or it will not catch and hold a spark. Here's how to make the best charred cloth and in sufficient quantity to last you for several weeks. Obtain a tin can of one- or two-pound capacity — the kind that has a tight fitting press-on type lid. Twist a wire around the can and leave a doubled, three-foot length of wire for use as a handle with which to change positions of the can and to lift it in and out of the fire. Punch a 1/16″ hole in the top center of the lid and another one in the bottom center of the can.

Using pure 100% cotton cloth, such as found in undershirts and in cotton flannel shirts, cut the material into four six-inch pieces. (Note: Only 100% cotton material can be used. If it has even a trace of synthetic material in its composition it will not charr properly but will completely burn, shrivel, and disintegrate when handled.) Drop the pieces of cloth, one at a time, into the can and press on the lid. Build a fire and let it burn down to a hot bed of coals. With the wire handle on the can, place it on the coals. Change the position of the can every one or two minutes so the cloth will be evenly cooked. During the charring process you will note that a jet of smoke and unburned gases are emitted from the holes in the can. From time to time these gases ignite and burn with the sound and flame of a small blow torch. When the smoke from the holes diminishes to an occasional puff as the can is turned to a different position, remove it from the fire, plug both holes with twigs and set it aside to cool. If the holes are not plugged, or if

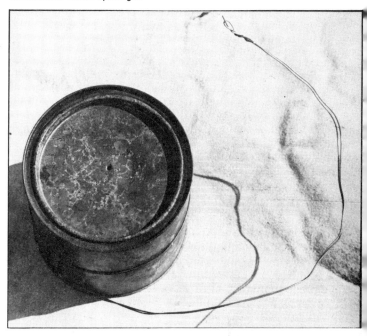

A can like this can be used to make charred cloth. Note the small hole in the top which allows the gases formed by the process to escape. Let the can cool before opening it.

the lid is removed too soon, the cloth may completely burn and disintegrate when oxygen enters the can.

After the can has been allowed to cool for five minutes, pry off the lid, lift out some of the cloth and examine it. The color should be uniformly solid black. Test its strength; a single piece of the charred cloth should offer very little resistance (less than one ounce) when you pull it apart. If areas of the cloth are brown colored, or if it did not tear easily, it did not cook long enough and will have to be put back on the fire. If it disintegrates in your hand, it was cooked too much and you will have to start over. The final conclusive test, of course, is made with your flint and steel. If the cloth has been properly charred it will catch and hold a spark on the first, second, or third strike.

For many years I have searched for a natural substance that will, without any preparation beforehand, catch and hold a spark. Thus far I have been unsuccessful. I have tried such materials as cattail down, bug dust, decayed wood, pulverized wasp nest, punk, puff ball spores — all without success. I came to the conclusion that if a mountain man in need of charred cloth couldn't talk his squaw out of her old calico dress, or if he had already used his last cotton flannel shirt, then he would be forced to char materials found in nature — buffalo chips, grass, fungus, decayed wood, etc. I tried some of these materials and was happy to find that they would catch and hold a spark although not as readily as does charred cotton cloth. In an emergency, materials that will ignite can be found in dead camp fires and around old forest fire burns.

At the July, 1979 rendezvous on Henry's Fork of Green River in Wyoming, I asked Walt "Grizz" Hayward if he had ever found anything in nature that would be used in place of charred cotton cloth. He replied that he hadn't but that he had heard Stefan "Dutch" Ott talking about a substitute he had found. Dutch is a copper miner by necessity and a sculptor and mountain man by inclination. It doesn't pay to drop by his home near Tucson, Arizona unexpectedly because he just might be off on a 200 mile riding and pack horse *jornada* south of the border or to the mountains and deserts of Arizona and Utah. I wrote to Dutch and in due time received a reply. Upon opening the envelope I was happy to find a letter enclosed and four pieces of odd looking material that had the appearance and texture of soft brown leather. The pieces measured approximately 1½" × 1½" and their thickness varied from 1/16" to ⅛". As I got out my flint and steel to test this material I was understandably dubious for I had been following a cold trail for several years and I half expected this to be another one. But both of the pieces I tested caught and held a spark on the second and third strikes. "Held a spark" is an understatement. It was nearly impossible to smother out once the ignited area had started to spread. Then I tried igniting a handful of dry tinder with this material. In this test it again performed as well as charred cloth. When a spark is caught on it, it cannot be blown out — the harder you blow, the more it spreads and the hotter it gets.

The brown leather-like material I tested was undoubtedly a type of fungus. One of the problems now is, can we find it anywhere else except Mexico? — for that is where Dutch said it came from — and it is found inside hollow live oak trees. Various species of evergreen live oak trees grow on California's Pacific coast and back in her more arid canyons, in Mexico, and on the Gulf coast from Texas to Florida, and north as far as Virginia.

Can this fungus be found in trees other than the live oak? Are there other species of fungus that will catch and hold a spark? Are there other materials in nature that will catch and hold a spark? These riddles are only a sampling of the kind we will not quit working on until they are solved. Some may not care for such riddles but I find great satisfaction in following these trails that have been growing cold for the past century and a half.

Good tinder is easier to come by than flint, steel, or charred cloth. Whether east of the Mississippi River or west of it, tinder for a fire can usually be found nearby. At home in Kentucky I prefer a thin, broad leaf grass called spangle grass that I find growing in small patches along a creek in the woods. It is no good until bone dry so I don't collect it until after winter has set in, or until early in the spring before the new grass grows high. I hang a bunch or two in trees at the edge of the woods and another bunch in a storage area inside the house.

Another good tinder is the tissue-thin outer bark of the juniper tree, which is the so-called "cedar" tree in most localities. It hangs dry and loose on the tree and can be stripped off in long strands. You will find it necessary to rough it up and tear it apart with your hands in order to improve its ignitability. Most any kind of dry grass ingites quickly as do thin dry leaves and the dry inner bark of cottonwood trees. In wet weather you can find dry tinder in the old nests of birds and mice, inside hollow trees and logs and under cliff overhangs. Plenty of dry wind-blown leaves can almost always be found in the entrances of caves and under cliff overhangs. In order to discover which tinder works best for you, try using various natural materials that are found in your area. Whenever you are in a different part of the country make it your business to find the best tinder there.

Starting a fire is easy when you have good flint, steel, charred cloth, and tinder. In the common method of starting a fire you take a double handful of tinder, form it roughly in the shape of a six-inch diameter bird nest and place it on the ground. Position enough charred cloth on the tinder to cover most of its surface. With one hand hold the flint, one long sharp edge exposed, approximately four inches above the center of the cloth. With the steel in your other hand, strike the sharp edge of the flint a series of glancing downward blows. Don't quit striking the flint until you see a glowing ring of fire on the charred cloth, then fold the tinder around it, take a deep breath and start blowing steadily into the bundle of tinder. When all conditions are favorable, the tinder will burst into flame within three or four seconds.

There is another way to start a fire that follows the same basic procedure just described. While it is no faster — possibly not as fast — it has the redeeming feature of being a more natural way for two-legged animals to start fires than the first method described. Instead of kneeling on the ground, possibly in mud or snow, you stand on your hind legs like a grizzly bear and hold all the fire making materials in your hands.

To make a fire while you are in an upright position, proceed as follows: Hold the tinder, charred cloth, and flint in one hand. (If you wish, wrap the cloth completely around the flint so sparks are almost sure to land in it.) With the other hand holding the steel, strike glancing blows across the sharp edge of the flint. When a spark catches, set the flint and steel aside or drop them upon the ground. Take a deep breath and blow into the center of the bundle of tinder until it bursts into flame.

First — Hold the tinder, charred cloth and flint in one hand.

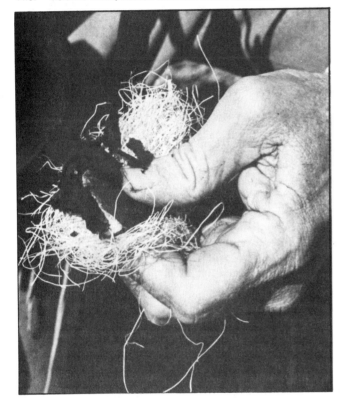

Second — Hold the steel in the other hand and strike glancing blows across the edge of the flint until a spark catches.

Third — Blow into the tinder until it bursts into flame.

When you are in a timed fire making contest, every second counts so try to make your fire in the least time possible. But when you are in the relaxed atmosphere of the outdoors and time is of no consequence, take your time! When a spark catches in good charred cloth, it is not going to die out until it has burned the entire cloth. You are free to arrange the tinder around the burning cloth, or to place the flint and steel back in your fire kit. If it seems likely that the cloth may be consumed before the tinder catches fire, stop and add more cloth before it goes out.

Before entering a timed contest, especially in damp weather, place your tinder and charred cloth near a fire for a few minutes to drive out accumulated moisture.

There are several ways to start a fire without a flint and fire striker, but the quickest, most convenient way is with the firearm you carry, either flintlock or caplock. These methods are not recommended except in emergencies because they are wasteful of powder and caps, and, with a flintlock gun, causes unnecessary wear of the frizzen and flint. To use a flintlock for this purpose when it contains a powder charge and ball, the touch-hole must first be plugged with a small twig. Fill the pan with as much powder as it will hold and lower the frizzen over it. Cock the gun, point it up in the air and while supporting it against your shoulder with one hand, use the other to hold a small bundle of good tinder as close to the pan as possible. When you squeeze the trigger the flash of powder in the pan will ignite the tinder.

A fire starting contest with flint and steel is usually a timed event and requires skill to win.

To make fire with a caplock gun, pour a *small* charge (five grains should be enough) down the barrel and press a frayed cotton patch down on top of it. Cap the nipple, aim the firearm straight up over your head and squeeze the trigger. The frayed patch should ignite as it leaves the barrel and fall close to where you are standing. Depending upon the caliber of your firearm, whether pistol, rifle, musket, or shotgun, you should experiment to find the proper quantity of powder to use.

A fire can sometimes be started by covering a pile of powder with tinder and firing a small charge into it. This is not a good way to start a fire because the tinder and powder is too often scattered to the four winds. A better way is to pour a small pile of powder onto the ground with a powder train leading away from it for about three feet. Cover the mound of powder with tinder. Now when you fire a small charge into the end of the train it will ignite the main charge at the other end of the train and not scatter the tinder.

CAUTION: When using this method, never allow your hands to be near the powder train as they would be if, for example, you were to strike flint and steel into it. The flash of powder in the train is certain to burn your hands.

KEEPING WARM
IN COLD WEATHER

It's a cold mid-December day. Since first light you and the other mountain men have been paddling down a wild but shallow river, getting out of the canoes occasionally to wade riffles where the water is too shallow to float. To reach this place before sundown you have stopped only once for the midday meal and once to reload gear after a canoe capsized. As you climb the steep bank to a line of cliff shelters a cold wind and stray flakes of snow are blowing out of steel-blue clouds in the northwest. Judging by the light where the sun should be, it is nearing five o'clock and already getting dark.

149

Upon reaching the cliff face your party breaks up into groups of three or four and sets about making camp. You and two others select one of the shallow cliff-front shelters and drop your bedrolls and packs inside. Past winds have already found and delivered your mattress, an eight-inch bed of dry leaves from the forest of trees that fills this hollow. While your two companions set about gathering a supply of dry firewood you take on the task of making a fire. It will be a small fire at first, just large enough to accommodate two small frying pans and a coffee pot.

You select a location for the fire that will place it slightly in front of the vertical rock face which rises above the shelter. In this position, heat will warm the interior of the shelter while the smoke, when not influenced by the wind, is free to climb the face of the cliff. This is just an overnight camp and it is getting dark; no time or need for a V-type fireplace; an ordinary slightly elongated fire will do. Over a handful of dry leaves you form a tepee-shaped cone of small twigs. Gripping tinder, charred cloth and flint in one hand and your fire steel in the other you strike a sharp edge of the flint several times in rapid succession. A glowing dot of fire appears on the blackened cloth and increases in size even as you fold your tinder over it. When you blow into the center of the tinder it bursts into flame. Placed in the leaves under the cone of twigs they ignite with a bright flare that glows on the cliff face above and brightens the interior of the otherwise dark shelter. From the supply of timber being brought in by your companions you add increasingly larger pieces of dry wood until the fire is burning briskly, then let it die down to a proper sized cooking fire.

On a cold night when the mercury dips down into the teens one always needs at least twice the quantity of firewood a Pilgrim would think should be enough. While others are cooking the meal, you cut and drag up enough wood to double the size of the pile already collected. You also cut seven straight lengths of timber approximately five-feet long and four-inches in diameter. These are to be used for a heat reflector which you begin to erect at the far side of the fire by driving two three-foot long stakes into the ground. By driving the stakes so they angle away from the fire at about 20° from the vertical, the straight lengths of wood can be placed one above the other to form a reflector that is approximately 28-inches high. In addition to reflecting heat back into the shelter, this wall of wood provides two other benefits: It causes a draft that diverts most of the smoke away from the shelter entrance and also serves as a windbreak.

After the evening meal has been eaten and the utensils washed, larger chunks of wood are put on the fire and the flames leap higher. Now the wet leather moccasins and wool socks are removed from cold feet and are placed over wooden stakes near the fire. While these are drying, spare moccasins and socks from the pack are put on and you start to feel down-right comfortable.

Spread your canvas and blankets on the leaves, Brother, and the best part of the day has arrived. While the pungent odor of hot cider and rum drifts in the air, true stories and innocent lies are bandied around the fire until it seems like time has been pushed back to the days

of the Beaver Men. I'll bet if Old Bill Williams or Jed Smith came up out of the bottom right now they wouldn't see anything strange in us. Their first comment might very well be, ''I don't recollect seeing you boys before. Air ye free trappers or workin' fer the comp'ny?'' Your dreams mingle with the rising smoke as you follow old trails and make new ones.

Not everyone knows how to really relax, but for those who don't there is no better place to learn than here where you are free of all modern inconveniences. Only natural sounds break the stillness: the water flowing over rocks far below, the quiet hissing of hominy snow as it glides through winter leaves, the popping of the campfire with now and then a rustle of embers as they burn through and move lower in the fire. With time reckoned in eons you have missed living with the Beaver Men by the flick of an eyelash, but before you drift off to sleep you thank the Great Spirit for at least allowing you to be here in this place at this time.

People who are not familiar with the lives led by their ancestors 150 years ago have not the foggiest notion of outdoor survival in below freezing temperatures. Those who do have some understanding of the problems involved assume that it can only be done by using modern camping equipment, such as a closed pop-up tent with sewn in floor, a gasoline cook stove and lantern, insulated boots, kapok or down-filled underclothing, coat, mattress, electric socks, and a butane hand warmer. But these technically advanced products were not necessary on the frontier. In fact, had they been available they would have been a hindrance rather than a help because the service and supply problems would have been too great with respect to the rough usage incurred by clothing and equipment. Bear in mind that this was in an era when matches were not yet trusted and the caplock rifle was tolerated by only a small percentage of the mountain men.

A knitted wool voyageur's cap will keep your head warm during the day and can be worn while sleeping to retain body heat.

150

Your cold weather clothing will consist of all, or most all, of the following items: leather moccasins or moccasin boots, heavy wool socks, felt liners or inner moccasins made of rabbit skin or sheep skin, long woolen underwear, or if you are allergic to wool, cotton underwear, buckskin trousers, wool blanket shirt, wool blanket capote, a buckskin or elk hide hunter's coat, and a fur hat that can be rolled down to protect the ears and back of the neck. For sleeping at night carry a knit wool voyageur's cap, or one of the type called a ski cap or toboggan. It is the job of this cap to keep warm not only your head but also the back of your neck and even the tip of your nose while sleeping. Your pack should also contain spare socks and moccasins and an extra suit of long wool underwear.

Most capotes have hoods which can be pulled over your head in cold weather.

This 'skinner is dressed for cold weather in a wool capote and buffalo mittens. For colder weather, a fur hat and heavier moccasins would be warmer.

Whether you travel by canoe, horseback, snowshoes, or on foot, it is important that you do not let your clothing become soaked with sweat. When, because of strenuous exercise you are likely to become too warm, either remove some of your outer garments or open them up for ventilation. When you feel you are getting too cold, put them back on or button up again. It is better to be a little cool during the day than too warm when you are working and sleeping outside in cold weather.

Besides looking good, fur hats will keep your ears and the back of your neck warm.

At night after you have finished cooking, dry out all clothing that got wet during the day. Place moccasins, boots and other leather articles, where they will warm slowly but not get hot, otherwise the leather will harden and crack. Rub warm waterproofing into the dried moccasins and boots and let them rest a day while you wear another pair from your pack.

Study of mountain man literature indicates that, summer and winter, one and sometimes two blankets was part of the trapper's standard equipment. At least one voyageur proudly proclaimed in later years that, regardless of the weather, he never carried more than one blanket into the wilderness. Be that as it may, let's not overlook the fact that these men were in the fur business and they usually had hides or furs in their packs. In addition, mountain men, with their *remuda* of pack animals and riding horses, always had an *apishamore* (saddle blanket), which could do double duty at night as a ground cloth or bed cover. The outer garments of the trappers became their bedclothes at night. Whereas most of the northern men preferred a blanket coat called a capote, the southwestern trappers working out of Taos, Santa Fe, and Bent's Fort frequently wore *serapes* or *fresadas*. These were thick and warm and, like the Navajo blanket, impervious to all except the heaviest downpours of rain.

You, just as were the old-time mountain men, are restricted as to the amount of bedding and shelter material you can pack on your back. If you are making a *jornada* on horseback and have pack animals to carry your gear, or if you are travelling by canoe where no portages are required, you will be able to carry enough bedding and waterproof canvas to make a warm, dry night camp. This material, for example, might include three heavy wool blankets, a fur robe (buffalo or other hides), and enough canvas for shelter and ground cloth. But when you are packing everything on your back, two blankets, a shelter and ground cloth, in addition to food and the rest of your gear, is the maximum you should expect to carry. With only these items and the clothing you are wearing you will be able to survive the coldest of nights. You will note that I said *survive,* for you will not be comfortable on the coldest nights. You must expect some discomfort but if comfort is your object, stay in your home where you can bank the fire and sleep under plenty of bedding.

Yes, you must have rest and as much sleep at night as possible in order to conserve and restore your energy. Do not go to sleep troubled by the old wives' tale that you will freeze and never awaken. Make a fire and sleep with the assurance that you will wake up — several times in all probability for when your body temperature drops too low you will stir around to find a warmer position, or you will get up to add more wood to the fire. Death in the wilderness by freezing is always a definite possibility and we should know how to deal with this threat. Usually freezing and death occurs only when the victim is hungry, completely exhausted, and after prolonged exposure to cold temperatures. It can also occur rather rapidly as, for example, after a ducking in water that is near freezing. Consciousness may last only four to seven minutes and death occur in fifteen to twenty minutes.

Strange though it may seem, fire poses a worse threat to the cold weather camper than freezing weather. Fire strikes when least expected and in the space of a few minutes can destroy clothing, bedding, and equipment, and can inflict serious injury and even death to the wilderness camper. Why is this? I believe it is because we tend to put too much wood on the night fire and then lie too close when it is growing in size and intensity. Also, some woods tend to pop and blow out burning embers more than others. As a general rule, avoid the use of soft woods (the evergreens) for the camp fire; many pop and spit fire and they do not last long as a fuel. Tuliptree (yellow poplar), box elder, and sassafras are also dangerous campfire woods.

From the days of Rogers Rangers to the present time, members of raiding parties behind enemy lines have found it necessary to bivouac together for reasons of security as well as for ease of communication when ready to move. Under these conditions the individual is restricted in his choice of an area where he can bed down. It is not possible for him to continue to travel until an ideal spot is found. A lone traveler, however, is free to move about until he finds natural features of the terrain and the materials needed to make a warm night camp.

As a consequence of the kind of life the mountain man led — the endless travel over all types of terrain, his continuous exposure to all kinds of weather, and his constant association with other experienced frontiersmen — he learned how to take advantage of the natural features of the land so that with only the materials at hand he could soon provide himself with a makeshift shelter wherever his wanderings took him. It is not possible here to describe, or even to enumerate, the various types of shelters it is possible to make. I shall, however, describe a few of the most primitive kinds of shelters you can make with only the materials you would find in the woods or mountains. A little practice in building these and other type shelters that you may improvise will go a long way toward increasing your confidence in your ability to survive outdoors regardless of the weather or terrain.

The reader has already been advised of the obviously good shelters provided by a cave or cliff overhang. Unfortunately, these cannot always be found when and where we need them. In most areas of North America the most obvious shelter is the traditional lean-to, or, as it was also called by the frontiersmen, the

Figure 3 illustrates the construction of a half-faced shelter. This type shelter was often constructed by the early frontiersmen.

half-faced camp. In November of 1771, Simon Kenton and two partners, while searching for the elusive cane-brakes of Kentucky, were forced by approaching winter to stop and build a permanent camp. They built a half-faced camp on the east bank of Great Kanawha River in what are now the environs of Charleston, West Virginia. Here they lived until April of 1772 when they left for the settlements with their furs.

When making this type camp, or any other winter shelter, it is imperative that a location be found that is as much out of the wind as possible. This wind-free area might conceivably be a narrow arroyo, an under-cut stream bank, the crevice between two hills, a dry wash, the leeside of downed timber, or in the angle formed by large chunks of fallen rock. Let's say that the best location you have found for a camp is on the leeward side of a high creek bank. Let the bank serve as the rear of the shelter. Brush away or tramp down the snow where the floor and campfire are to be located. For a two- or three-man lean-to cut 2" or 3" diameter poles in the approximate lengths listed below. (See Figure 3.)

Pole No.	Qty.	Length
1	2	6'-6"
2	6	8'
3	2	10'

Poles cut to these dimensions will provide a shelter measuring six feet high by seven feet wide in front, two feet high in the rear, and nine feet deep, i.e., from front to rear. Note that the lengths specified allow six inches at junction points for tieing with rope or cord.

With your tomahawk, cut to points the lower ends of poles Numbers 1 and 3. Select a Number 1 and a Number 3 pole and lash them together within six inches of their blunt ends. Do the same with the second set of Number 1 and Number 3 poles. Lash the eight foot crosspiece, Number 2, in the crotches of the Number 1 uprights as shown in Figure 3. Push the pointed ends of the Number 3 roof poles into the vertical bank at a point two feet above floor level. If possible, force the pointed ends of the Number 1 poles into the ground. Lash the remaining crosspieces on the roof so they are approximately equidistant from each other.

Cover the roof frame with branches of evergreens; use balsam, fir, juniper, small cedar, or spruce branches (the needles of pine foliage are too thinly distributed to be of much use). Starting at the lower edge of the roof, lay the branches in rows like shingles so that each upper row overlaps the preceding row. Western cedar and eastern juniper branches can be cut to leave a stub end that will hook over one of the horizontal poles, but branches of the other evergreens are shaped like flat sprays and must be placed flat side down on the roof. If your location is completely out of the wind the roofing material will lie securely in place, but if the wind is blowing, hold the branches in place with rope or cord, or by placing additional cross poles over the completed roof.

To further improve the half-faced camp, tie bracing poles over the open sides of the shelter and cover them with branches as you did the roof. A layer of snow can now be added to the roof and more snow heaped up against the two sides to provide you with a windproof shelter. Now build a long fire in front of your shelter and a heat reflector back of it and you have what amounts to a heat barrier against cold air coming from that direction.

The steep cut bank or cliff face provides us with yet another way of erecting a snug shelter. Lean the two long roof poles directly against the vertical bank or cliff face. Finish the roof and one side of the shelter as detailed in preceding paragraphs but leave one side open for an entrance and build a fire in front of this.

All things considered — your physical condition, clothing, bedding, shelter — the greatest heat loss incurred when sleeping outside is caused by lack of insulation between your body and the cold damp ground. For this reason, you must cover the floor of your shelter with armloads of evergreen branches. Carefully arrange this material shingle-fashion to a depth of at least 9 or 12 inches. Start the first row at what will be the head of your bed and continue with succeeding rows to the opposite end of the shelter. You may wish to place small logs around the edge of your bed in order to hold the branches in place. All natural vegetation compresses badly so if you intend to stay more than one or two nights you may find it necessary to add more branches to your bed after the first night's use.

At this point, a few words are in order about vegetation other than evergreens that can be used for roofing and flooring material. Look around you in the winter woods; what other options do you have? Standing tall and sear throughout the long winter months are what I call the "long plants" and they offer us a snug roof and a warm mattress just for the gathering. There are still to be found the cattails, rushes, reeds, flags, sedges, and wild grasses waiting to serve you just as they have served mankind since time immemorial. Look for the sedges and tall wild grasses in forest clearings and along stream banks. Rushes, reeds, flags, and cattails are found in the frozen shallow backwaters of ponds and lakes. The common winterkilled leaves and grasses also make good bedding material but the only leaves that cling to their parent trees throughout the winter months are those of the young beech and some of the oaks. The Great Spirit, doubtless for some reason unknown to us, lets the young beech keep most of its leaves until the arrival of spring when they are finally pushed off by the new arrivals. It is thought-provoking, yet sad, to see here and there in the eastern forests a young beech tree standing like a small grey ghost among his larger neighbors, still clinging to his funereal shroud of winterkilled leaves.

Western sage brush works fairly well as a mattress material if you trim the branches from the main stem. Use them and you will find as I did, that you can sleep on nothing more aromatic unless it be foliage from the previously mentioned balsam fir. I never leave the land of sage before first cutting a few of its sprigs and rolling them up in my blankets. Weeks later, their smell triggers mental pictures of rolling sage-covered hills, flat-topped mesas, and blue skies.

The loose outer bark of cedar and juniper trees has long been a source of material for thatching and bedding. Collect it by pinching a loose end between your thumb and forefinger and pulling it away from the tree. If you have the time and patience to collect a large quantity it makes a warm, though inflammable, mattress. As a roofing material, handfuls can be tied together in bundles and applied to the roof and sides of your shelter.

In the spring when sap starts to rise, slabs of bark can be peeled from the hardwood trees. Rainproof roofs can be made when this bark is available, but when all the trees are gripped by winter it is not feasible to use bark in building an emergency survival shelter. While the icy fingers of frost probe deep into the wood it is impossible to rob the bark without first cutting the tree and heating the logs in a fire.

The winter of 1848-1849 was an extremely bad one in the southern Rockies. Despite the fact that all signs presaged a severe winter, Old Bill Williams, that master trapper, cagey Indian fighter, and pathfinder extraordinary, allowed himself to be talked into guiding Captain John C. Fremont on his Fourth Expedition to the Pacific coast. Somewhere after crossing the Sangre de Cristo range and the San Luis Valley in present Colorado, Old Bill had an argument with Fremont and from there on, other less experienced pilots took over as guides.

On a high summit ridge of the La Garita mountains, engulfed by blinding clouds of snow and screaming winds, the expedition came to a slogging halt. The rest of the story is tragic history. Before the survivors reached the safety of the nearest settlement, 10 men were dead and 23 were crippled, some permanently. In addition, 120 mules died and most of the equipment and personal possessions of expedition members was lost.

How Fremont and 22 of his men managed to survive a mid-winter crossing of the mountains is a classic story of survival. Tom Breckenridge, who was one of the survivors, later wrote that while trapped for five days and nights on top of the ridge, buffeted by sub-zero winds that cut like cold steel, they tramped deep holes in the snow, made a fire in the center of each and sat or lay where they could absorb the heat.

While trappers and voyageurs are known to have used this method of getting out of the wind and keeping warm, they also knew a technical refinement of the method which makes it possible for a person to survive Arctic weather without blankets or protective clothing other than what he is wearing at the time. Here's how it's done. Let's say you are hunting in the high country. You are not wearing especially warm clothing because the days have been sunny and the air dry. You thought you were heading back toward camp but as the shadows lengthen you realize you are lost. A storm is blowing in from the northwest that promises to be a freezing blizzard; finding your way through the nighttime blizzard would be impossible; to stop with no blankets or shelter would be fatal.

You've got to act fast. Far down below timberline you find a sheltered spot between two rock buttresses. The natural protection afforded by the rock and the surrounding fir trees baffles the wind to near zero velocity and, like a snow fence, causes the flakes to settle here in a thick blanket. Tramp down the snow within a circular area of eight or ten feet. Make the pit at least four feet deep and then build a good-sized fire in its center. Drop several four-inch diameter firs and trim off their branches. Place four or five of the poles across the hole from rim-to-rim and directly over the fire. After you have stockpiled plenty of wood for nighttime use you can lie down on the poles above the fire. Heat reflected from the sides of the pit and heat rising from the fire beneath you will keep you alive throughout the night no matter how cold and exhausted you were the night before.

The next time you are out in cold country without enough bedding and not much time to make a shelter, try the following trick. Brush away the snow to expose the surface beneath. If it is rocky, fine; if it is not, collect rocks and cover the cleared area with them in a rectangular pattern three feet wide and six feet long. Build a fire that covers the entire surface of rocks. After the fire dies down, brush away the embers and cover the rocks with lengths of timber placed close together. Lay branches and brushy material over the timber so you and your clothing will be well protected as you sleep above the heated area.

HOW TO THROW
THE TOMAHAWK

One of the most useful items you can carry into the wilderness is a sharp, lightweight tomahawk. It is handy for cutting fire wood, shelter poles and tent pegs. It's the most logical choice when it comes to blazing a trail in trackless country or quartering big game such as elk and moose. My friend Skeeter Vaughn (Grey Otter is his Indian name) was taught how to throw both the tomahawk and the knife by his Cherokee grandfather who used them when he was a warrior for the Confederacy during the Civil War when he fought under the great Indian General Stand Watie. During the depression of the 1930's, Skeeter used them to provide wild game for the family table at a time when he couldn't afford rifle and shotgun ammunition. Today, Skeeter Vaughn lives in North Hollywood, California, and he has the distinction of being one of the foremost professional knife and hawk throwers in the country.

Tomahawk throwing, like many other frontier skills, was commonplace in former times and could be learned from a relative or from the nearest neighbor; like hunting, or tracking, or finding your way without a compass, it was not deemed worthy of being put into print. Consequently, the old books and manuscripts will not provide you with a detailed step-by-step de-

The three forged tomahawks pictured here are typical of those carried by the early frontiersmen. Hawks served as a weapon as well as a very handy tool.

155

scription of how our pioneer ancestors learned to throw the hawk, but in an old book of mine with the imposing title, *Notes on the Settlement and Indian Wars of the Western Parts of Virginia and Pennsylvania, From 1763 to 1783, Inclusive,* I learned how the author, Joseph Doddridge, practiced and improved his throwing skill. In writing about sports on the early frontier, Reverend Doddridge says in part: "The tomahawk with its handle of a certain length will make a given number of turns in a given distance. Say, in five steps (using a short handled tomahawk) it will strike with the edge, the handle downwards; at the distance of seven and a half, it will strike with the edge, the handle upwards, and so on. A little experience enabled the boy to measure the distance with his eye, when walking through the woods, and strike a tree with his tomahawk in any way he chose."

This skill, which was learned as a youth, stayed with the frontiersman all his life. At weddings, cabin raisings, game surrounds, and corn huskings he had ample opportunity to develop his skill to the full extent of his natural abilities. While still a boy of 12 or 14 years of age he was assigned a loophole at the neighboring fort and from then on might be called on to accompany military expeditions, relief parties, and rescue missions during those troubled times on the border during the Revolutionary War and in the years that followed.

Wherever men gathered, whether at the forts and military encampments of the East, or at the Forts and trapper rendezvous of the West, they brought the means of protection, and amusement, with them — their tomahawks, knives, and guns. Today, at rendezvous and shoots all over the country at places like Fort de Chartres on the Mississippi River below St. Louis, and at Fort Bridger in Wyoming, men, as well as women and children, find hours of amusement in tests of skill with these time-honored weapons.

The mechanics of throwing the tomahawk and making it stick in a target block are not as difficult as you may have been led to believe. The main requirements are that you have good eyesight, normal muscular coordination, and a good sense of timing. I have taught a great number of men, women, and children how to throw the tomahawk and nine out of ten of them were making it stick in the block after the first few throws. Follow the instructions given here, practice every day for awhile, and at the next gathering of buckskinners you can be a serious threat to other contenders in the tomahawk matches. If you are already an experienced thrower, you may be able to show me a point or two that will improve my score. But read the instructions anyway and try out some of the ideas. One good idea might enable you to advance to a higher level of proficiency.

A word of warning: Until you gain proficiency in throwing, you are sure to miss the target block occasionally, so make sure the entire area behind it and for 15 or 20 feet on each side is clear. Watch out for children and pets who have the unnerving tendency of suddenly darting into the danger zone. Also, don't use a live tree for a target. A glancing blow will send the hawk flying dozens of feet in an unpredictable direction; besides, deep wounds in the tree make it susceptible to infection and eventually may cause its death.

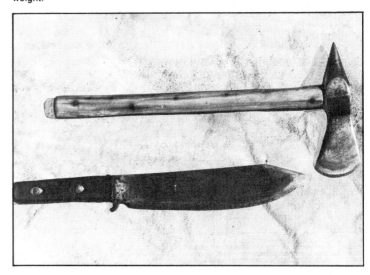

The author's personal throwing knife and tomahawk. Both were designed by Boughton and are very near the same weight.

Assuming that you eventually will want to learn how to throw both the hawk and the knife, it is important that you first consider the following theories which I have developed and proven over the years:

1. The correct throwing distance from you to the target is dependent on the length of your arms and legs, and the length of your knife, and the length of your tomahawk handle.
2. The end-to-end length of the tomahawk handle should be the same as the end-to-end length of the knife.
3. The overall length of the tomahawk and knife should equal the length of your forearm as measured from the knuckles of your clenched fist to the tip of your elbow.
4. Your knife should weigh approximately one ounce for every inch of overall length.
5. Your tomahawk and knife should be of equal weight.

These ideas are not difficult to put into practice. With your fist clenched and your elbow resting on a table, measure from the top surface of your knuckles to the tip of your elbow. Remember this figure. This is the approximate length that both your knife and tomahawk should be.

What is the logic behind the five rules?(1) A short tomahawk or knife will turn over in the air a greater number of times in a given distance than a long tomahawk or knife. (2) When measuring distance from the target to the throwing position, a tall person takes longer steps than a short person. Therefore, (3) By paying attention to the five points listed above and making any necessary modifications of equipment, the variables of lengths and weights are nullified. A verbal or written explanation of how to throw will now apply to either a short person or a tall person. Then too, (4) If your hawk and knife are of different weights and lengths, you, the thrower, will find it more difficult to learn to throw from, say, the one complete turn distance because you will be forced to throw the knife from one distance and the tomahawk from another. To learn to throw from the farther one and one-half turn distance you will have another set of figures to remember and estimate correctly. On the other hand, if your tomahawk and knife are the same length and weight, I can tell you how many paces to walk from the target block and you will find that particular distance correct for both the tomahawk and knife.

A cross-section of tree trunk makes an ideal target block. If possible, obtain a two-foot diameter section of wood from a pine, spruce, fir, sycamore, or poplar tree. The cutting edges of knives and tomahawks will easily penetrate and stick in these soft porous type woods, especially if the section is cut from a tree that has been dead for some time or after the block has become weathered. A section two feet in diameter by eight or twelve inches thick will last two or three years before having to be replaced. If you can't find one elsewhere, a good source for a block is someone who deals in firewood. Mount the block about chest high on a wooden tripod made, if possible, without nails or other metal parts, but held together with wooden pegs in drilled holes.

The actual throwing of the hawk is simple and straightforward. Fasten a small piece of cardboard or a playing card to the center of your tomahawk block with a splinter of wood. Starting with your back to the block, take seven steps forward, then turn and face the target. (NOTE: From what has been said before, you must realize the importance of taking NORMAL STEPS, not measured paces). Lightly grasp the last four inches of the handle. Let the tomahawk hang straight down alongside your leg with the cutting edge facing to the rear. Crouch slightly and shift your weight to the ball of your right foot (left foot if you're left-handed). From here on the act of throwing is a blend of free-flowing, simultaneous movements. Twist your body slightly to the right and start drawing your arm back as if you were going to throw a ball. While keeping your eye fixed on the target, move your left foot forward almost a full step and bring the hawk up over your head, then forward in a full sweeping arc. As the tomahawk comes forward

The three pictures below illustrate the proper form in throwing the tomahawk. As "Hawk" begins the throw (left photo) note flexed knees and weight on right foot. In mid-throw (center photo) note the stride with the left leg while the right arm is fully extended coming forward. The follow-through (right photo) is very important to accuracy. It is especially important to note Boughton's total concentration on his mark during the entire throw.

release the handle smoothly and allow your hand to follow through to your left side.

If you have trouble making the tomahawk stick in the block, stop for a minute and go through the motions you would make when throwing a ball. You do not keep both feet side-by-side when you throw a ball. And if you are right-handed you do not put your right foot forward when you throw. At the proper instant when you throw, let the handle slip out of your hand as if it were an icicle. It is during the last few micro-seconds before you release the handle that guidance is affected. For this reason, it is important that you don't flip the handle or otherwise try to put ''English'' on your throw. Knowing the precise point in the arc at which time you should release the handle is something you will learn with practice and experience. Rest assured, after this knack is acquired, you will release it at the correct instant without further conscious reasoning.

If you have followed the instructions thus far but still have trouble making the hawk stick in the block, here's one sure way to discover what you are doing wrong. Normally when you throw, you should keep your eyes fixed on the target at the precise point where

''Hawk'' Boughton illustrates excellent form in throwing the tomahawk. Once the basic technique is learned one need only to practice to become very proficient with this weapon.

158

you want the blade to strike. But if it is striking and not sticking, try this: Keep your eyes on the target until the instant the hawk leaves your hand, then, while it is in mid-air, quickly focus your eyes on the hawk and follow it to the target block. At the instant it hits the block, take particular note of which part contacts the block first. From a position directly over your head to the target block, the hawk should turn 360°. If you saw the end of the handle strike before the head came up, this indicates that you threw from a position too *near* the block and the hawk did not have time to turn a full 360°. To correct this error, *increase* the range approximately one step.

On the other hand, if the upper end (the poll) struck the block first, this indicates that you threw from a position too *far* from the block and the hawk turned more than 360°. To correct this error, *decrease* the range one step.

You found the normal starting position for the one turn distance by taking six steps, plus an additional one which is used when you step and lean forward to throw. The correct one and one-half turn starting position is six steps, plus three steps, plus one step. Similarly, the correct starting position for throwing the two turn distance is six steps, plus six steps, plus one step, a total of 13 steps.

HOW TO
THROW THE KNIFE

Most all of the modern mountain men and buckskinners I know agree that it was easier for them to learn how to throw the knife after they had developed skill in throwing the tomahawk. I know this was true in my case, but even after you have mastered the hawk, you may have beaucoups of trouble learning to throw the knife unless you have one of proper design.

The three principal design features to look for in a knife are:
1. The balance point, which is determined by laying the knife flat side down on your index finger or on the edge of a ruler, should be within one-half inch of its center.
2. For reasons explained in the preceding paragraphs on tomahawk throwing, your knife should be of approximately the same weight and length as your tomahawk.
3. The knife must be capable of standing up under the rugged use encountered in throwing and in everyday use on the trail and in a wilderness camp.

It is quite possible that after you buy a knife you will find it necessary to modify it in order to make it conform more closely to the three design features listed above.

Most commercially produced knives come with scales (commonly called grips or handles) made of synthetic materials which were unknown in 1840. Some scales are made of wood or antler and these are not satisfactory either because they are brittle and will break after a few throws against the hard face of a target block. You can remedy both of these shortcomings by removing the original scales and replacing them with two narrow slabs of leather. Leather of proper thickness can be bought from your local cobbler; he keeps it on hand for re-soling shoes. Fasten the scales to the knife handle with two-piece screws made especially for that purpose, or use rivets made of brass rod or pieces of soft iron nail. Use brass washers at the ends of each rivet. Countersink the rivet holes in the leather so the washers and peened-over rivet heads will project only slightly above the scale surface, otherwise they will catch on your hand and cause throwing errors.

More often than not, a knife that is out of balance is handle-heavy. When this is the trouble it can usually be made to balance better by removing the scales and drilling several holes through the metal handle to remove the unwanted weight. The holes remain hidden by the scales and the lessened strength of the handle is negligible.

Another more drastic way to remedy a handle-heavy knife is to reshape the blade. Reduce the blade's width by grinding its cutting side so it gradually tapers back toward the handle. Do not remove any metal from the point; begin the grinding about three inches back of it. Grind slowly and carefully so as not to remove the temper from the steel. Stop grinding every few seconds and dip the heated blade in cold water. After you have ground it to the desired shape, grind and resharpen the cutting edge.

A third way to achieve better balance, especially if your knife has a thick blade, is to reduce the blade's thickness. File or grind both sides of the blade beginning about three inches from the point and gradually tapering all the way to the end of the handle. Don't reduce the thickness too much. The metal when measured at the end of the handle should be at least 1/16″ thick. As cautioned before, grind slowly and dip the blade in water every few seconds.

The knife is thrown in much the same manner that the tomahawk is thrown. Fasten a target to the wood block. Take seven normal steps directly away from the block. This is the same position from which you throw the hawk. Face the target and grip the knife by its handle. While standing with the knife hanging straight

The author is equally proficient with the knife or hawk. Here he illustrates his stance as he begins the knife throw. The basic procedures are the same for throwing either weapon.

down, let the handle slip through your fingers until its end is about one-half inch below the crease in your skin at the junction of your hand and wrist. Use the same throwing technique you used in throwing the hawk. Keep in mind as you throw that you want the knife to make one 360° revolution from the time it leaves your hand until it sticks in the target block. Again, as with the tomahawk, if the knife strikes the block and doesn't stick, force yourself to watch the knife as it leaves your hand and note whether it has turned too far when it reaches the block or has not turned far enough. Correct your throwing accordingly by stepping closer to, or farther from, the target.

The knife can be thrown from various distances by changing your grip from the handle to the blade. For example, when throwing from the one, two, and three turn positions, the knife is grasped by the handle. When throwing from the one-half and the one- and one-half turn positions, the knife is grasped by the back of the blade at its widest part where it starts to taper to the point. The distance and degree of accuracy you achieve in throwing are limited only by the amount of time you spend in practice and by the natural abilities given you by the Great Spirit.

IN CONCLUSION

The space allotted for this chapter does not allow me to continue with other of the many skills of the mountain man and frontiersman. I hope, however, that you will learn these and other skills and practice them whenever you can get out into the woods and the wide open spaces. There is no graduation from Wilderness College, or "Rocky Mountain College," as the original mountain men called it.

In your camps and rendezvous at least a small part of the total time there should be used in teaching, or learning from others, some of the skills of the mountain man. Suitable to the occasion would be the subjects of how to keep from getting lost; edible and medicinal plants; tracking man and animals; evasion; crossing streams with your equipment; tanning; trapping; making primitive weapons; and making snares, pitfalls, and deadfalls. Regarding this last subject, remember that snares, pitfalls and deadfalls should not be used where children or domestic animals might be caught in them.

Most states have outlawed their use in favor of steel traps except where the trapper can prove that their use was occasioned by a life-or-death emergency.

Learn to identify the tracks of animals in your area in wet sand, mud, and snow, then practice following them and reading sign in the woods and grasslands. You and a few like-minded friends may have a lot of fun by organizing a frontier war game in which you can practice the arts of tracking, sign reading, ambush, and evasion.

I suppose that even though we barely missed the frontier period in our nation's history, we should be grateful that we are privileged to live in the present age while there are still hundreds of clear running streams and millions of acres of woods and grasslands. Even so, the possibility of future war and our dwindling natural resources makes our preoccupation with mountain man survival skills an investment in the future and will help to ensure us the position of last place on the endangered species list.

Bibliography:

Adair, James. *The History of the American Indians.* London, 1775.

Angier, Bradford. *Field Guide to Edible Wild Plants.* (Illustrated in color.) Harrisburg, Pennsylvania: Stackpole Books, 1974.

Angier, Bradford. *Field Guide to Medicinal Wild Plants.* (Illustrated in Color.) Stackpole Books, 1978.

Arnow, Harriette S. *Seedtime on the Cumberland.* New York: The Macmillan Company, 1960.

DeVoto, Bernard Augustine. *Across the Wide Missouri.* Boston, Massachusetts: Houghton Mifflin, 1964.

Doddridge, Joseph. *Notes on the Settlement and Indian Wars of the Western Parts of Virginia and Pennsylvania From 1763 to 1783, Inclusive.* Albany, New York: Joel Munsell, 1876.

Eckert, Allan W. *The Frontiersmen.* Boston and Toronto: Little Brown and Company, 1967.

Hafen, LeRoy R., ed. *The Mountain Men and the Fur Trade of the Far West.* 10 vols. Glendale, California: The Arthur H. Clark Company, 1965-1972.

Mails, Thomas E. *The Mystic Warriors of the Plains.* Garden City, New York: Doubleday and Company, Inc.

Morgan, Dale L. *Jedediah Smith and the Opening of the West.* University of Nebraska Press, 1971.

Peatty, Donald Culross. *A Natural History of Trees of Eastern and Central North America.* New York: Bonanza Books, 1964.

Peatty, Donald Culross. *A Natural History of Western Trees.* New York: Bonanza Books, 1953.

Women
in Buckskinning

by Shari Wannemacher

SHARI IS A MEMBER of the NMLRA, and has watched her husband, Whitey, be a 'skinner for the past four years. She has attended rendezvous and shoots in many parts of the country and is temporarily settled in Colorado Springs where she earns her share of the income by singing with a band in the local night clubs. In her spare time she sells Mary Kay cosmetics and writes articles for the MUZZLE-LOADER. On the days that contain more than twenty-four hours, Shari enjoys competing in matches with her percussion rifle, sewing calico mountain man shirts that sell at Brent Arms (a black powder shop), and reading books of every shape and size.

I. LIFE WITH A BUCKSKINNER

You know your old man's been shooting his black powder rifle out on a range each Sunday with his friends, but you're unprepared for the day he comes home with a dead varmit crouched on his head and announces that he's going to be a buckskinner. Your first decision is whether you'll go to the rendezvous with him next weekend or stay home with the kids, or stay home and send the kids with him. However, don't think that by staying home you'll escape all involvement in this new life-style of his! Your firmest intentions may well crumble at the pathetic look of helplessness in his eyes when he hands you his new Hudson Bay blanket and an envelope of directions for making a capote coat. He can't understand the directions. Would you please make his coat for him so he'll be warm at the rendezvous? And while you're at it, could you please make him a mountain man calico shirt? All right. You'll find time to make just these two things, but he's on his own with the rest of the stuff he needs.

It doesn't end there. The grimy person wearing an oversized grin, bounding through the doorway in his own little cloud of dust — this must belong to some other household! He's full of stories about all the wives and families there and all the fun you missed. He needs you to hold up his new brain-tanned hides and cut them to the shape of trousers. Then he lays them on your wormy maple dining room table and while gluing them together, he glues them to the table as well. The wooden barrel he brought home is floating in the bathtub — so it will swell up and hold water, he tells you. Something that looks like an ax is soaking in the toilet, and while the diapers you use for rags have been disappearing from the closet, you notice a growing pile of ashes on top of the refrigerator. This is his "char" for starting a fire with flint and steel, he tells you. If you're really unfortunate, on the first cold night, he insists that all the windows be left wide open and he goes to bed in his buckskins. You dream you're lying beside an armadillo in a cow stall. Whether you want to be or not, you're involved. Every part of your life is affected by his decision to be a buckskinner — a life-style that he takes on with serious commitment to live out each day.

Every time he goes to one of these black powder meets or rendezvous he returns with more plunder, more stories, more information, and you're beginning to wonder if he just might be having more fun going than you are staying behind. At last your common sense and curiosity lead you to consent to go and see for yourself. (I slept in our van through all the rendezvous for the first few years, so for me it was a matter of deciding to wake up and look around.)

There are some plans and preparations to make now that the whole family is going. Your old man can't live in his buddy's tipi anymore, and you won't want to wear blue jeans. No one will expect you to arrive on the scene entirely primitive and historically accurate your first time out (or second or third!). That's a standard to work towards achieving. But if you plan to live in the primitive area of the camp, then you'll definitely need a pre-1850 lodging; you'll want to begin establishing an identity for yourself within a given historical period; you'll need your cooking materials and menus planned and organized; and depending upon the identity you've chosen for yourself, you'll want appropriate clothing. "Rendezvous women" also suggest that once you become involved in the life-style of your buckskinner husband, you may begin searching for an activity or craft to specialize in.

Now don't think you'll be suddenly swamped with a lot of new things to do. "Do it yourself" is the buckskinner's motto, and there's a lot your husband will want to do for you. A friend of mine acquired her Indian outfit by driving to the rendezvous, while in the passenger seat her boyfriend finished up her moccasins and leggings. Since the decision-making and planning can be yours to the extent that you choose, I'll be discussing in this chapter the major areas mentioned above and offering suggestions from the experience of other wives and from my own research to give you a head start in the right direction.

II. LODGING

The two major pre-1850 lodgings are lean-tos and tipis. Each has its own method of dictating your pleasure and pain. My friend, Joyce Levins of Rockford, Illinois, looks at the small opening flap of her tipi every morning and says to herself, "I'm not going to make it out of here!" She and Al are looking for a lean-to to buy. My husband, Whitey, and I are looking at tipis, after slithering all over each other in our lean-to for the past two years trying to find the things we need. Ours lives up to its name — it leans sideways. In high winds and storms it looks like a parachute in a hurricane, and you can forget about trying to build a fire for warmth. Even with the flap down, there's very little protection from

Today more and more women are attending rendezvous with their husbands and boyfriends. At a rendezvous in Michigan this lady 'skinner enjoys a cool refreshing drink from a crock jug.

wind, though we do stay dry now (after twenty different people waterproofed the seams twenty different ways!). The advantages in owning a lean-to are that it's less expensive, the poles needed are shorter and fewer, it's easier to put up, and I like it because I can sit in its shade and still observe the camp doings.

In the cool evenings or in high winds and storms, the tipi is warm and secure. The fire blazes undisturbed, the stew bubbles in the pot, friends enjoy each other in comfortable, roomy surroundings. Only the owners remember the trouble they went through to transport it and set it up. Most tipi owners drive a pick-up truck, but I've known some who successfully carried the poles on top of their vans.

Marilyn Hering, who with her husband, Bruce, makes lean-tos and tipis and other primitive, authentic shelters, has sound advice for the would-be do-it-yourselfers. Don't try to make these shelters yourself. A 16-foot tipi requires 91 yards of heavy canvas fabric, enough to instantly mummify four large grizzlies. Your new fancy sewing machine will beg for mercy, request last rites and expire before you've finished the first seam. Although awning makers have proper equipment and a system for dealing with tons of fabric, they don't know what a primitive shelter is, so you'll wait a month while they do research in the public library. The easiest way to obtain your choice of shelter is to buy one already used or order a new one from an outfit that specializes in making them.

While wandering through a primitive camp you may be asking yourself if you really want to sleep on the damp, hard ground with crickets eating up your expensive Hudson Bay blankets and spiders spinning webs in your ears. Well, the part about the crickets and spiders is true, but look a little closer inside the lodgings and you'll probably see heavy canvas material covering the ground and over-lapping up the sides. And notice how the wool blankets and furs are raised a few inches above the ground as though there's something under them. Well, take a peek and you'll probably see a warm zippered sleeping bag on a thick foam rubber pad. So it isn't all that difficult to get a good night's sleep. As long as you keep everything covered with authentic stuff no one has to know what a "softie" you are.

To help us set up our lodging correctly, we took photos of others like ours and studied where the poles were placed. Then Whitey devised his own system of poles and guide ropes, totally *unlike* any of the photos. The first night, just after we finally got to sleep, it all fell down on top of us. The next day he devised another of his original systems, which somehow works.

If you'll remember to set up your camp at a respectful distance from your neighbor, you'll really look like an experienced buckskinner, even if it's your first time out.

No matter which lodging they live in, primitive campers know that life is simpler, more relaxed, and the family is more vigorous, healthier and happier in the fresh air and a life-style that goes back to the basics.

III. ESTABLISHING YOUR HISTORICAL IDENTITY

There are two things you can do that will make you feel instantly at home at a rendezvous. First, build a fire at your new residence. The second is to arrive with a sense of your place in history. Show me a man in buckskins, his noodle held together with a red bandanna and it's no trick to know his occupation, lifestyle, his image to the civilized world and the probable components of his personality within a historical context. We can do the same for ourselves by understanding the full definition of a buckskinner and then determining the races and social conditionings of the women who shared their lives.

Cathy Bauman, shown with her husband Rick, dresses Taos or Mexican-style.

Most women attending rendezvous choose to dress Indian style as shown here by Gloria Smith. Gloria made and beaded her dress leggings and accessories.

From the beginnings of the white man's culture in the Eastern United States, there were white men who wore buckskins and strongly identified with the Indians, trapping and trading and pushing through the frontier boundaries, opening them up to white civilization. These Eastern frontiersmen had wives battling right beside them. When fur-bearing animals became scarce in the East, the trappers and pioneers were forced westward to continue their hunting and trading with the Indians. The rendezvous became an annual event in the western regions, and because there were no white women living in the West prior to 1836, the trappers chose Indian and Mexican women for companions. Thus, it is not historically accurate for white women to attend a rendezvous, (nor is it accurate for

rendezvous to be held in the Midwest or East). This is why most women at the rendezvous dress as Indians. However, the reality of our modern-day rendezvous is that our buckskinner-husbands are mostly married to white women. It's a get-together of all of us as we are now, seeking an alternative life-style that is not a "retreat to a different era, but an attempt to gain perspective on our lives by living by a different set of rules," to quote Tom Malinoski in his editorial in *Muzzle Blasts,* March, 1980. As wives of buckskinners, our historical identity could be taken from any year of the Fur Trade Era at any place in the country. Here are some choices:
1) A white buckskinner woman, such as Mrs. Edward Pentry. Dressed in a "close-fitting tunic of deerskin reaching to the knees, with leggings to match," she

Whether it be taking part in a rifle match (above) or participating in a knife throwing contest (below), there's usually plenty for a woman to do at rendezvous.

accompanied her husband and two other men to the wilderness shores of Maine's Moosehead Lake in 1672 where they hoped to establish a trading post with the Indians.

2) A white wife of an Eastern frontiersman.

3) The Mexican wife of a Western trapper or mountain man.

4) The white missionary wives, Narcissa Whitman and Eliza Walker who, although they weren't buckskinner's wives, did attend the last Green River rendezvous in 1836, enroute to their mission settlement on the Walla Walla in Oregon.

5) The Indian wife of a Western trapper, living and traveling with him, or remaining with her tribe and occasionally joining him for brief periods.

6) The white girl on the wagon train heading to Oregon who ran off with the trapper in the 1840's, as related by Frances Parkman in his book, *The Oregon Trail*.

7) The white wives remaining behind in frontier settlements such as St. Louis while the husbands pushed westward. Harriet Sinclair, daughter of James Sinclair, independent trapper and trader, stayed behind with her mother in the settled towns.

Most buckskinners' wives try to coordinate their clothing to their husbands'. For example, if he is dressed as a Western mountain man, she still has the choice of being Mexican, Indian or white within a time period of the late 1700's to early 1840's.

IV. THE WAY WE WERE

If you were a white frontier woman, perhaps moving your family further westward every few years at the urgings of your husband, what would you be like? Bedraggled? Martyred? Rigidly pious? Kneading bread to your own squeaky strains of "When the Roll is Called up Yonder I'll be There"? Would you be subject to the will of your husband? A piece of his personal property like his horse? From the movies we know the brave, hardy, confident saloon women of the Gold Rush Era, their voluptuous bodies poured into tell-tale (excuse the pun) satins and sequins. Were their female predecessors a special breed of woman?

To answer these questions we have to begin with the Puritan women of Colonial America from 1620 to about 1760. They were in short supply and large demand. The ungainliest of women, who in Europe would be disgraced old maids, found themselves in the Colonies married and badly needed, not only for their ability to work, but for the creation of large families to do the farm chores. Because their work was a direct contribution to the basic survival of themselves and their families, they had strong feelings of self-worth and confidence. They poured their skills and knowledge into every aspect of colonial life from midwifery to shopkeeping. Eleven colonial women ran printing presses; ten of those published newspapers. They stood side by side with their husbands, enjoying a freedom of expression without worry of being unattractive. Page Smith in *Daughters of the Promised Land* notes that "The most notable New England wives were daughters of vigorous and devoted fathers," who treated their daughters as though they were a "living mind" rather than a toy. Margaret Fuller wrote a classic account of a father-daughter relationship: "He called on her for clear judgement, for courage, for honor and fidelity. . . . Thus nurtured she took her place easily. . . ."

In the 1780's and 90's, everything changed for colonial women. They were no longer in demand; no longer needed for the family's basic survival; their importance diminished. Small communities emphasizing marriage and family, gave way to large, impersonal cities. The rise of capitalism and the Industrial Revolution was upon them. Marriage became a game to enable ambitious men and women to climb the ladder of social success through union. To ensnare a man, women adopted behavior and dress according to what men themselves specified they wanted in a woman.

In the spirit of capitalism, husbands were out getting rich while their wives and daughters became fragile, delicate children, preoccupied with good manners and social graces. The new mores forbid females to employ any overt sexual allurements, the result being repressed sexuality. Men married "good girls," while "bad girls" filled their sexual needs. It all happened fast. In 1790 young John Quincy Adams returned to New England after spending three years in France to find American girls "superficial," "affected" and "simpering".

The families living on the frontiers, pushing westward didn't know of the fate of their New England sisters. Husband and wife, man and woman remained partners in work and survival. Women were still scarce, valuable and appreciated for their real skills and true

Joyce Levins, of Rockford, IL, tells her husband, Al, exactly what she thinks of the hat he's about to buy.

169

Today's buckskinner camps probably look much like the temporary camps of the early settlers. Here both men and women pitch in to take care of the camp chores.

Artist Ronnie Boren of Vernal, Utah, sells her drawings and paintings at rendezvous. When you see her, you'll know why she's called "Eyes Talking".

sexuality. It isn't surprising that the Western states were the first to acknowledge women's right to vote.

In summary, the white frontier women were hardy, confident and self-respecting. Because they were highly valued for themselves, and there was no pressure on them to be attractive to the opposite sex, they were free to reveal themselves as the unique individuals they were. They possessed all the frontier skills their physical strength would allow them to accomplish. There's a lot to be said for the fortitude and bravery of these women and for the men who shared their lives as partners.

Without really wanting to boast, I'm sure I'm a descendant of the frontier woman, from the fortitude and bravery I've displayed in the past. I've been known to run for miles with the speed of buffalo in stampede to escape flying insects. I've noticed too, that my need to be attractive to men diminishes in proportion to the extent of my fear.

In general, women's roles in Indian cultures were more varied and established, depending upon the tribe. If you've chosen an Indian identity, then you'd want to study up on the women in the tribe. It should be noted that Indian women who left their tribes for periods of time to travel with their husbands found new freedom of self-expression and a different sense of personal value.

V. A WORD ABOUT CLOTHING

Once you've decided on an identity, you'll want to do research on clothing for yourself and your family. I prefer going to original sources with pencil and pad and sketching what I see. Museums are a good place for looking at authentic clothing. Old photographs and sketches can be found in books in libraries as well as in collections in your state's Historical Society. Also in the library you can find books of paintings and sketches of Indians and pioneers by famous artists of the era,

171

Susan Fecteau shown at rendezvous. Very knowledgeable about Indian women's clothing, Sue has researched, written and published a book about primitive Indian dresses.

such as Bodmer, Weyeth, George Catlin and Alfred Jacob Miller. This type of research is fun to do and you'll have a real sense of accomplishment when the outfits are completed and you know they're authentic.

For a fast-start, find Wilson and Hanson's *Feminine Fur Trade Fashions* (see bibliography at the end of this chapter) and take your pick of Indian, Mexican or white fashions. Indian fashions, consisting of tunic, leggings and moccasins, are easy to understand and construct. On the other hand, white women's clothing might appear complicated until you understand a few basic concepts. Their slips were always showing. These same slips also doubled as nightgowns, and they wore their corsets on the outside, over the slip.

Imagine yourself in the 1700's. Your house is cold in the mornings, so you don't want to take off your nightgown. Around your waist you tie a petticoat of boned hoops (basket reeds), and over that you put on your dress. Now the lacy sleeves of your nightgown are hanging beneath the shorter sleeves of your dress, and the drawstring, ruffled neckline of your nightgown is peeking above the lower neckline of your dress. It rained the night before, so to keep from getting the skirt of your nice dress muddy, you lift it off the ground on your walk to the well for water. Your legs mustn't show, so you leave your nightgown-slip (chemise) to drag in the mud. This was how and why the outer skirt of many costumes became draped and pulled up as a permanent arrangement. If you were wearing a skirt over your chemise, you could wear a laced corset for your top outer garment, much like we would wear a vest over a blouse today. In the 19th century undergarments became underwear, something to be hidden.

VI. COOKING

No doubt as Head Female Honcho of the Household, you're also Captain of the Kitchen. This means that the bulk of organization and menu decisions for your primitive outings will be up to you, even if your husband is an excellent open-fire cook. Mine isn't. It took me five years to decide to cook in the out-of-doors. Until then we ate from the booths or nearby restaurants or mooched off neighbors. Of course, if the latter occurred, I always had extra food to throw in their stew pot if they volunteered to feed me, too. (On those nights Whitey drank water for dinner. He won't eat anything unless it's spaghetti.) Finally at the Mid-America Rendezvous in Arkansas, 1980, I decided we'd "go for it". Whitey's breakfast every morning was a bologna sandwich. His lunch was a bologna sandwich, and by suppertime the neighbors were feeling sorry for us, so my dinner came from someone's stewpot.

A month later I announced to Doc and Dee Carlson at the Western Rendezvous that I was *really* cooking at this one. Doc said he was so glad — he felt sorry for Whitey, eating out the inside of Aspen tree bark in Arkansas.

The more I learn about kitchen organization and menu planning from experienced rendezvous women, the more excited I get about *really* going for it — next year! Marilyn Hering was the first to show me her system. She's an organization expert, who, before becoming a buckskinner, camped and cooked in the outdoors with the most elaborate and modern equipment. She says primitive-style cooking is so much easier. Whether your meals are going to be modern foods, such as steak and potatoes, barbecued chicken and fresh lettuce salad, or the more primitive, authentic foods, such as corn meal cakes and beans, has to do with what your family will eat and what your bodies will tolerate. Most of us have to be back at the office the day after we arrive home from a rendezvous and if our diet has been too radically different, we could end up with a week-long tummy ache. Marilyn and her husband, Bruce, prefer the modern menus.

Their main food storage container is a large, well-insulated ice cooler with the lid opening on top. It's covered with white canvas and stored outside their lodging. A week before the rendezvous Marilyn buys and freezes all the meat they'll be eating. This meat is then stored in zip-lock bags in the bottom of the ice chest at the rendezvous. A large plastic container in the chest keeps lettuce and other foods from getting in contact with the melting ice. Other perishable foods, such as butter, are kept in plastic refrigerator containers with lids. Inside the door of their lodging, Marilyn keeps a dipper and a porcelain bucket with a lid on it filled with water. For her, this is easier than struggling with the heavy water barrels. Her dry foodstuffs are kept in a deep wooden box with a top-opening lid. These are never unpacked from one rendezvous to the next. Here you'll find flour and coffee in oiled tins, seasonings neatly organized in bottles, and every necessity of the kitchen where it can be instantly found.

Cathy and Rick Bauman of Haven, Kansas, have kept their supplies and menus as primitive and authentic as possible. In fact, if it weren't for the beer Rick likes to have at rendezvous, they wouldn't need an ice cooler at all. Much of their knowledge of food, utensils and menus of the Fur Trade era can be found in Hanson and Wilson's *The Buckskinner's Cook Book,* which Rick and Cathy sell, along with a complete supply of buckskinner needs at their store, Ne Shutsa Traders.

The meats they eat at rendezvous are sugar-cured

This sumptous mealtime fare is beaver tail and beans.

Cathy Bauman's "keep".

ham, bacon and dried tongue. One large cloth bag holds many smaller cloth bags containing black-eyed peas, coffee beans, black beans, pinto beans and lentils (early beans). For beverages Cathy serves authentic Lapsang Souchong tea — a long-leaf China tea with a "tarry" flavor (*everyone* knows what a "tarry" flavor is!), fresh-ground coffee, and a Mexican chocolate drink called "Chocolate Atole". To make this she mixes together and heats over the fire: 1 cup brown sugar, 3 one-ounce squares of chocolate, 3 cups milk (canned or dry-powdered), and 2-3 cups of water, along with several sticks of cinnamon. Cathy uses canned evaporated milk for recipes requiring milk. She also serves cheeses which she keeps in the shade, wrapped in cheese cloth and an old diaper-type cloth.

175

Jean Johnson shows a Sioux Indian dress she has almost completed. It is made of blue selvage edge trade cloth with a dentalium shell cape.

The quill work on the toe of this moccasin is perhaps the finest being done in the country right now. The artisan: Jean Johnson.

In the opposite photograph you can see Cathy's simple, yet complete "kitchen". Like Marilyn, she carries and stores her basic foods and utensils in one rustic wooden box. The pan for dishwashing rests in the top of the frame.

Pat Croft of Kansas City, Missouri, makes biscuits to go with any meal by adding water to self-rising flour for the dough and deep-frying spoonfuls, like a donut. For apple or other fruit fritters, add a little sugar to self-rising flour, mix water in to make the dough, and in the middle of each ball of dough put in finely-ground apples, cinnamon and nutmeg, or other fruit. After deep-frying, shake in a paper bag containing powdered sugar.

Campfire cooking can be very simple for you if

Elayne Hedin of Arvada, CO displays her beautiful rosettes and other items she's made by hand.

you'll follow my advice: let someone else do it! Frances Scurlock consented to go to her first rendezvous only after her husband, Oran and son, Bill, promised to do all the cooking. That's being smart! Of course, when I met her, she was doing the cooking because Oran and Bill were so busy. It was the first time she had ever cooked over a campfire, but she was so expert I thought she'd been doing it forever, so it must be a simple skill to learn.

If you are the chosen one to cook, don't do what I did. A bucket of water sitting on the coals in the fire will take three days to boil, if it ever does. If you try moving it to a hotter spot in the fire, chances are you're going to dump it and suddenly you won't have a fire at all, which is what I did, not once, but twice at the same meal. When I finally got the water boiling, (thanks to a tripod arrangement David Wright loaned me, which allowed the bucket to hang from a rope directly over the fire) I threw in the spaghetti. The bucket tipped threateningly. Flames licking the edge of the bucket caught the tips of spaghetti on fire like sticks of incense. The mess in our plates looked like porcupine quills and I'd learned a lesson: let him eat bologna sandwiches.

VII. SPECIALIZING

Once you've been to several rendezvous, you're going to find something special to do that you'll enjoy developing into a real skill. This could be leather work, some form of art, quill work, beading, sewing, woodworking, cooking, writing, the study of a particular

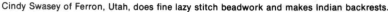
Cindy Swasey of Ferron, Utah, does fine lazy stitch beadwork and makes Indian backrests.

A close-up of Cindy Swasey's lazy stitch beadwork.

person or historical era, tomahawk-throwing, knife-throwing, gun-building or shooting a black powder rifle or pistol, to name just a few.

I would like to see women at rendezvous teaching other women the skills they've learned. When Elayne Hedin of Arvada, Colorado showed me how she made her beautiful beaded rosettes, I was sure I could do it, too, as long as she was sitting beside me talking me through each step the first time.

I didn't realize how difficult it can be to learn a skill, such as beading, from a book until I watched Whitey try to do it for the first (and last) time. In the first three minutes he had: knotted the short end of the thread, broken the needle, sewed beads and leather to his lap, put beads on the needle without pulling the thread through any material, spilled beads everywhere, and given up in authentic, primitive frustration. That's when I decided that a living person who had already learned the hard way would teach me what I want to learn.

Those ingenius buckskinning moms. Tommy Struebing models his unique combination of diapers and buckskins.

Capote Woman (Barbara Struebing, Wauwatosa, WI) gives her friend, Shell Woman, an affectionate smile after placing the feather in her hair.

179

VIII. EPILOGUE

The sun burned orange in the late afternoon. Mothers, fathers, and children, maybe twenty in all, gathered in an open meeting place between the lodges. A buckskinner, dressed in his Sunday-best fur hat and coat, stood and addressed his friends in a firm, gentle voice, in simple language so the children would understand. "Today we're giving a new name to Phyllis Horn. At home, in everyday life she will still be called Phyllis, but wherever buckskinners and families get together for rendezvous, I would like her to be called 'Shell Woman' from this day on."

Shell Woman sat cross-legged at his side, her head held high, a look of pride in her eyes. Her garments were of the softest hides and her long hair hung in two thick long braids.

Then Shell Woman's friend, Capote Woman, stood up and walked to her side. There were tears in her eyes as she placed a large feather in Shell Woman's hair, and her voice choked when she began to speak, "This is our husbands' way of honoring us for sharing this part of their lives with them."

It was a simple, moving ceremony. Our husbands have found a way of showing us their appreciation for coming along to keep them company. They want us with them. Those old values of marriage and family still live in the modern buckskinner's heart. We'll make history all over again.

Bibliography

Eckert, Allan, "Winning of America" Series, beginning with *Wilderness Empire*.

Gray, Dorothy, *Women of the West*, Millbrai, CA, Les Femmes, 1976.

Grimm, William Carey, *Indian Harvests*, New York, McGraw-Hill, c. 1973.

Hanson, James A. and Kathryn J. Wilson, *The Buckskinner's Cook Book*, Chadron, Nebraska, The Fur Press, 1979. (A *Must* for every buckskinner's library)

Hanson, James A. and Kathryn J. Wilson, *The Mountain Man's Sketchbook*, Vols. 1 and 2, Chadron, Nebraska, The Fur Press, 1976.

Hays, Wilma Pitchford, *Foods the Indians Gave Us*, New York, Ives Washburn, c. 1973.

Healy, W. J., *Women of Red River*, Women's Canadian Club, 1923.

Humphrey, Grace, *Women in American History*, Bobbs-Merrill Co., c. 1919.

Kavasch, Barrie, *Native Harvests; Recipes and Botanicals of the American Indian*, Vintage Books, New York, 1979.

Klinger, Robert Lee, *Distaff Sketch Book*, A Collection of Notes and Sketches on Women's Dress in America, 1774-1783, Union City, TN, Pioneer Press, 1974.

Koch, *Dress Clothing of the Plains Indians*.

Kreidberg, Marjorie, *Food on the Frontier*, Minnesota Cooking from 1850 to 1900 with selected recipes, Minnesota Historical Society Press, St. Paul, 1975. (Not Fur Trade, but definitely Frontier food.)

Laubin, Reginald and Gladys, *The Indian Tipi*. (Hardback revised edition much improved over original)

Lowie, Robert H., *Indians of the Plains*, New York, The Natural History Press, 1963.

Lyford, Carrie A., *Quill and Beadwork of the Western Sioux*, Boulder, CO, Johnson Publishing Co., 1979, reprint of 1940 edition.

McClellan, Elizabeth, *History of American Costume*, Book I, 1607-1800, New York, Tudor Publishing Co., 1969.

Miller, *Four Winds Indian Beadwork Book*.

Niethammer, Carolyn, *American Indian Food and Lore;* 150 authentic recipes, New York, Collier Books, 1974.

Olsen, Larry, *Outdoor Survival Skills*.

Orchard, William C., *Beads and Beadwork of the American Indians*, Museum of the American Indian, Heye Foundation, New York, 1975.

Smith, Page, *Daughters of the Promised Land*, Women in American History, Boston, Little, Brown, c. 1970.

Stiller, Richard, *Commune on the Frontier*, The Story of Frances Wright, New York, Crowell, c. 1972.

Terrell, John Upton and Donna M., *Indian Women of the Western Morning;* their life in early America, New York, Dial Press, 1974.

Thomas, Dian, *Roughing It Easy*.

Van DerBeets, Richard, *Held Captive by Indians*, Selected Narratives, 1642-1836, (Includes personal accounts by Mrs. Mary Rowlandson, Elizabeth Hanson, Mary Kinnan, and Mrs. Rachel Plummer), Knoxville, University of Tennessee Press, 1973.

Weiner, Michael A., *Earth Medicine;* earth foods, plant remedies, drugs and natural foods of the North American Indians, New York, MacMillan, 1972.

Wilson, Kathryn J., and James A. Hanson, *Feminine Fur Trade Fashions*, Chadron, Nebraska, The Fur Press, 1976.

Worrell, Estelle Ansley, *Early American Costume;* Fashions from 1580-1850. Harrisburg, PA, Stackpole Books, 1975.

The Crafts

by David Wright

DAVID WRIGHT'S FIRST INTRODUCTION to muzzleloading came at the ripe young age of five when his older brother Don (then seven years of age), bought a percussion musket for 50¢ from one of the neighborhood boys.

Born in the small town of Rosine, Kentucky in 1942, Wright moved to Tennessee in 1952 and grew up on a farm outside Goodlettsville, where upon graduation from high school, he decided art was to be his lifelong career. While in art school, Wright spent the summer of 1961 studying in Italy. During this time, he purchased his first black powder gun, an original French Charleville Musket, model 1777. For the next few years he hunted squirrels, rabbits and quail with the Charleville and then "retired" the gun because of its excellent condition.

Finishing art school, he started his career in art only to be interrupted shortly by Uncle Sam. Drafted into the Army in 1964, he found himself 11 months later in Vietnam serving as an "advisor" to a small group of ARVNs (Army of the Republic of Vietnam) and flying as a door gunner on a helicopter gunship.

Upon his discharge from the Army in 1965, Wright resumed his profession as an artist. In 1968 he bought a muzzleloading rifle and actively started shooting black powder again and has been at it ever since.

In 1973 Wright joined Gray Stone Press, a publisher of limited edition art prints. Before long, limited editions of his works were distributed nationwide and abroad.

David Wright is fortunate enough to share his love for buckskinning with his profession of art. Fellow buckskinners have become models for his paintings, and he feels that "skinning" has given him a little insight into painting the mountain men and longhunters of those days past.

He is a member of the Tennessee Longhunters and belongs to the American Mountain Men. With his wife Charlotte and his two children, Shannon and Shawn, David Wright resides in Cross Plains, Tennessee.

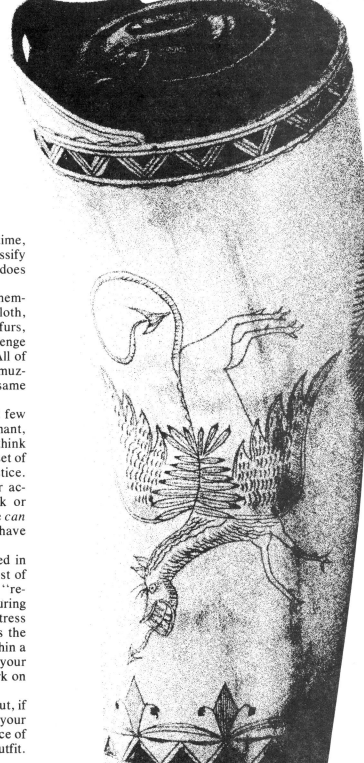

I DOUBT THAT ANY OTHER sport, pastime, hobby, livelihood, or whatever you prefer to classify buckskinning, fosters the variety of craftsmen as does the sport of buckskinning.

For those who are interested in making items themselves, the materials are varied, such as leather, cloth, wood and iron supplemented with beads, feathers, furs, horns, antlers, teeth, claws, etc., offering the challenge of creating (or recreating) a multitude of items. All of these materials were used originally during the muzzleloading gun era and, for the most part, these same materials are still available to us today.

With the growth of muzzleloading in the past few years, we've seen many talents that were dormant, emerge, only to discover that one who would not think of sewing clothing before can sure whip out a fine set of skins after some serious studying and a little practice. Whether it be building guns, making clothing or accoutrements; beading, blacksmithing, quillwork or scrimshawing powder horns, we've found that we *can* do things that a few years ago we would not have thought of attempting.

Since most serious buckskinners are interested in recreating a specific era in American history, most of the time when we make an item, we are actually "recreating" something that would have been used during that particular time. For that reason I am going to stress one point here that I feel is very important. It is the value of research. If you *want* to be authentic within a certain historical period of time, then research your subject as much as possible before beginning work on any item.

You can be the finest craftsman in the world, but, if your beautiful finished work of art doesn't fit into your historical time frame, then you will have a fine piece of work, but not one that correctly goes with your outfit.

If possible, visit museums. Nothing can replace a first hand look at details.

It's a shame, for instance, to see a buckskinner outfitted representative of the fur trade era (1820s to 1840s) carrying a bag adorned with beadwork done in the intricate Sioux style of the late 1800s.

Possibly you feel I am being too critical; maybe so. But, it is just as easy to bead something in the style of the 1820s to 1840s as it would be to do it in the styles of the 1870s to 1900. Research will make all the difference.

While the majority of today's buckskinners tailor their outfits and arms to fall within the western fur trade era (i.e. 1820s to 1840s), others choose to emulate people of other areas and time periods in our history. Groups such as Rogers Rangers, the longhunters and the voyageurs are all seeing their following grow as more historical materials become available.

Luckily for all of us the increased popularity of the sport of muzzleloading has caused many new books to be written and many old, out-of-print books and journals to be reprinted. These give us a more detailed look at what occurred during the days when the longhunter and the mountain man were roaming the American east and west. These sources help us to gain new insight into the clothing, guns and customs of these people of yesteryear which before have been available only on a more limited basis. In addition, the four major black powder publications offer many historical articles, as well as fine how-to articles.

An excellent source for books on the fur trade, both eastern and western is THE OUTFIT, Box 111, Lafayette, Colorado, 80026. The proprietor, Terry Johnston has an extensive selection of books and journals, many of which are reprints of original materials. A letter will bring you a well described listing of available books and prices.

(At the end of each section in this chapter is a list of some books and sources that I feel will be a help to all interested buckskinners, be it an old-timer or a newcomer. This is not to "plug" any one company or publication, but to share sources I've found to be a help to me and hopefully help eliminate the hours of efforts that I've spent in locating them.)

In this chapter, beadwork, scrimshawing a powder horn and some simple blacksmithing will be covered. These are crafts I think all of us can handle without necessarily being a master craftsman. Additionally, the items produced by these crafts are commonly used by every skinner.

I would like to add one last thing before proceeding on to the craftwork. What I am passing on to the reader are techniques that I have found to work best for me through research and plenty of trial and error. This is not to say that it will necessarily work best for you. Most everything can be improved upon. In any case, I hope that you will take what I am relating to you, make it better, and pass it on to someone else.

Lance Grabowski at the 1980 Western Rendezvous. Lance makes his own clothing and is shown here in an early plains Indian outfit adorned with quillwork and hairlocks.

INDIAN STYLE
BEADWORK

In the old days, it seems that the most common ways mountain men liked to spruce up an outfit was to adorn it with Indian quillwork and beadwork. Both Indians and white men wore clothing and accoutrements that were adorned with pony beads, real beads, seed beads, and other numerous kinds of trade beads that became available when trade with the Indians flourished.

Unfortunately, for those of us whose interest lies in the 1760s to 1850s time frame, most existing specimens of beadwork in museums today are referred to as originating during the late period. Try to tie down a museum curator on just what constitutes "early or late" beadwork and you will have more luck trying to corner a cat in a round room.

However, most experts seem to agree that the earlier period of Plains Indian beadwork (pre-1850s) was simpler in design, utilizing mostly blocks, rectangles and triangles with fewer colors. Later beadwork introduced more intricate geometric designs with many colors of beads. Of course, there are always exceptions, but I've seen work that was dated as early as 1805 composed of what appeared to be number 13 beads, a very small seed bead that was prevalent in the late nineteenth century.

The most preferred colors in the earlier works tend to be red, blue, white and black; however, other colors *were* used.

Much Indian beading was done directly on buckskin; however, I've seen specimens beaded directly on trade cloth, canvas or duck material as well as other cloth fabrics.

The Indians tanned their skins using the animals' brains (hence called brain tan). A good brain tanned skin is "suede" on both sides and softer than today's

A fine example of beading on fabric. This beadwork by RoseAnn Wright, done in the Crow style was beaded onto red wool which was then sewed to a gun cover.

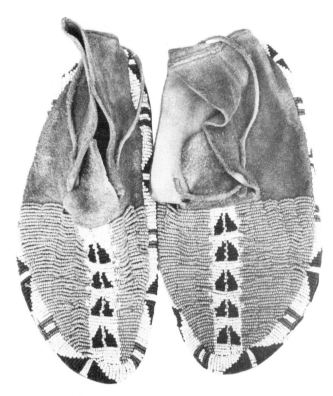

The author's first attempt at beading done several years ago. And it looks it. Note the "sag" in the runs of beading as mentioned elsewhere in the text. This is caused by putting too many beads on a run.

chrome tanned skins. When beading, the Indians, as a rule, did not sew through the entire thickness of the skin but only through half of it. I would recommend this method when beading on buckskin, but you will find it harder to push a needle into chrome tanned leather than you would brain tanned buckskin. If you decide to bead in this fashion (The backside of your leather will be free of exposed threads.), be sure you get a good "bite" with the thread so it won't pull out.

A much easier way of beading (and authentic too) is to bead directly on to a piece of fabric, later sewing that fabric to the article. By tucking the edges of the fabric or by running a border of beads around to cover the edges, you can virtually eliminate any fabric from being seen.

The two techniques of beading that I will cover in this chapter, the lazy-stitch and applique techniques, will deal with the use of seed beads. Seed beads come in different sizes with common sizes being size 10 to 16. The larger the number is the smaller the bead will be. Most beadwork you see will be made up of sizes 10 through 13. For the beginner, I would recommend size 10s, as they are easier to work with. The smaller beads

Most, though not all Indian pipe bags exhibit beaded panels above quilled sections.

A small tobacco pouch made by the author. Sometimes partially beading an object is just as effective as full coverage.

produce a finer design but it will take longer to cover an area.

Most good beads today come from Czechoslovakia and can be bought through many of the reputable dealers who advertise in the black powder publications. They may also be obtained from traders at rendezvous. Usually they are sold by the hank, a string of beads measuring approximately 220″ to 240″ in length.

Tools and Materials You Will Need
BEADS. Size 10's or 11's for starting out.
NEEDLES. Beading needles, #10 for size 10 beads and #12 for smaller beads. Purchase regular length, not the long loom needles.
THREAD. Use beading thread, generally nylon. Do not use regular cotton thread as it will break through

normal wear. Size varies from A to F. The size needed for size 10 beads is F. A is the finest. I like to use artificial sinew split into fine threads. It's very durable and "looks" like sinew in your beadwork. It will work easily with size 10 or 11 beads.
SMALL PAIR OF NEEDLE NOSE PLIERS. You will need these to break unwanted beads after being sewn on.
SCISSORS OR KNIFE. Use to cut thread.
MATERIAL. Buckskin, light weight canvas or duck, or any fairly heavy fabric.

The Lazy Stitch and Applique Methods
The two beading methods that I mentioned earlier were used most by the Plains Indians. Most of their geometric designs were executed by lazy stitch with floral designs being done by the applique method. Loom beading is rarely seen among the Plains tribes, though the woodland Indians utilized both loomwork and applique.

Let's Start
Lazy stitch is shown in Figures 1 and 2. The thread is knotted and is brought up through the fabric. It is then

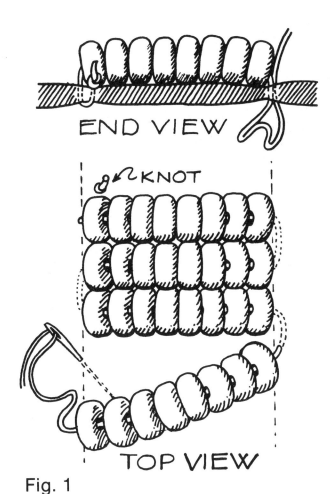

END VIEW

KNOT

TOP VIEW

Fig. 1

INDIAN METHOD
partially through buckskin

through fabric

Fig. 2

block and/or triangle pattern without lots of fine lines. (Besides, this type of pattern should fit right in with the style prevalent during the western fur trade.)

Your design should be marked on the material in some fashion. Whether you draw directly on the fabric or draw the design out on a sheet of paper to transfer will be up to you. I recommend working out your design prior to transferring it to the fabric. Graph paper works well for drawing out your design. A good transfer sheet is fabric carbon. It can be obtained where you buy fabrics. I wouldn't recommend regular carbon paper because it is messy and makes a wide line. Your drawn lines should be fine to help when you commence beading.

strung with the correct number of beads. The needle is pushed straight down along side the last bead, then brought up again a sufficient distance away to be in line for the next row. Ultimately it should form neat rows of beads.

For your first design I would recommend a simple

Fig. 3

for rosettes (Embroidery Hoop)

for pipe bags & breech clouts

for shirt & leggings strips

Before you actually start beading, the fabric should be tacked to some sort of frame. This is especially important when large areas are to be covered. Hat bands, legging and shirt strips can be beaded easier if the fabric is kept taut. A frame can be made of thin crate lumber or something similar nailed at the corners. Your work can be thumb tacked to it. (Fig. 3). An embroidery hoop works well for small items and rosettes. In the case of leather, don't stretch it overly tight. When taken off the frame it probably will return to its original size and may distort your beadwork.

Fig. 4

(from pipe bags at the Buffalo Bill Historical Center, Cody, Wyoming)

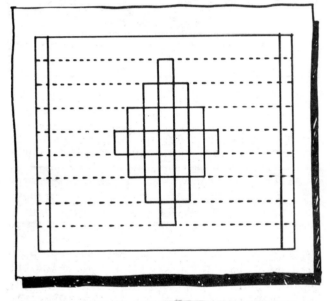

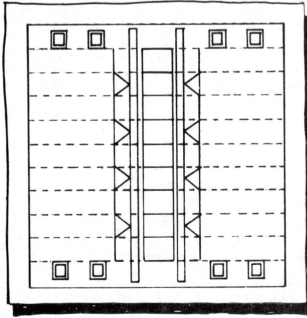

When laying out rows for your design, a width of six to eight beads is easiest to handle. Measure the width of your rows and mark this on your design. (Fig. 4). This will help keep your rows straight. An even width makes a neater job.

When you come to the end of the thread, there are two ways to secure it. If you are not going all the way through the leather with the thread, then run the thread back through the last one or two rows of beads. Run the needle in a zig zag a couple times under the threads then knot. Cut it off or bring it out the back of the material.

If you need to take out a bead at any point after a row has been sewn down, you can do so with the flat nose pliers as shown in Figure 5 without breaking the thread. A word of caution here. Look away as you break the bead to protect your eyes from flying particles of glass.

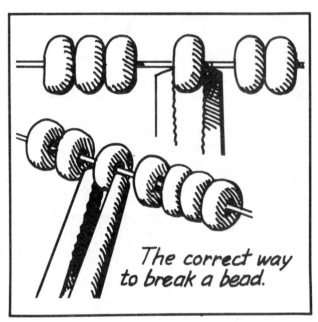

The correct way to break a bead.

Fig. 5

Applique beadwork can work for geometric designs but primarily is used for floral work. In this method, a string of beads is appliqued to the fabric. By the method described you can bead curved lines or fill in large areas. Some people prefer to use two threads and some use only one as shown in Figure 6. Experiment to see which method works best for you.

The design is put on the fabric as described previously and the fabric is tacked to a frame. The thread is knotted and fastened, and the beads are strung on the thread and sewn down. Depending on the curve of a particular run, you may sew only one or two beads at a time. On straighter runs you may get up to four or five beads but I would not go more than that as a run begins to sag under its own weight.

When doing curves such as a vine, the smoothness of the curve can often be helped after beading it by using a separate thread. Tying it off at one end of the curve, run the thread through the whole string of beads. (Fig. 7) Pull tight and knot it off. This will help smooth out the curve.

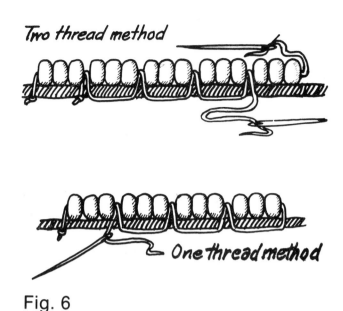

Two thread method

One thread method

Fig. 6

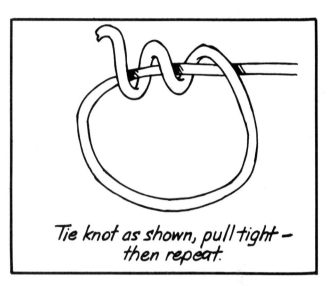

allowing it to burn down almost to the knot. This melts and forms a knot in the sinew that will prevent the end of the sinew from slipping through the tied knot.

Tie knot as shown, pull tight — then repeat.

If you choose to knot your thread on the front side of your work, do it in an area that will be covered by beading. If you are using artificial sinew, tie the knot as shown in Figure 8, cutting the sinew about ¼ inch from the knot. Light the end of the sinew with a match

Fig. 7

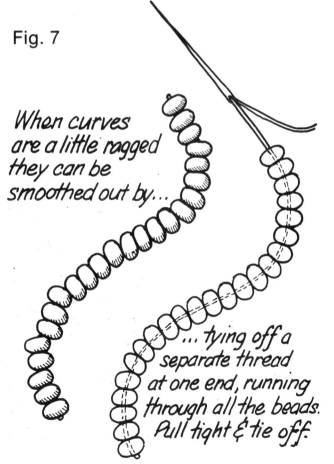

When curves are a little ragged they can be smoothed out by...

... tying off a separate thread at one end, running through all the beads. Pull tight & tie off.

Beading Rosettes

You may wish to bead a rosette to go on your fur hat. If so, you will need a base on which to bead. An old felt hat brim works fine for this. Draw out your design. Then attach the felt to a frame. Begin in the center with one bead tied down. Thread four to eight beads for the first row using the applique method. For this first row sew down every bead to get a smooth circle. Start your next row the same way using whichever color has been selected. Sew down every second or third bead. Each row should be sewn as closely to the other row as possible without forcing them. Repeat this procedure until the rosette is completed. When each circle of beads has been completed, your thread should be pulled through the first one or two beads to pull the ends together without leaving a gap. The rosette should be perfectly flat when finished. If it is loose or irregular it means that beads may not have been carefully picked to fit in. When finished beading, cut a leather backing the same size as your rosette and sew it to the back. This will cover the exposed threads and will strengthen the rosette.

Good beadwork takes practice and patience. But with a little of both, anyone can do a nice piece of beadwork. It's very gratifying when someone asks, "Where did you get that beadwork?," to be able to answer, "I did it."

Reference Books on Beads and Beadwork:
Quill and Beadwork of the Western Sioux by Carrie A. Lyford. Johnson Publishing Co., Boulder, Colo.
Beads and Beadwork of the American Indians by William C. Orchard. Published by the Museum of the American Indian-Heye Foundation 1975 — New York, N.Y.
Crow Indian Beadwork – A Descriptive and Historical Study by William Wildschut and John C. Ewers. Published by Museum of the American Indian-Heye Foundation, New York, N.Y.

SCRIMSHAW
THE ART OF ENGRAVING A POWDER HORN

A fine scrimshawed horn by Don Wright. This horn was
made in the style prevalent during the French and Indian
War of the eighteenth century.

Powder horns have been around for centuries. Long before they were introduced to America from Europe, men used cow horns to store and transport gun powder. They are natural containers because they are light, durable, non-flammable, will not break if dropped, will not rot and if sealed properly, are waterproof. In time, men sought to decorate their powder horns by engraving words or pictures on them.

Actually the art of scrimshaw originally applied to the engraving of nautical subjects and scenes on ivory, horn, whales' teeth and animal tusks. It became popular sometime around the American Revolution. However, today we refer to the engraving on powder horns as scrimshaw, so, technically right or wrong, most people today are familiar with the term "scrimshaw" in reference to decorating a powder horn. I will refer to it as such in this chapter.

Though there were professional engravers of powder horns in the eighteenth century, probably the majority of horns were scrimshawed by those who used them. Soldiers, hunters, trappers and others scratched or cut names, dates or records of events and scenes into their horns.

Geographically most of the engraved horns in today's collections were made east of the Mississippi River with the large majority being made during times of war. However, those who went west carved on their horns as well. Those horns generally were not engraved to the extent of the earlier horns. Even horns that were not professionally engraved have a certain charm about them and definitely take their place as a true form of folk art.

As in any art form, scrimshawing a powder horn would be as individualistic as the person doing it. However, certain subjects were more popular and consistently were used. They included maps, forts, façades of towns, animals, (both real and mythical) birds, ships, soldiers, Indians, trees, flowers and floral vines. Rhymes were popular. The name of the owner was frequently followed by the words "HIS HORN," and sometimes a date. Many times the guide lines for lettering were cut into the horn, becoming a part of the overall design.

Upon observing these horns you will find that some were engraved with deep, bold cuts and others with fine lines. To accentuate the scrimshaw, shoe black, grease, gun powder or soot was rubbed into the lines.

These are all things to take into consideration as you scrimshaw your horn. If you want to build a horn that looks like the horns carried in the eighteenth and nineteenth centuries, study original horns, either in museums or in books and periodicals. At the end of this

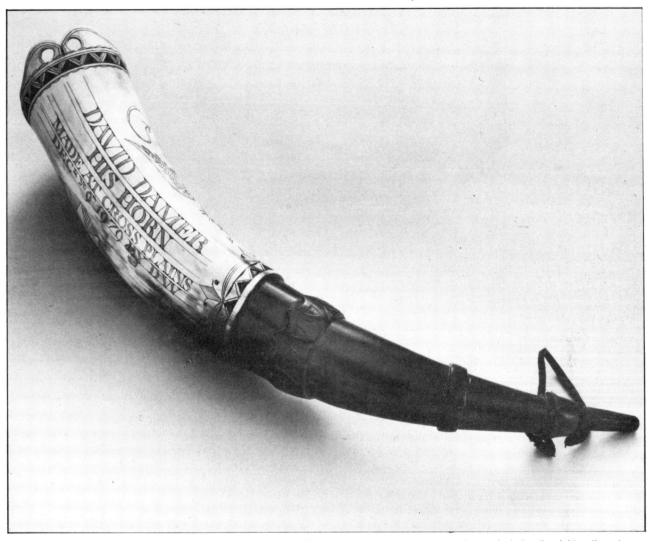

Two views of a powder horn made and scrimshawed by the author. This horn is similar to those horns being made during the eighteenth century.

section is a list of some excellent references for those interested in building and scrimshawing powder horns.

I have found the following list of supplies and tools to work best for me. For the actual cutting of the horn I have used pocket knives, scribes and X-Acto knives with different blades. I have even modified some of those blades. But through trial and error I have found the one knife listed below to work best all around for me.

Tools and Materials

KNIFE. An x-acto with heavy duty handle and a #28 blade as shown in Figure 1. I have found this hooked blade will "hang in" on a curved surface. It is also less likely to slip than other blades. These knives may be found at arts and crafts supply stores.

SANDBAG. I find that resting a horn on a sandbag while working on it offers a steady hold at the same time allowing the horn to be moved into the many different positions needed when scrimshawing. To make a small

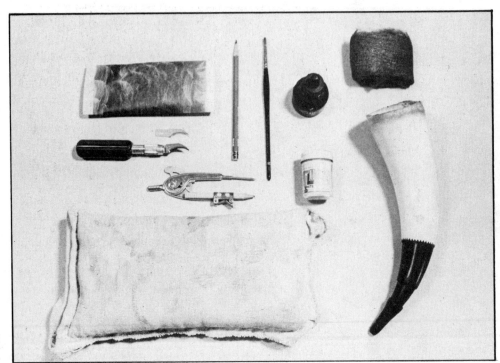

Fig. 1

Shown are items needed to produce a scrimshawed powder horn. Included is a transfer sheet, pencil, paint brush, black ink, steel wool, white paint, horn, sand bag, compass, X-Acto knife handle and #28 blades.

bag, procure some heavy fabric. Cut it to approximately 12″ × 14″. Fold it over to 12″ × 7″ and sew up the bottom and one side. Fill with sand and sew up the opening. While you are at it, make two. You will find that an extra one comes in handy at times.

PENCIL. Get one with a hard lead. The 2H to 6H series are plenty hard and work fine. These hard leads will keep a sharp point longer and the finer the pencil line the easier it will be to follow your design while cutting.

PAINT. An opaque white water base paint such as chinese or zinc white in gouache or tempera is best. This is used for coating the horn before drawing or transferring your design into the horn. The slick surface of a horn will prohibit the pencil lead from adhering well causing the graphite to rub off easily during handling. By painting on a smooth, thin coating, you can also see your drawing more clearly. The drawing should then last while you are working on the horn. These paints can be purchased at most any art supplies store.

PAINT BRUSH. Any inexpensive artist's brush can be used for applying the white paint, and then later, the ink.

INK. A waterproof black India ink works very well for rubbing into the scrimshaw to make the lines show up. For a brown color try sienna or brown ink. Be sure the inks are waterproof. I have found that magic markers work well, too. Black powder mixed with water to form a thin paste works well, also.

STEEL WOOL. 0000 grade.

THE HORN. It seems that of all original horns I have observed, none have had highly polished surfaces, nor did they ever appear to have polished finishes at any time. I prefer working on a horn with a finished surface that has been sanded or scraped smooth but not highly polished. It needs to be free of all "working marks" such as file marks and sandpaper scratches as these will pick up the ink when you rub it into the cut lines. I rub down a horn with a fine grade of steel wool prior to scrimshawing the horn.

Let's Start

I usually work out my design on a piece of paper before ever drawing on the horn. At this point, work out details, size relationships and all rough spots in the drawing. You should keep in mind that drawing on a flat surface is not the same as the curved tapered surface of the horn. After the drawings are worked out to your satisfaction, cover the horn with a smooth coating of white paint. (Figure 2.) A word of caution here: If you apply an overly thick coat of paint, the pencil will cut into it instead of marking upon it. At the same time a too-thin mixture will tend to bead up on the surface.

Wiping the horn down with lighter fluid, alcohol or benzine prior to painting will remove oils left from handling which can also cause the paint to bead. Also mixing a little soap with the paint will make it adhere

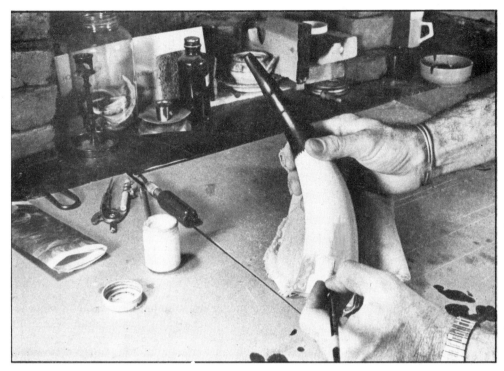

Fig. 2

better to the horn.

Because of the slight difficulty of transferring a design to a horn, I prefer to draw directly on the horn. However you may want to transfer your previously drawn design. Here's how to do it. To make a transfer sheet, use a sheet of tracing paper or onion skin (approximately 6″ × 6″). Cover one side as dark as you can using a soft lead pencil or stick of graphite as shown in Figure 3. Then using a cotton swab saturated with lighter fluid or benzine, rub over the whole area in circular motions. (Fig. 4). Some of the pencil may be picked up by the cotton, necessitating repeating the procedure. Once this is done you will have a transfer sheet that can be used many times. Rubbing the graphite with the fluid keeps the graphite from smearing quite so easily. Your transferred lines will also be finer and cleaner. It will be impossible to wrap your whole design

Fig. 3

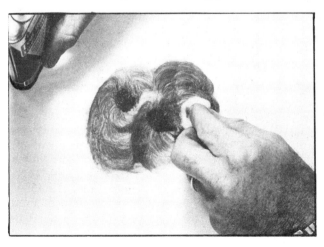

Fig. 4

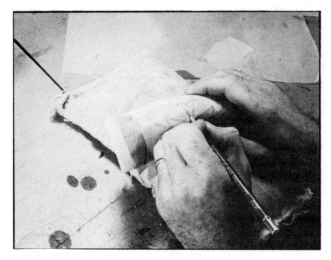

Fig. 5A

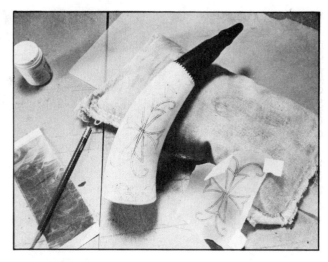

Fig. 5B

around the horn without a great deal of wrinkling. For that reason, you will find it necessary to cut apart your design and transfer sections as best you can. Usually the smaller the section of paper the better it will conform to the contour of the horn. Tape the tracing at the top and put it into position on the horn. Slip the transfer sheet under it (pencil side down) and trace the design onto the horn (Fig. 5A and 5B). Use the hard lead pencil and keep it sharp. The traced lines will be finer.

Now that the design is on the horn you can begin to cut. Grasp the knife down close to the blade. Use your thumb as a guide and also as a stop (Fig. 6) to prevent slipping. Practice awhile on another horn to find out what is most comfortable for you. Place the horn on the sand bag and hold the horn in a position that allows you the most control to make the cut. Turn the horn whenever necessary to utilize the most comfortable position. Whenever you feel you are coming into an

Fig. 6

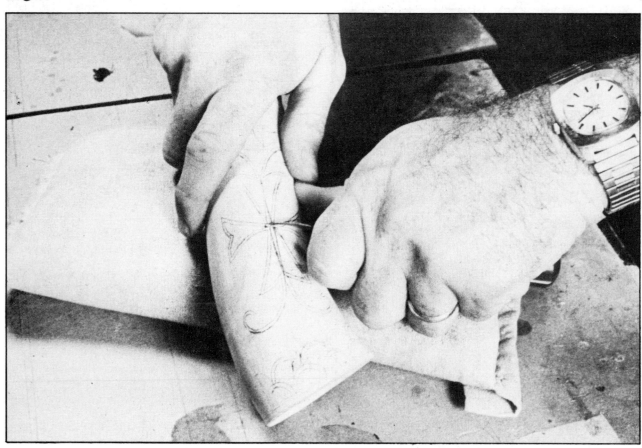

uncomfortable position, stop cutting and reposition the horn to a better advantage. Always try to cut with the knife blade held at a 90 degree angle to the surface of the horn. (Fig. 7) Angling the blade (Fig. 8) sometimes will cause unwanted results such as flaking or chipping. Sometimes with a difficult or intricate cut, it is easier to make a light guiding cut, then go back over it, cutting deeper with each subsequent cut.

To draw circles, use a compass. For straight or slightly curved lines, a flexible plastic ruler works well. Sometimes a slip or unwanted cut can be scraped out, depending on how deep the cut is and how much area around it can be scraped without affecting the other scrimshaw.

When finishing scrimshawing, wash the paint off the horn with cold water. Brush ink into the cuts and allow to dry. Then steel wool the surface of the horn.

A word on proper lighting. It is a must because of the difficulty of seeing the finely cut lines. I like a strong light source close to the horn. This casts a strong shadow (Fig. 9) that helps in picking out exactly where some of those fine lines are.

This should complete your scrimshawed horn. Probably while you were working on it you learned a few things that work better for you than those methods mentioned. That's fine as nobody's method is the last word.

Reference Books on Horns and Scrimshaw:
American Powder Horns by Stephen V. Grancsay. Published by Ray Riling Arms Co., Philadelphia, PA. *Engraved Powder Horns* by Nathan L. Swayze. Published by Gun Hill Publishing Co., Yazoo City, MS.

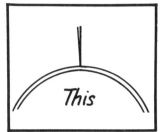

This   Not this

Fig. 7   Fig. 8

Fig. 9

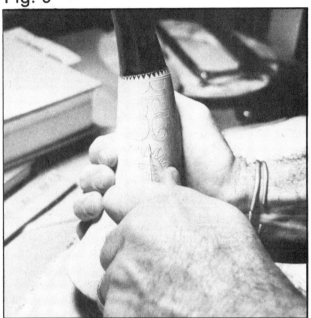

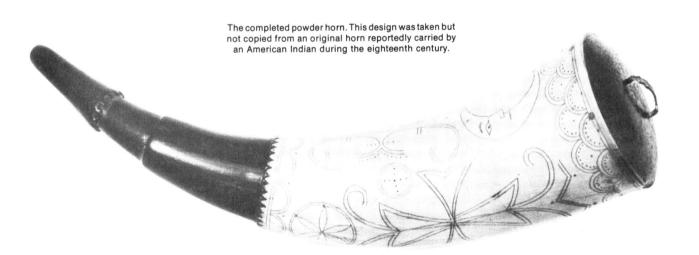

The completed powder horn. This design was taken but not copied from an original horn reportedly carried by an American Indian during the eighteenth century.

196

SIMPLE BLACKSMITHING —
MAKING A SCREWDRIVER

The art of blacksmithing has been in existence since before recorded history. The invention and introduction of much modern machinery and materials have all but sounded the death knell for the professional blacksmith. But with the revived interest in handcrafts that our society now exhibits, the skill of working at the forge is making a comeback. The sport of muzzleloading is contributing its part in this revival by adding great numbers of people who are interested in procuring hand forged goods.

I am going to introduce you to some "simple" blacksmithing. I refer to it as simple because the art of blacksmithing, like all arts, is a craft that requires a great deal of learning and a development of skill, judgement and feeling. Should your interest in blacksmithing go beyond what I cover here, it is possible that, with the right training, you could become a very proficient blacksmith. My article, however, will touch only the tip of the iceberg, so to speak, and will deal with making an item with very simple tools that most everyone should have around the house.

I have chosen to make a tool that most buckskinners have a need for and one that many of us carry in our pouches: a screwdriver. Whether to change a flint or to remove a lock, when the time comes to need a screwdriver, it's handy to have one right at hand.

Since most buckskinners would not want to be caught dead with one of those modern plastic handled jobs in their pouch, I will show you how to make a small utilitarian screwdriver, just right for carrying in your hunting pouch, and I will do it with some very simple tools.

Most of us do not have professional blacksmithing tools around the house. Since I don't consider myself a professional blacksmith, I will use tools that most everyone would have in their basement or garage shop. The only exceptions are the anvil and homemade forge that was used in the pictorial sequence as follows. The other tools are common to most households. I will tell you later what to substitute for the anvil and forge.

To photograph the step-by-step process or making the screwdriver, I asked my good friend, Glenn Sheppard, if he would do the blacksmithing while I photographed the procedure. Glenn has made his own forge and has been turning out needed items for years. So while he forged, I photographed.

The group of tools as shown includes a hammer crescent wrench, key stock (stock for the screwdriver) pliers, file and a vise. Also needed is a heat source and an anvil or substitute.

Tools
> 32 oz. ball peen hammer
> 8″ crescent wrench (or vise grips)
> Pliers (here again vise grips will work)
> 8″ mill file
> Vise
> 12″ length of ¾″ diameter round stock
> Cold chisel
> Bucket of water
> Propane torch with pencil burner tip

Stock
We'll use 3/16″ square key stock which can be purchased at most any hardware store.

A good shop vise will work in place of an anvil. A length of round stock locked tightly in the vise will suffice for the horn of the anvil. (This is the rounded tapering point on an anvil) Various sizes of round stock may be desired to achieve different results.

We used Glenn's homemade forge in which to build our fire with coal. However, with mild steel such as we chose to use, the heating can be accomplished by using a propane torch with a pencil burner tip. You will find that it will take longer to get the heat up to the desired color.

With the tools mentioned and the following illustrations and photographs, one can turn out small items.

These procedures and illustrations are intended only to show how something *can* be done rather than to demonstrate the *only* way.

The beginner will find that it usually requires several "heats" (reheatings) to accomplish any one step. The steel should not be worked after the visible heat glow has disappeared, but can still be safely bent. Also probably many corrective actions with the hammer will be required. Don't let this discourage you. In time they will come easier and faster. *One word of caution:* While hammering any metal, it would be a good idea to wear safety glasses or at least squint your eyes to protect them from flying steel particles or oxide scales. Use your own judgement.

198

Fig. 1

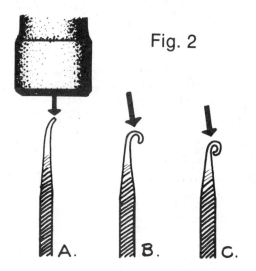

Fig. 2

A.   B.   C.

Fig. 3

Let's Start

Using 12″ of key stock, heat approximately ¾″ of one end to bright red. With rapid hammer blows, flatten the end to a thin spade shape about ½″ wide as shown in Figure 1.

To make the small decorative curl, reheat the flattened portion. (You can hold the stock at the other end with your hand since the heat will not spread that far up the stock. However, should you want to cool the stock, simply immerse it in the bucket of water.) Stand the stock straight up and tap lightly with the hammer as shown in Figure 2, curling the flattened tip to the desired curl.

Once accomplished, proceed on to shaping the handle eye. Heat about 1½″ of the handle end of the screwdriver to bright red. Then lay the stock over the horn (or ¾″ diameter steel rod locked in the vise.)

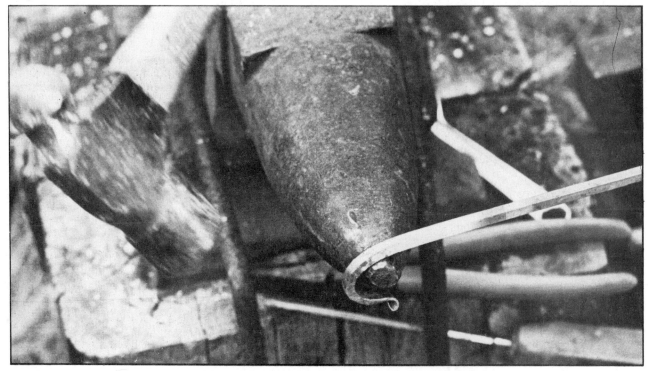

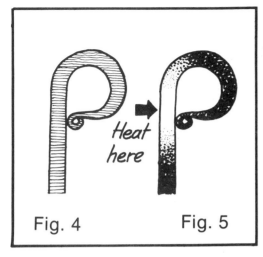

Fig. 4   Fig. 5

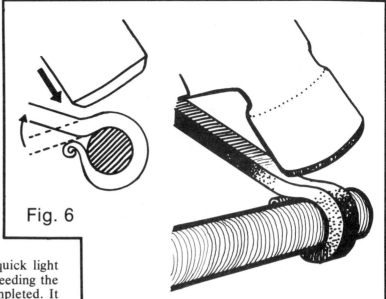

Fig. 6

Starting right behind the small curl, use quick light blows to bend the stock around the horn, feeding the stock as you go (Fig. 3) until the eye is completed. It should look as shown in Figure 4.

To center the eye over the shank, apply heat at the base of the circle (Fig. 5). Then fit it over the tip of the horn. A couple of blows on the side (Fig. 6) should center the eye as shown in Figure 7.

Next we will proceed to the ornamental twist in the shank. Heat the shank to bright red. Quickly lock the eye in the vise and attach the crescent wrench (vise grips will work fine) to the stock approximately where you will want the blade of the screwdriver to be. Hold the end of the stock in one hand and rotate the wrench the desired number of turns (Fig. 8). Pulling lightly with the hand holding the stock while rotating with the wrench helps keep the shank aligned with the eye.

At this point we are ready to cut the screwdriver from the rest of the stock. Lock a cold chisel in the vise, cutting edge up. Cut off the screwdriver with several quick blows of the hammer, being careful that the final hammer blow is not as heavy to keep from damaging the cutting edge of the chisel. (Fig. 9)

Fig. 8

Fig. 7

Fig. 9

Fig. 10

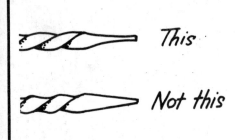

This

Not this

Fig. 11

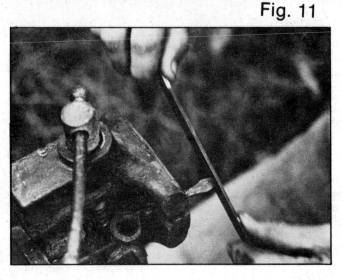

Fig. 12

Now we are ready to shape the blade of the screwdriver. Heat ½" of the shank (You will now have to hold the stock with pliers or vise grips.) and flatten with quick heavy blows as shown in Figures 10 and 11. You should now have a tapered flattened area approximately ¾" in length. Quench in water to cool. All that is left to do is to square off the blade with the mill file (Fig. 12) and that should be it. You have now hand forged a screwdriver.

As a final closing thought I will leave you with a reflection made by Glenn Sheppard while making the screwdriver: "You know, sometimes the difference between handmade and homemade is whether you do it for a living or not."

If you are interested in pursuing the art of blacksmithing further I recommend, for a start, picking up the book *The Modern Blacksmith* by Alexander G. Weygers, published by Van Nostrand Reinhold Co. It is an excellent book for beginners and is very well illustrated.

In conclusion, the three crafts covered in this chapter represent only the "tip of the iceberg" so to speak, of the many crafts involved with buckskinning. Even these three have not been fully discussed as an entire book could be written dealing with an indepth look at the many different crafts. It is this writer's hope that what has been covered here will get you through these projects that you may want to do but also that maybe your appetite has been "whetted" to make you want to learn more and to put what you learn to practice.